letters for life

Guidance for Emotional Wellness from the Lubavitcher Rebbe Rabbi Menachem M. Schneerson

זצוקללה"ה נבג"מ זי"ע

LEVI Y. SHMOTKIN

LETTERS FOR LIFE
Copyright © 2024 by Chabad.org

718-735-2000
editor@chabad.org
For inquiries and comments: lettersforlife@chabad.org

Published by
EZRA PRESS
770 Eastern Parkway, Brooklyn, New York 11213
718-774-4000 / Fax 718-774-2718
editor@kehot.com

Order Department:
291 Kingston Avenue, Brooklyn, New York 11213
718-778-0226 / Fax 718-778-4148
www.kehot.com

All rights reserved. No part of this publication may be reproduced, stored in a retrieval system, or transmitted in any form or by any means, electronic, mechanical, photocopying, recording, or otherwise, without prior permission from the copyright holder.

Excerpts of Letters by the Lubavitcher Rebbe and Selections from Igrot Kodesh, are copyright by Kehot Publication Society®.

 EZRA PRESS is an imprint of KEHOT PUBLICATION SOCIETY®.
The Ezra logo is a trademark of KEHOT PUBLICATION SOCIETY®.

1 3 5 7 9 10 8 6 4 2

ISBN: 978-0-8266-9014-2

Printed in the United States of America

Preface

THE QUEST FOR PEACE of mind is universal. It spans every age, class, culture, and background. This book looks for answers in the counsel of a revered Jewish sage and Chasidic master who lived in our times and drew his wisdom from a river stretching all the way back to Mt. Sinai.

The Rebbe, Rabbi Menachem M. Schneerson, of saintly memory, is widely known for his central role in reviving Jewish life in the wake of the Holocaust. After living through czarist pogroms and the rise of communism, he escaped the Nazi inferno and established his home in New York City, where he shared the secrets of Jewish mysticism and the riches of traditional Jewish practice. As the seventh Rebbe of the Chabad-Lubavitch dynasty, he taught spiritual values of self-refinement, love, and prayer, and mentored hundreds of thousands who came to his humble synagogue in Brooklyn to imbibe his Chasidic wisdom and piety.

In posthumously awarding him the Congressional Gold Medal, the United States Congress praised the Rebbe for "exemplifying the highest ideals of scholarship, teaching, ethics, and charity," for "inspiring people to a renewal of individual values of spirituality, cooperation, and love of learning," and for creating "over 2,000 educational, social, and rehabilitative institutions touching millions of people from all walks of life in every corner of the globe."

Much has been written examining the Rebbe's innovative teachings and transformative campaigns. This book, however, hones in on a lesser-known area of his vibrant legacy: His insights into emotional health communicated in one-on-one audiences and correspondences.

To my friend forever,
Moshe Yehuda ben Golda

—George Rohr

TABLE OF CONTENTS

Introduction IX

PART 1
Essentials For a Healthy Life

Essential Outlooks

Chapter 1 See Others................................... 3

Chapter 2 Know You're Not Alone 17

Chapter 3 Recognize Your Unique Role............ 39

Lifestyle Essentials

Chapter 4 Build Healthy Habits..................... 57

Chapter 5 Be Spiritually Anchored 83

PART 2
Overcoming Darkness
Brief Introduction.. 105

Common Challenges

Chapter 6	Discontent 107
Chapter 7	Worry 123
Chapter 8	Bad Moods................................ 139
Chapter 9	Self-criticism 147

General Tools

Chapter 10	Don't Battle; Pivot........................ 161
Chapter 11	Transcend Isolation...................... 181
Coda	The Courage to Change................ 195

Guide for the Endnotes 213
Endnotes...................................... 215
Essay: A Vision of Wholeness 327
Acknowledgments........................... 335

Introduction

IT WAS AN ORDINARY evening in 1960, and several students and educators from Hillel (a Jewish campus organization) sat in the Rebbe's study. A new world was dawning, and their minds were plagued by pressing existential and practical questions.

Do I have free choice or is everything predestined? What are the strengths and limits of reason? Where can I find G-d in this cold and physical world?

The questions went on. For our purpose, I want to highlight one snippet from the wide-ranging conversation.

"I observe from your library that you are well-read," a Hillel director said. "So I want to ask you: Must we address how Judaism aligns with philosophy and science when teaching today's erudite college students?"

"I'll give you an example from a professor I knew," the Rebbe responded. "He was a professor of medicine, and, at one point, he was immersed in studying the anatomy of the leg. He delved into the research to understand the function of all the muscles and how they perfectly coordinate when a person walks. However, he later told me, while he was engrossed in the details of walking, he found that *actually walking became more difficult*. With every step he took, his mind would analyze the workings of each muscle and joint, complicating his natural gait.

"Similarly, when introducing students to Judaism, talk of the essentials without trying to convey all the complex philosophical intricacies... It will save time, and it will be clearer in the student's mind."

This book is not an anthology of abstract hypotheses. To borrow from the above metaphor, this book does not explore the Rebbe's extensive theoretical insight on the "anatomy" of the human psyche—the complex workings of the mind, the harmonic interplay of divergent emotions, the delicate relationship between faith and reason, and so on. Instead, it is a collection of practical tools, culled from the Rebbe's counsel to regular individuals in real time, on how to actually walk through life with confidence and serenity.

Thus, the letters in this book speak in a clear and direct tone. A sense of immediate relevance, almost urgency, is felt throughout their lines. Unlike other areas in the Rebbe's corpus, they are not characterized by intellectual journeys into the transcendent world of Chasidic ideas. They seem focused on extracting and applying the core of those ideas to help people live their daily lives with health and purpose.

An exploration of the Rebbe's thought on the psyche's "anatomy" merits a book of its own. This is a book on walking.

INTRODUCTION

On a personal note:

I never met the Rebbe, nor received a letter from him. Yet, I am a direct beneficiary of his timeless guidance.

At a certain point in my teenage years I hit upon emotional turmoil common to adolescents. An apathetic attitude gradually took root inside of me: Nothing is worth getting upset over, nor is anything worth getting excited about. Have no expectations of life and life will have no expectations of you. A passive cynicism morphed into my default disposition. To take life seriously was for those who didn't get the memo, who hadn't grasped the tragic comedy of it all.

It was then that I discovered the Rebbe's letters.

I'd been aware of them before. I'd even read many of them. I found them intellectually stimulating—and then promptly returned them to the shelf. Conveyed with such straightforward simplicity, the real depth of the Rebbe's advice had eluded me. Until now, when I rediscovered them through the prism of my lived experience.

An alternative world opened up before me. New perspectives on life and its complexities, new methods of thought, new strategies to approach internal struggles.

Slowly, and almost imperceptibly, apathy was replaced by optimism and purpose. My painful emotions and thoughts, so pervasive just a little while back, were gradually fading out of consciousness. In their place a sense of inner freedom emerged. After a period clouded by negativity, the Rebbe's letters gave me a sense of gratitude and tranquility in a manner I'd never experienced before.

I was enthralled by the candidness of the Rebbe's counsel. Without evading their dilemmas nor relieving them of responsibility, he would urge each person to adopt the necessary perspectives, habits, and practices to transform their own state of being.

As I internalized more of these letters, I started to detect patterns of advice and recurring themes. Instinctually, I organized these points in my mind, forming them into a series of principles. I then began applying these tools to my own mind and heart.

Since then, these tools have remained at my side, to use and use again: flattening hills, avoiding pitfalls, and continually pushing me toward a life of purpose, happiness, and true freedom.

These tools are in the book in front of you.

Levi Shmotkin
18 Iyar, Lag Ba'Omer 5784
Brooklyn, NY

Note: *This book does not address mental illness and cannot replace professional consultation. Indeed, the Rebbe often clarified that his advice to one may not apply to another. Most letters quoted herein are only excerpts, many are free translations, and some are archival copies missing the Rebbe's final edits. In the end, this book is inevitably a subjective take on a vast body of material and all responsibility for error is mine alone.*

Part 1

Essentials for a Healthy Life

CHAPTER 1

Chapter 1
See Others

IN A CANADIAN OBSERVATORY in the year 1971, an astronomer watched a faraway star orbiting a massive object some sixteen hundred light-years away. The object itself remained invisible, but he could see that it mysteriously caused the star to wobble. After months spent ruling out various possibilities, it became clear that he was witnessing the elusive phenomenon known as a black hole. Scientists had been speculating about this theoretical possibility for decades—an object with a mass so dense that nothing, not even its own light, could escape its gravitational pull.

A few years after this discovery, Professor Herman Branover, a respected physicist in the field of solar energy, was scheduled to address a conference of scientists. Before he left for the conference, the Rebbe asked that his presentation include a life lesson that could be learned from the sun and black holes, and suggested the following:

The black hole turns everything inward, drawing all of its energy toward itself. The sun, on the other hand, radiates its energy outward, illuminating other beings in the solar system. If the sun heated only its own mass, who would pay any attention to it? It is upon us to emulate the sun's example and turn our energy outward. We must make an effort to radiate our light and warmth to others.[1]

KABBALAH TEACHES[2] THAT THE entire cosmic order is constructed according to a system of "sun and moon"—an interplay of giver and receiver. The sun, being the source of light and energy, represents giving. The moon, being the recipient and reflector of the sun's rays, represents receiving.

This system of give and take begins in the spiritual worlds. Like terraces in a cascading waterfall, each *sefirah*—divine attribute—acts as both the recipient from the *sefirah* that precedes it and the source of the succeeding *sefirah*.

The same dynamic can be found in the composition of the human psyche. For example, emotions receive guidance from the intellect and serve as the stimuli for speech and action. And it is ultimately reflected in the structure of the physical world. For example, plants receive energy from the earth, water, and environment, and contribute food and oxygen.

This same model applies to human relationships.[3] In our inherent design, we are both moons and suns, both receivers and givers. Receivers of the wisdom, teaching, and advice provided to us by our elders and friends, and givers who contribute our energy to brighten the lives of others. If we forget our responsibility to be a sun to others, and instead live like a moon, only taking from others—or, like a black hole, disengaging and focusing entirely inward—we are bound to experience emotional discomfort.

"A brief reflection," reads a letter to a college student who wrote of his low spirits,

> will clearly reveal that the universe we live in is ordered in a system of give and take, and the personal universe of the individual (the microcosm) must likewise conform to this system of reciprocal relationship. Consequently, when one disrupts or distorts this system [by thinking only of their own needs], it must necessarily bring about a distortion in one's immediate surroundings, and especially in one's inner life.[4]

You Get What You Give

THE VALUE OF TURNING one's mind and heart toward others was a central theme in the Rebbe's counseling.[5] In addition to fulfilling the Torah's foundational dictum—"Love your fellow as yourself"[6]—he believed it could have a transformative effect on one's personal wellbeing.

Marc Wilson, a syndicated columnist and community activist in North Carolina, was facing a grim period after the collapse of his second marriage and the disintegration of his career as a congregational rabbi. "These events just plunged me into a black hole of depression and despondency," he recalled. A friend advised him to go see the Rebbe. With little to lose, he traveled to New York.

It was the early 1990s, and the pressures on the Rebbe's time were greater than ever. Thus, their meeting was brief. "Sometimes," the Rebbe counseled Wilson, "a devoted layperson can do incalculably more good than a rabbi. You should teach something, perhaps Talmud, even if it's only to one or two people in your living room."

A year passed with no action. "It was, all told, a dismal, dark year, full of sickness and grief and self-recrimination," Wilson later wrote. Most of his day was spent in bed watching television or penning articles about his bleak life. "There are plenty of depressed people who like reading stories about depressed people," he thought.

Finally, at the urging of a friend, Wilson began to act on the Rebbe's advice. He started leading a class in Talmud, and, as he later put it, it was then that his restoration to soundness and self-respect began. "The Rebbe obviously understood that to heal from depression, I needed to start giving to others," Wilson concluded.[7]

Similarly, a handwritten response to a woman who evidently went through a lot in her life reads as follows:

> Many people whose life experiences are similar to yours (with regard to suffering, etc.) have found relief through regularly and consistently devoting their energy, time, and *emotional attention* to assisting others who find themselves in distress or in a state of confusion. This has helped them perceive and value their life in an *entirely* new way (their joy of living increased, their self-confidence increased, they found new meaning in life, etc.).[8]

A Liberating Effect

ONE OF THE IMPORTANT ways helping others can improve our wellbeing is by freeing our minds.

"You are much too wrapped up with yourself," reads a letter to a young man who wrote of his dark ruminations,
> with your own emotions and feelings and aspirations.... You must get away from yourself, and begin to think of others. It is time to begin an active participation in society; to give, and give generously. The opportunities are many, and the need is great.[9]

Our minds can sometimes get locked into negative, self-absorbed thought patterns. We may obsess about our real or imagined shortcomings ("I'm so lazy and incompetent"). We may overthink our relationships ("Do they really love me?") or our unfulfilled dreams ("I thought I would be in a different place by this age") and so on. It can be hard to break out of these ruminations.

But thinking of what *other people* might need and how we can actively help *them* has the potential to set off an internal liberation. It lifts us from the narrow tensions of our own little worlds and transports us, for the moment, to the broader horizons of giving to others. As our minds become absorbed with enhancing the life of a friend, the chains of our own psychological prisons begin to loosen.

IN THE WINTER OF 1950, Berel Junik, a Russian-born twenty-two-year-old, finally made it to New York. He had just escaped the Iron Curtain by the skin of his teeth, and was now planning to study under the auspices of Rabbi Yosef Yitzchak Schneersohn—the spiritual leader of the Chabad movement at the time.

Rabbi Yosef Yitzchak had been sentenced to death in 1927 by the Soviets for his efforts in keeping Judaism alive, but after a worldwide uproar his sentence was commuted and he was compelled to leave the country. This geographic distance created a nearly impenetrable wall between him and his many disciples, who were still engaged in a desperate struggle for survival in the Soviet Union. While the Soviet Chasidim managed to maintain a secret line of communication with their mentor, Junik and his friends had never actually met Rabbi Yosef Yitzchak, and they dreamed of the day they would be together in person. Now, at long last, this dream was coming to fruition.

However, only ten days after he arrived in New York, Junik's world collapsed: Rabbi Yosef Yitzchak passed away.

In the ensuing months of mourning, the Rebbe (who was Rabbi Yosef Yitzchak's son-in-law and confidante) adamantly refused to take on the mantle of spiritual leadership. To those who exhorted him not to "leave the flock without a shepherd," he would explain that he felt unworthy to take the place of his revered father-in-law.

But Junik wanted guidance. So, despite these refusals, he mustered the courage one night to knock on the Rebbe's office door and declare that he sorely needed a *yechidus* (a term reserved in Chasidic tradition for a private audience with a Rebbe). Upon hearing his request, the Rebbe became very serious. He walked over to the window, closed the blinds, sat down by the table, and began to cry.

Junik has since passed, but his journal contains a transcript of this audience along with the Rebbe's edits on it (evidently he gave his transcript to the Rebbe to ensure he had understood what had been said correctly). The following is an excerpt (the Rebbe's edits are in italics):

> I relayed that while I have good periods, other times I find myself feeling down over my [spiritual] state of being. The Rebbe responded,
>
> "If there are changes above (i.e., even in Heaven), will there not be changes below (i.e., in a human being here on earth)?
>
> "This is a problem for many of our young people—they analyze themselves too much. It is necessary to think about others for at least an hour a day. *This was one of the ideas the Rebbe [Rabbi Yosef Yitzchak] exhorted [us to do] in his teachings and letters, etc.—to work with others.*
>
> "When a thought about your state enters your mind, *and you see that it is disturbing you from what you should be doing, increases a feeling of dejection, etc.—* you should push the thought away. *If you do not have a way to dispel the depressing thought, because you're not in a good state [and so you have reason to be dejected], you should remind yourself of the obligation to help others.* Think about others *and how you can make things better for them.*"[10]

Junik is advised here to spend time bettering a friend's life for two reasons—as an imperative in its own right ("exhorted in teachings and letters") and as a means to liberate his mind from the shackles of his depressing thoughts, by turning his attention (for at least an hour a day) to someone else.

And there are always people who can use our help.

Practically Speaking

"THERE ARE MANY PEOPLE," concludes a response encouraging a widowed woman to discover the healing power in helping others, "in *every* city and circle who need support (materially or spiritually). Even though some of them are embarrassed to speak of their needs—those individuals deserve even more compassion."[11]

There are people around us ("in *every* city and circle") who need financial assistance—getting set up with a job, a loan to buy a house, help with covering medical bills, and so on. Others might need emotional support—companionship to dispel loneliness, a listening ear, a mentor to help fight an addiction, or simply to be seen for who they are. Still others can use spiritual help in their existential journey for meaning and faith in a turbulent and confusing world. Some might ask for help, but many will be too ashamed to even reach out ("those individuals deserve even more compassion").

We don't need to get creative, travel abroad, or make awkward cold calls to find opportunities to help. A little sensitive reflection on our extended family, friends, and neighbors will usually open our eyes to those who can really use assistance. As one response puts it:

> As much as possible, try to minimize thoughts such as, "How am I feeling?" "Am I afraid of something?" *and so on*. Replace these thoughts with *contemplation* as to how you can assist and see to the needs of your neighbors or relatives; surely you will find many such matters. And one who acts with kindness toward one's friend is rewarded with G-d's kindness to a much greater degree.[12]

Another effective option can be to volunteer or work for an institution dedicated to helping people in need.

"Although I have made the suggestion to you before," reads a 1952 letter,
> I want to repeat that you ought to engage in some social or welfare work to bring benefit to others. The usefulness of this kind of work is two-fold: a) It is the best therapeutic treatment for nerves, through diverting attention from the self to the needs of others; b) G-d regards all mankind as his children, and when one tries to do good to His other children, He compensates such a person manyfold by blessing them and their children.
>
> Needless to say, this is not intended to rule out medical advice. But the best medicine is preventive medicine, and such medicine has the additional benefit of doing good even in ill-health.
>
> I am sure that if you make up your mind earnestly, you will find such useful work, and in dealing with other peoples' problems you will soon forget your own and certainly will be capable of resolving them.[13]

Let's conclude with a story:

Taibel Lipskier was born to a Russian Jewish family in the tumultuous first years of Communist Russia. Her mother died at a young age, leaving her to care for her younger siblings. Eventually she married, and after years of hardship, the couple and their children escaped the Soviet Union. After spending time in various displaced persons camps, they finally made it to the United States.

Life as new immigrants wasn't easy. After a failed attempt at farming in New Jersey, they relocated to Brooklyn. Making a living sufficient to sustain a family was a constant challenge—by then there were ten children. Naturally, the upheavals of her life took their toll on Lipskier, and she suffered from anxiety and depression. She decided to consult the Rebbe for guidance on how to improve her psychological and emotional state.

The Rebbe gave her unexpected advice: "Go to as many weddings as possible and dance, and inspire other people to dance too."

As it happens, Lipskier was an exceptionally skilled dancer. She followed the Rebbe's advice, and for decades she would go to every possible wedding and dance the night away.

"She lived in Brooklyn," her grandson explained, "where at the time there were many young women getting married who had little or no family in attendance. My grandmother would show up and dance, sometimes for hours, with the bride and her friends, bringing immense joy to the wedding."

Rishe Deitsch was a young girl of fourteen when she moved out of her parents' home in Massachusetts to go study in Brooklyn. The pace of New York living, and the frenetic energy of its weddings, were entirely new to her.

"One night," she later recalled, "I was at a wedding and I was wallflowering it. I didn't know these dances, and the speed and noise were all new to me. I knew I couldn't keep up, so I didn't even try. Suddenly this older woman, this whirlwind dancer, grabbed my two hands with her two hands and pulled me into the center of the circle. I tried to pull away and explain I'm-from-Worcester-I-don't-dance, but she couldn't hear me anyway. And she had me with an iron grip. So I took my only option, other than to faint: I danced!

"It would not be an exaggeration to say I had more fun in that one dance than I had ever had in my whole life up until that point. She whirled me around, she flipped me this way and that way, and I just followed her lead, since I had absolutely zero choice in the matter (remember: iron grip). After it was over, she asked me my name. I was way too shy to ask her name, but later someone told me it was Mrs. Taibel Lipskier.

"I always remembered the dance, but I didn't know there was something deeper to it. It was only many years later that I heard the story of what she went through and the Rebbe's guidance to her."[14]

"It wasn't like she was outgoing by nature," her grandson observed. "It was actually quite contrary to her nature. But she constantly did it, and she did it with every fiber of her being. And ultimately, we saw how the joy she brought to hundreds and thousands of people over long decades came back to her; we saw how it gave her so much joy and strength and fortitude and resilience."

Thinking about it all these years later, he reflected: "Many of us are dealing with unresolved wounds. We want to extricate all that darkness from our system, from our psyche, from our environment and home. But sometimes the most effective solution is not to fight the darkness, but to kindle a flame of joy—by dancing and inspiring other people to dance. In that dance, with the pure intent of bringing joy to others, a passion of fire and warmth is created in us and around us, allowing the darkness to dissipate and be banished."[15]

RABBI MENACHEM M. SCHNEERSON
Lubavitch
770 Eastern Parkway
Brooklyn 13, N. Y.

HYacinth 3-9250

By the Grace of G-d
15th of Kislev, 5730
Brooklyn, N. Y.

Greeting and Blessing:

    I duly received your letter in which you write about your daughter. Please write to me also the Hebrew name and mother's Hebrew name of her fiance, and I will remember them in prayer when visiting the holy resting place of my father-in-law of saintly memory, in accordance with the contents of your letter.

    I do not know whether the doctor has such a pessimistic view, but there have been similar cases where positive results were accomplished through getting the person interested in some outside activity to help others. Thus, it would be well if some suitable youth group or organization would approach her with a request to help out in its activities, in an area compatible with her ability, appealing to her for her help. This would give her a stimulus to overcome her present frame of mind, even if she would not make the effort to get out of her own shell for her own sake. Perhaps it would be advisable to discuss this with your family doctor, in order to ascertain what activity would be most suitable for her. Needless to say, this should be done in a way that would not arouse her suspicion that it was all prearranged, but that she should really believe that her aid is needed. As a matter of fact, it may well be possible to find an activity where she could really make a positive contribution.

    Needless to say, especially as you are a communal worker, you are no doubt aware of all that is going on in the community.

    Judging by your writing, it is unnecessary to emphasize to you at length the need to spread Torah-true Yiddishkeit in your immediate environment, as well as in the community at large. Indeed, this is the obligation of every Jew, for we are commanded to keep all things of holiness on the ascendancy. And no matter how satisfactory things may be at any particular time, there is always room for improvement in matters of goodness and holiness, which are infinite, since they derive from the Infinite.

CHAPTER 1

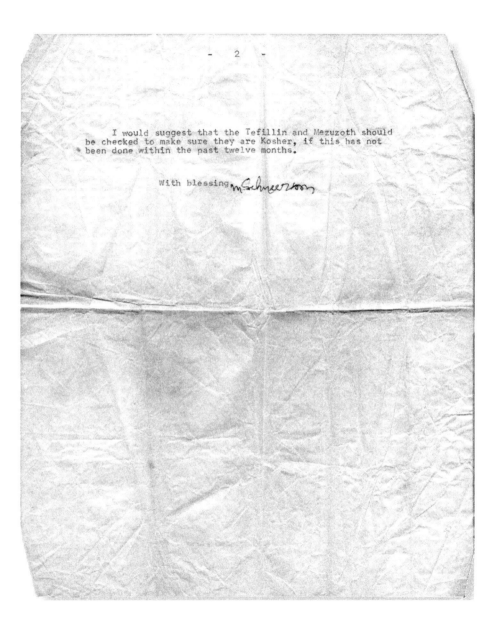

Takeaway

Becoming a giver is key to inner health and resilience.

Open your mind and heart to see those around you. Be sensitive to their needs, and try to brighten their lives.

If you feel down or dispirited and inclined to retreat inward ("Once I feel better about myself I'll be able to start thinking about others"), caring for others is an effective way to refresh your own emotional state.

(Needless to say, this is but an *additional* benefit derived from fulfilling our intrinsic responsibility toward one another.)

But where can you find strength to be a giver? The next chapter will offer some perspective.

Chapter 2
Know You're Not Alone

ON A HOT SUMMER day in 1970, Israeli fighter pilot Menachem Eini was returning from a mission when his plane was hit by an Egyptian anti-aircraft missile. He was just fifteen seconds away from the border, but with his plane about to crash he was forced to parachute into hostile Egyptian territory.

Badly injured on landing, Eini saw the smoke of his ravaged plane, but found no sign of his co-pilot. In the distance, he saw a truck full of Egyptian soldiers coming his way. He feared his end was near. The soldiers searched him, sedated him, and took him into captivity. After some time in the hospital, he was placed in a cramped cell with nine other Israeli captives.

For three long years they lived together, hidden from the sun. On the few occasions they were allowed to leave their cell, they were blindfolded. Isolated from their family and friends and cut off from the outside world, the prisoners had no idea when, or if, their captivity would end. Finally, in 1974, after the Yom Kippur War, a prisoner exchange was brokered and the captives were released.

Some time after arriving home and reuniting with his wife and daughters, Eini accepted the Air Force's offer to return to base in a non-combat role.

"Outwardly I was productive and energetic," Eini later recalled. "In fact, I was held up as a model of recovery and resilience. Inside, however, I was hiding a terrible inner fatigue. I would look around and see people at ease with themselves, while I felt profoundly restless. Any noise would irritate me. Even music became an intolerable clamor. I could find no peace." A friend of his recognized that everything wasn't right and advised him to visit the Rebbe.

In the Rebbe's study, for the first time since his release a few months earlier, Eini unburdened himself. "The memories were very painful," he recounted, "and I think people who've gone through a traumatic experience often prefer to suppress the trauma as much as possible. Yet here I was recounting these memories, without feeling a drop of pain or shame, if there even was anything to be ashamed of."

As Eini exposed his months and years of trauma—the loss of his co-pilot, his fear of imminent death, the never-ending interrogations, the years in captivity, the shock of freedom, the anxious anticipation, the surreal reunion, the visits with families of friends who didn't survive—the Rebbe gently coaxed him to share more.

"He was absolutely and totally present, sharing my burden with me. I felt that he became my consciousness. I was speaking to him, but also to myself; I was bringing things to the surface from inside that I would never otherwise tell anyone else or even myself. His listening the way he did helped me heal from the experiences of captivity. I even had my first healthy laugh. I discovered that a person can be addressed fully through silence and listening alone.

"I needed this meeting like oxygen. When I left, I felt more reflective, more connected to myself. I was able to revisit my time in captivity, and begin to relate to it without fear. I felt like a stone had rolled off my chest."

Eini went on to spearhead the multi-billion dollar project to develop the Lavi, a fighter jet for Israel's Air Force. But before concluding their meeting, the Rebbe advised Eini to write a memoir of his time in captivity. "Unfortunately," he explained, "you will probably not be Israel's last prisoner of war, and others who will be taken captive will benefit from reading about your experience."

EINI RECOUNTED A PARTICULARLY poignant moment in this fateful meeting:

"I told the Rebbe that one of my challenges while in captivity was the pressure from the incessant togetherness. Even as I engaged in personal work, like drawing or writing poetry or journaling, I knew I wasn't alone and others could always look at what I was doing. 'It was always crowded in the room,' I said, 'being together all the time, without even a minute to yourself…'

"After a moment of silence, the Rebbe remarked: 'And yet, despite the togetherness, everyone was left with their own loneliness.'

"I looked at him for a moment and thought: How does he know that?! But I knew he was right. And I also realized that he had insight into how a person could overcome this universal loneliness.

"Today, many years later, I sometimes think that the Rebbe would want me to find this path, too..."[16]

Alone in a Crowd

ON AN ELEMENTARY LEVEL, when we think of loneliness we think of the absence of human interaction; the craving we feel to be with others when we're all alone.

However, as Eini experienced, feeling lonely can mean something deeper than simply wanting to be with other humans. Even when surrounded with many friends it is possible to feel alone on life's journey—that no one is really *with* us; there's no one who truly knows and pays attention to what's going on inside our hearts. Despite the best intentions of the people we spend time with, we might still feel like we carry the burden of life entirely on our own.

When studying the Rebbe's letters, it appears that addressing this core human loneliness sat at the center of his counseling. He sought to provide an antidote to the sadness, the emptiness—the sheer, utter aloneness—that so many endure. He believed that filling this void was critical to becoming a healthy human being. As he wrote to a teenage boy:

> To feel not alone in life (with only you on
> one side, and the entire world on the other)
> is the most important thing of all. A person's
> entire sense of fulfillment and contentment is
> dependent on it...[17]

When the Rebbe assumed leadership in 1950, the world

was still reeling from the devastation of the Second World War and the atrocities of the Holocaust. People were displaced and broken, and many were struggling to find their place—literally and figuratively—in a world that had treated them so brutally. People were thoroughly *alone*. A letter from 1951, addressed to a couple who survived the war, describes this:

> The tremendous upheavals of our generation, which shattered various spiritual foundations and tore many away from deeply rooted traditions—both familial and national—have caused many people to feel like they're suspended in mid-air.... They go about their days thinking they are alone, and each one draws conclusions from these [lonely] thoughts in accordance with their own individual natures and personalities....[18]

Though the world we live in today is far removed from the traumas of the first half of the 20th century, these words still seem to accurately depict the experience of many. Despite living in an age of round-the-clock connection, people feel increasingly isolated.

Clearly, we are all yearning for something more than simply to be with others (physically or digitally). It appears that, ultimately, *"despite the togetherness, everyone is left with their own loneliness."*

So what can allow us to fill this gnawing void?

There are various approaches, ranging from the soberly practical (see chapter 11) to the profoundly existential. In this chapter, we will explore a spiritual response to this most perennial of questions.

The Great Divine Achievement

CHASIDIC TRADITION RECORDS[19] THE following moment:

Once, in the years between 1784 and 1787, the early Chasidim sat together in conversation. Their topic of discussion: What did our Rebbe (Rabbi Shneur Zalman of Liadi) accomplish for the individual by teaching Chasidut? What lack in the individual's subjective experience of life did he fill?

It wasn't Torah study, they agreed, because Torah was already being studied in depth. It wasn't a lack of internal spiritual work—people hadn't known it was necessary to feel it was lacking. It wasn't material wealth—"no one had wealth before and it wasn't necessary; no one has wealth today and it remains unnecessary."

Finally, they hit on it.

"The Rebbe accomplished that we are no longer lonely.

"In the past, the teacher was lonely and the students were lonely. The Chasidic path taught by our Rebbe brought about the great divine achievement that the teacher is no longer lonely, and the students are no longer lonely."

The words of these Chasidic pioneers require explanation. They tell us that the "great divine achievement" of Chasidic teachings is that they profoundly alleviate human loneliness. But how?

In a 1962 letter to a woman who struggled with loneliness (she seems to have been a teacher in her twenties), the Rebbe explained:

> Surely you know the saying that "Chasidut accomplished that a person not be lonely." If this was said even regarding the relationship between a Chasid and his Rebbe [seemingly a relationship of reverence, which conjures

distance], all the more so is this true regarding the relationship between one person and another. And certainly regarding the [loving] relationship between G-d and the Jewish people.

This is better understood in light of the foundational teaching of our Torah, the Torah of life, about G-d's individual providence—which means, quite literally, that G-d closely oversees every detail of a person's life with individual attention. And His providence and His blessings and His nurture are one and the same, because they are sourced in He Who is simple oneness.

From these ideas emerge—and these ideas inform—a person's practical, emotional, and intellectual approach to life: Every individual finds themselves in a world (composed of human, animal, plant, and inanimate kingdoms, each consisting of multitudes of beings) that he or she influences, and is simultaneously influenced by them as well.... Thus, every being is full of meaning, at least potentially, and it is up to the individual person to activate this meaning so that it moves from potential to actuality....

Especially in your case, where divine providence has put you in the field of educating children.... Every good step you take with your students creates an eternal closeness between you and them, a spiritual and sacred bond that is also tangibly positive and meaningful. When it comes to such a bond, the distance of space does not and cannot create a barrier, and no severance of this bond is possible (which is why it remains eternal).

In other words, when you sit in your room and find yourself overcome with loneliness, and at the very same time one of your students reviews a lesson they heard from you, or makes a blessing as you taught them, [physical distance notwithstanding,] this increases the vitality and light in your bond with each other; and it is impossible that your divine soul not feel this increase, because it is part of your soul's very essence; and the soul, in turn, is the deepest, innermost part of a person.[20]

IT SEEMS, THEN, THAT this was the meaning of the early Chasidim:

A surface-level perspective on existence sees each person as a lone creature in a vast and unfeeling world. We're all particles flying through space; we're all people whose interests, nefarious or noble, happen to converge. In the end, when you look reality hard in the face, you are all alone.

The Chasidic masters sought to change that. They opened people's minds to a higher perspective: There is a divine presence in the world. There is a divine presence in your life. There is a divine presence in your relationships with others. You are always in the company of G-d. You are truly connected to the people in your life. In the end, when you look reality deep in the face, you are never alone.

The aforementioned letter to a teenager proceeds to drive this point home:

For those who think deeply into their personal world, the only way to truly counter the sense of being alone in life ["only you on one side and the entire world on the other"], is with an awareness of the Creator and Conductor of the world, who is ever present in the world, even today—in the expression of our Sages, "within ten *tefachim* of the ground"[21] [i.e., within our own lived reality].[22]

Let's unpack this a little more.

"G-d is Your Friend"

FOR MILLENNIA, PHILOSOPHERS, THEOLOGIANS, and thinking individuals have mulled over the foundational questions about G-d and His relationship with the world.

Some have posited that the Creator of the universe has abandoned it to fend for itself, leaving it and all its inhabitants to navigate existence on their own. Others have opined that He is only involved in the great world events that alter the course of history, or in the fundamental principles that govern nature, but the petty details of any one individual's life are too inconsequential for Him to be concerned with.

The Chassidic masters thought differently.[23] They taught that far from abandoning the universe, G-d is intimately involved in the world. He is always present at the side of every individual, no matter their spiritual level or place in society, and all the occurrences in their lives are intrinsically important to Him.

The following two Chasidic principles are repeatedly found in the Rebbe's counseling:[24]

First, G-d is directly involved in even the smallest details of our lives.

Second, as he once put it to a young man: "G-d is your friend."[25] G-d is not out to get us. He is the essence of goodness and kindness and always looks out for our best interests.[26]

Reflecting on these two ideas can help us replace our fears of being alone in a brutal world with the serenity of being in the company and care of G-d, Whose greatness surpasses every challenge and Whose kindness is total and unwavering. Unlike many human relationships that falter and sometimes fail, often leaving us feeling even more alone, G-d's presence and interest are constant. He has no external reasons for being in your life. It is you He is interested in.

Irving Block was a philosophy student at Harvard University in the mid-1950s when he was drawn to the Rebbe's teachings and came to study under his tutelage for a period. Throughout Block's time in New York, the Rebbe would often ask him about his mother, who had been widowed at a young age and lived in Nashville, Tennessee.

One day, Block's mother traveled to New York and told her son that she wanted to meet the Rebbe he had told her so much about. Block was able to arrange a meeting, but she told him not to accompany her; she wanted to go in alone. After the meeting, she told him what she had discussed with the Rebbe: that she had two sisters, both married, but that she was alone. "On Friday nights when I light the Shabbat candles, I'm all by myself, and I feel very lonely."

Block was embarrassed by his mother's words, feeling that this was an inappropriate emotion with which to approach the Rebbe, particularly at a first encounter. But the Rebbe, it turned out, didn't feel that way at all. He simply told her, "You don't have to feel lonely. *Der Aibershter is alle mol mit dir*—G-d Almighty is with you all the time."

Block recalls: "My mother came out and she was calm." After that day, whenever he asked his mother how she was feeling, she would answer, "Come on now, G-d is always with me." Indeed, she told her son that from the time that the Rebbe told her those words, she was not lonely in the same way anymore.[27]

BEING MINDFUL OF G-D'S presence does more than ease loneliness.

When you truly know and feel that you're not alone, when you internalize that the Master of the universe, the benevolent Creator of all things, is eternally with you—it can transform your whole approach to life. The way you move through the world and participate in society takes on a different spirit.

The fragile vulnerabilities so inherent to the human condition—the insecurities, the fears, the need to impress—are significantly diminished. In its place, a quiet confidence emerges. Importantly, as the Rebbe would emphasize, this healthy backbone does not manifest in arrogance toward other people.[28] It puts you *and others* at ease to navigate life with strength, fearlessness, and kindness.

Following are a few examples.

With a Head Held High

1927 WAS A VIOLENT year in Soviet Russia. Stalin had all but solidified his hold on power, outmaneuvering his rivals for absolute dominance of the Communist party. In February, the infamous Article 58, authorizing the prosecution of anyone suspected of counter-revolutionary activities, was passed, and the savage elimination of all "enemies of the people" was in full swing. For the Jewish community, this meant the destruction of centuries of painstakingly built Jewish infrastructure.

On June 15th, after midnight, the authorities raided the home of Rabbi Yosef Yitzchak Schneersohn (the sixth Lubavitcher Rebbe, 1880-1950) who was running an underground network of Jewish life. They took him to Spalerno prison—a facility notorious for its wholesale executions, torturous interrogations, and sadistic cruelty. From the first minute of his arrest, they unleashed on Rabbi Yosef Yitzchak the full scope of their physical brutality and abusive mind-games. In a journal he wrote a year after his imprisonment, he recorded what went through his mind upon arrival at Spalerno:

> What is happening in our home now? I thought.
>
> This question overwhelmed me. Knowing thoroughly the character, nature, and behavior of each individual, I was able to imagine the general picture—
>
> The tears of my honorable mother. The pale, apprehensive face and the deep inner anguish of my wife, and her silent cry. The broken hearts and terror of my bewildered daughters.... And who knows what is happening with all of our friends, the Chasidim. How are they doing? This image swept over me and a stream broke from my eyes. Hot tears rolled down my face. My whole body shivered....
>
> Halt those ruminations! These words flashed

in my mind and lit up my thoughts like a bolt of lighting—What about G-d? True, I am a son, I am a husband, I am a father, I am a father-in-law, I love and I am loved; they are all dependent upon me, but I and they in turn are dependent upon G-d Who spoke and created the world.... At this moment I was liberated from the mire and dread of my situation. I ascended to the starry heavens with thoughts beyond the confines of finite, physical existence. I was bolstered by pure faith and absolute trust in the living G-d....

These thoughts revitalized my spirit and strengthened me immensely. I forgot my present state and I sat in complete calm. My thoughts began to settle.... I came to the firm resolve to be strong and courageous, without fear. To speak with a clear voice and to disregard my surroundings. This determined resolution raised my spirits and self-respect. I sat like I was in a garden, or strolling in the breeze. The sunlight lit up the white wall across me....[29]

Fifty years later, the Rebbe (Rabbi Yosef Yitzchak's son-in-law and successor) shared this account with a woman who expressed that she is alone:

I want to respond to what you wrote that you are alone. We would often hear from my saintly father-in-law, of blessed memory (whose fiftieth anniversary of liberation [from Soviet prison] we celebrated this week...), that one is never alone; the Almighty G-d oversees each and every person individually, even over the smallest details of their life....

In the journal he wrote about his imprisonment, my father-in-law describes how this idea—that the Creator and Conductor of the universe watches over everyone individually—gave him the strength and courage to rise above despair even while being in an awful prison, in a terrible situation.... And this fortified him to endure all the interrogations and suffering with his head held high and with pride.

His intention in committing these memories to writing, which he requested to be published, was that every individual [who reads] these records learn from them and act similarly in their own lives. And although who can compare themselves to his exalted persona... nevertheless, after he granted us a living example and paved the way for us, this is now accessible to every individual in their own personal situation. Especially since the difficulties we face in our lives do not compare to the type of adversity he overcame.[30]

I Shall Fear Not

SOMETIME IN THE FIRST millennium BCE, a young King David composed the following, while hiding from mortal enemies in the wilderness of the Judean hills:[31] "G-d is my shepherd; I shall not want.... Even when I walk in the valley of darkness, I will fear no evil—for You are with me.... Only goodness and kindness will follow me all the days of my life" (Chapter 23 of Psalms).

In 1968, a woman wrote to the Rebbe that she was extremely anxious about other people and what they might be saying about her. In addition to advising her to take anti-anxiety pills if recommended by a professional, the Rebbe suggested:

> Study Chapter 23 of Psalms until you are well versed in its content (not necessarily the exact words; and it also does not matter in which language you study it).... In the future, pay no attention at all if somebody speaks about you; don't even ask them about it [i.e., if they spoke about you]. For (as stated in the chapter of Psalms) "G-d is with you" and "only goodness and kindness will follow you." Consequently, no one at all can—Heaven forbid—have power over you.[32]

ON A PERSONAL NOTE, I once met someone who lived a lifetime with these words from King David.

It was on a Chasidic holiday a few years back. A few friends and I—all teenagers—knocked on the door of a modest home in an Israeli town. Here, we had heard, lived someone worth listening to.

A short, vibrant old man opened the door. "Come, come inside," he said. "On a special night like this, I want you to sit with me." He invited us to find seats around a little dining room table, upon which rested an open Chasidic manuscript. "This is the Chasidic discourse I'm in the middle of committing to memory," he said, in the way one makes small talk about the day's events with a new friend.

His name was Avrohom Lison. He was 92 years old.

Lison was born in 1922 to a Chasidic family in Ponevezh, Lithuania. With the outbreak of WWII, his blissful childhood came to an end, and at 17 he was forced to escape Lithuania by himself. For years he wandered alone through the endless Russian terrain, trying to outpace the German advance, the Luftwaffe's incessant bombardment, and pervasive hunger. In the meantime, his entire family was slaughtered by the Nazis. After the war ended, he ultimately made it to Israel where he went on to establish a large family.

"Children," he told us in Yiddish, "I've seen a thing or two in life, and I want to tell you something: Money comes and goes. Honor comes and goes. It all gets blown away by the wind. The only thing that stays with you for a lifetime is a little bit of *pnimiyut*,[33] a little depth of spirit. And this you can acquire through working hard to internalize the teachings of our Rebbes.

"When I came to the Rebbe, I sensed the aura of Paradise; I felt what it means to live a passionate life in awareness of the benevolent divine presence."

He then taught us a song. The tune was an old Chasidic melody. But he had melded it with the original Hebrew words of King David. He closed his eyes and sang:

"Even when I walk in the valley of darkness,

Ayayay...

I shall not fear, because you are with me.

Ayayayay..."

When I looked at his face, I saw a little tear in the corner of his eye.

"Okay, children, I'm not feeling so well, and you need to sleep too. This was rejuvenating. Be well, and be Chasidim."

Two weeks later, I bumped into him in the side room of a synagogue. His bike, which he rode till his last days, was parked right outside. I wanted to hear that song again, and I

asked him if he could perhaps sing it for me. "Sure," he said. He closed his eyes and sang with all his heart:
"Even when I walk in the valley of darkness,
Ayayay...
I shall not fear, because you are with me.
Ayayay..."
When he finished singing, he looked up and told me matter-of-factly: "Whenever I feel myself in danger—it might be a physical danger or a spiritual one—I sing this song to myself and it calms me. G-d is always with me, it reminds me. I have nothing to fear." Then he got onto his bike and rode away.

You Can Do Big Things

ONE LAST STORY:

As a young rabbinical student in the 1970s, Benzion Milecki traveled from Australia to New York to study under the Rebbe's tutelage. Like many people in their early twenties, Milecki had various spiritual dilemmas on which he wanted to receive the Rebbe's counsel. One of them was his lack of self-confidence.

"Throughout my school years, my teachers would write in my report cards that I didn't have enough confidence in myself; that I didn't have sufficient appreciation of my talents," Milecki recalled.

"This continued through my teens. It wasn't that I felt inadequate or weak—in my own personal life I was a high-achiever, setting goals and pursuing them successfully. But I was introverted. I perceived myself as a small guy who did small things in his own private world. I didn't consider myself someone who could make big things happen in the big world.

"In 1977, I finally had the opportunity to obtain a long-awaited private audience with the Rebbe. In the note I handed to him, I wrote about my lack of self-confidence.

"The Rebbe said to me, 'Regarding your lack of faith in yourself, you should study the beginning of Chapter 41 of *Tanya*, where it says that just as a person looks at you, so too is G-d looking at you.'

"'This thought,' he continued, 'will give you the confidence you need. Use it for good things.'

"This audience was transformative for me. I came out feeling like I could fly. Like I could achieve great things. I remained exhilarated for many days after.

"What I found most enlightening was how the Rebbe interpreted G-d's constant 'look.' In earlier Chasidic teachings, this concept is primarily taught as a meditation to inspire awe of Heaven, as a warning to keep one's behavior in check. But the Rebbe was teaching me that G-d's constant 'look' should inspire confidence! You're not alone in life. G-d is there for you, He cares about you, He is at your side. You can feel empowered. You can feel strong. My problem with confidence has basically left me since then.

"Even today, when on occasion I experience a loss of confidence, focusing on that 'look' and those moments with the Rebbe causes my confidence to return."

"To be honest," Milecki told me over the phone, "words are only containers. The transformative impact of that private audience was in the experience, in the way the Rebbe expressed it, in the way he looked up at me when he said, 'just as a person looks at you, so too is G-d looking at you.' Simply transcribing the words won't capture why that meeting changed me."

I responded that unfortunately I'm writing a book, which is made of, well, words...

"Try your best," he replied.

RABBI MENACHEM M. SCHNEERSON
Lubavitch
770 Eastern Parkway
Brooklyn 13, N. Y.

HYacinth 3-9250

רל שניאורסאהן
באויטש

מנחם מענדעל
וקלין, נ. י.

By the Grace of G-d
In the Days of Sel[i]
200th Anniversary o[f]
Histalkus of the Baa[l]
of blessed memory.
Brooklyn, N. Y.

Mr.

Greeting and Blessing:

With the approach of Rosh Hashan[a] begining of the New Year, may it brin[g] blessings to us all, I send you and a[ll] yours my prayerful wishes for a good [and] happy year, materially and spirituall[y].

With the traditional blessin[g]

כתיבה וחתימה טובה

Cordially M. Schne[erson]

I received your letter of the 6th of
and the previous one. In the meanti[me]
my reply was received to my letter to yo[ur]
father.

CHAPTER 2

- 2 -   In the Days of
         Selichoth, 5720

As for your moods and feeling of lonliness, etc., surely there is no room for it in the light of the teachings of the Baal Shem Tov and the true concept of Divine Providence which extends to each and every individual and in every aspect of life. The realization of this must instill a deep feeling of confidence and optimism, and you will do well to reflect on this subject.

I trust that you have taken full advantage of the auspicious days of the Season of our Rejoicing, to be inspired and to inspire others in the fullest measure, and to carry this joy over to last through the year.

I hope to hear good news from you.

Takeaway

Know that you are never alone. The Master of the Universe is always at your side.

He is your *friend!*

If you ever feel small or lonely inside our cavernous and impersonal world, or contend with the dispiriting notion that everything you do is, in the larger scheme of things, worthless—meditate on these simple facts:

G-d is with you as you negotiate life's challenges, and everything you do is important to Him, regardless of how people evaluate it. He is always available to you, even when you've messed up, and His love for you is unconditional.

To reflect regularly on these principles is to build a healthy psyche and unassailable self-esteem.

In the next chapter, we'll explore how this outlook can transform your perception of your own role in the world.

Chapter 3
Recognize Your Unique Role

There can be two approaches to life:
 (a) To consider it as a matter of pleasure—in which case every effort should be bent towards getting the most out of life, in terms of pleasure; and in every situation to seek the easiest way out.
 (b) To consider life as a challenge, and to help make a better world to live in, especially since the society we live in is far from perfection. In this case, every effort must be bent towards this end, even if it means the sacrifice of certain personal pleasures, and even if it requires a great deal of continuous physical and mental exertion.
 But, as a matter of fact, it is this latter approach that offers the maximum pleasure—real pleasure and gratification.[34]
 —Fall, 1961

KABBALAH TEACHES[35] THAT HUMANITY'S task is to transform the world from brokenness to wholeness, from darkness to light, from disparate pieces to divine oneness.

Every person's soul descends to Earth to play a distinct role in this shared mission. Each person is allocated a part of the world to uplift and sanctify, beginning with their own mind and body.[36] Providence orchestrates that everyone ends up in the exact place that's uniquely meant for them.[37] And there are no spare pieces in this cosmic plan.

Just as in a well-kept home everything is in its proper place, for a designated purpose, and there aren't random objects lying around—the same is true for the universe.[38] Nothing and no one is here by mistake. Everybody has a role that they—and only they—can fulfill.

In 1943, just two years after escaping a burning Europe and witnessing firsthand the destruction humanity can bring upon itself, the Rebbe wrote an opening letter for a Jewish calendar he was creating for American children. Addressing "My dear young friend," the Rebbe explained that the task of a human being is to actively work to make the world a better and brighter place, and thereby "bring true happiness to ourselves and to the world around us." The note continues:

> And let no one say, "What can I do to help in this lofty task?" For this world is a great royal palace, the palace of G-d, King of the universe, erected out of numerous component parts, big and small. Even the smallest particle of the great edifice would leave a gap if it were missing. Each one of us *must*, therefore, do our share….
>
> We trust that you will do your share with all your heart, and we wish you success.[39]

CHAPTER 3

༄

AN UNDERLYING THEME THROUGHOUT the Rebbe's correspondences is the attempt to expand people's self-perception, to help them view themselves as an indispensable part of something greater than themselves, to inspire them to recognize how within their own lives, circumstances, and talents lies an opportunity—and responsibility—to fulfill a unique purpose.[40]

To the rebellious young adult first charting their path in the world, he would explain that their youthful contrarian energy is a powerful, once-in-a-lifetime force that they can—and must!—harness for the good.[41]

To the businessperson, he would explain how they can make their work meaningful by finding opportunities to provide spiritual and material help to their colleagues and giving charity from their earnings.[42]

To the stay-at-home parent, he would explain how the imprint of the early days of childhood has a long-term impact on the future adult and how G-d has entrusted them with the tremendous task of nurturing and educating this child, thus shaping countless generations ahead.[43]

To retirees, he would explain how the easing of work pressures provides an opportunity to study and volunteer on a whole new level, and encouraged them to share their hard-earned life wisdom with younger generations.[44]

To all types of people, in every station of life, he would try to impart the recognition that their specific position offers a special framework for fulfilling their designated purpose. Three examples follow.

Marcia Greensite grew up in San Diego, California. After completing her degree in psychology at UCSD, she took a job as a research assistant studying autism at the UCLA Neuropsychiatric Institute, while being active after hours at the local Chabad house (a center for all Jewish needs). At a certain point she decided to write to the Rebbe.

"I began," Greensite recalled, "by writing how old I was and what I was doing. My secular job, I wrote, was at UCLA, and then I went on to say that I considered my activities at the Chabad house to be my real work. At the time, my passion lay in my work at the Chabad house, and I considered my research work at the Institute to be simply a job.

"Where I had written 'my secular job,' the Rebbe crossed out *secular*, leaving 'my job,' and expounded in the margin, 'the purpose of which is the emotional wellbeing and healing of children.' Clearly, he saw it as not simply a mundane occupation, but as a divine mission."

Today Greensite is the executive director of a behavioral therapy agency that serves over one hundred children with special needs as well as a family therapist with a focus on teenagers. "Working with children became my life's work," Greensite says, "so the Rebbe's message means a lot to me."[45]

BARUCH NACHSHON WAS BORN in 1939 in Haifa, Mandatory Palestine, to a traditional Jewish family of European emigrants. An artistic, individualistic, and some might say eccentric soul, he began to draw at an early age. (He credited his kindergarten teacher with discovering his talent; she explained simply, "If I wanted quiet in class, I had to give this boy a paintbrush.")

As an adolescent, he didn't do well within the rigid structure of school and would often roam the fields and hills nearby. "Classes were stifling," he recalled. "Their only redeeming factor was that they caused my mind to wander." For his military service, he herded flocks for the army.

While his academic studies felt cold and uninteresting, he made significant strides in his artistic aspirations. He studied with Shlomo Nerani, a pupil of the Post-Impressionist artist Paul Cézanne, and would watch him work for long hours. They grew close, and Nerani considered Nachshon his artistic heir. However, alongside his artistic growth, a dark inner void gnawed at Nachshon, and he struggled with depression.

At some point, he happened upon the teachings of the Chasidic masters, and something there touched him.

"When my future wife expressed interest in marrying me, I told her she must understand what I was up to. I didn't want to have children; I didn't want a family; I didn't feel a desire for anything. Everything looked black to me. The only thing I wanted was to travel to New York and go see the Rebbe. I sensed he was a man of truth amid this empty world of falsehood. If she was open to marrying a guy like that, I was down. Amazingly, she agreed."

The newlywed couple saved whatever money they could, and in 1964, they set out on a grueling two-week boat journey to America. Soon after arriving, Nachshon had a private audience with the Rebbe that lasted for three hours.

"I did most of the talking, opening up all the dark thoughts and doubts that perturbed me, while the Rebbe listened closely. As the minutes passed, I felt that I was being raised from all the mire and darkness, that I was being freed from my personal Egypt that had been enslaving me for so long. I was slowly feeling whole again.

"At one point in the meeting, I said that because of all the inner turmoil I'd gone through in life, it was hard for me to be joyous. The Rebbe proposed a deal: When I felt the need, I could smile at him and he would smile back. And that's what I would do. When I felt depressed, I would stand near the Rebbe's office when he was scheduled to leave, and I would smile. He would always respond to me with a big broad smile of his own that in turn would resuscitate my spirit.

"At the very end of my audience, the Rebbe told me something that has stayed with me my whole life: 'The talent of art has so often been misused; it is your task to elevate it.' He then advised me to stay in New York for a year or two, explaining that there were good art teachers there and that this would allow me to perfect my talent. I walked out of the Rebbe's study a different man."

The following lines, which dominate a page in the unruly notebook of drawings, sketches, and musings that Nachshon kept a few years after this audience, appear to express his existential shift:

Everything considered—It's all quite boring!
If there is nothing, one must create it.
This is all.
Signed,
Baruch Nachshon

After a few years of study in the U.S., Nachshon and his wife moved back to Israel. He spent the rest of his life drawing spirited paintings about the soul's yearning for divine connection, bringing into vivid color some of the foundational teachings of Torah and Kabbalah. Occasionally, after spending time with his many children and grandchildren, he would stand up and head to his art studio. Echoing the Rebbe's words to him, he would explain with a smile, "Sorry for leaving you; I have some 'elevating' to do."[46]

(I heard this story firsthand from Nachshon in his home, two years before his passing.)

AVRAHAM ZIGMAN, WHO SERVED for decades as a radio musical editor and program presenter, recalled the following from his own encounter with the Rebbe.

"During my audience, the Rebbe spoke with me about the best uses for one's G-d-given talents. If someone has a certain talent, no matter what his field of endeavor is, he should use it to spread the light of Torah. If he does not do so, he is harming creation. Why? Because G-d entrusted him to utilize his talents and strengths to do good in this world.

"The Rebbe went on to address the medium of radio specifically. He explained that radio waves are especially powerful because they penetrate closed doors and places that are normally hard to reach. He added that those who work in radio must be extra careful. We must never hurt others through this medium by insulting or slandering people, or even just by speaking badly of others. We must watch carefully what comes out of our mouths and keep our language clean of crude or obscene words.

"I took his message to heart. I knew well that many songs that we played on the radio used coarse language, curse words, and a style of expression that was not appropriate. Therefore, someone like me, who made decisions about what we would broadcast, had to be careful to choose only those songs that were clean. And ever since the Rebbe brought this to my attention, I have followed his guidance in this regard."[47]

What Does This Mean in My Life?

FULFILLING OUR TASK DOESN'T necessarily mean we have to do something earth-shattering.

The great Chasidic master, Rabbi Meshulam Zusha of Anipoli (1718–1800), was known to say: "When I get to heaven, they won't ask me why I wasn't Moses. They won't ask me why I wasn't my brother. What they *will* ask me is why weren't you Zusha?! To this I will have to answer."

"Generally speaking," reads a letter to a young woman,
> every thinking person, looking around and reflecting upon the important events that take place in the world, is inclined to think in terms of big personal accomplishments, which are sometimes beyond one's capacity.
>
> However, G-d—Who is the essence of goodness, and "it is the nature of goodness to do good"—does not expect anyone to do more than [they can] in accordance with the capacities which He bestowed upon the person, and which G-d desires [to] be utilized to the full.[48]

Similarly, a letter to a couple working in the army, who wrote of their despondent moods and how their lives felt gray and insignificant, offers this explanation:
> Some possible advice for your [dejected] moods: Reflect on the fact that every person is an emissary of G-d to do good and increase good in His world.
>
> This is typically not accomplished through revolutions or roaring self-sacrifice, but rather through living daily life based on *Shulchan*

Aruch [the Code of Jewish Conduct]; gradual self-education; and *activism* to help those in your surroundings, even if most of these activities are labeled by the world as "gray" and "insignificant." All of this is possible on the "gray" days in the army as well.

May G-d grant you and your husband success in bringing the potential *given to you* to actuality, and to serve G-d with joy.[49]

Of course, it is not always obvious how we can best fulfill our personal missions within our specific circumstances. It may be at work, after hours, or at home. However, there is certainly a way we can contribute, and when we know this with confidence, it animates our search. As this letter to an elderly man explains:

When we think about the world, we recognize that everything, even in the inanimate realm, is organized with strict laws, everything has its place and function, and there is nothing that exists without purpose. This is certainly true for human beings who have been gifted with intellect.... Therefore, there is no doubt that everyone has a mission and role in life.

True, it is not always easy to find the right field and channel, but we are guaranteed that "if you toil you will succeed." The complete confidence that there is something to search for and that we were given the ability not only to search but also to find helps ensure the success of the search and discovery. I am confident that with a proper search you will find your way of influencing and contributing to your surroundings."[50]

The impact we can make on our environments through our own personal growth should not be underestimated either.

Gordon Zacks was an American businessman, philanthropist, and presidential advisor. In his twenties, he had a long personal audience with the Rebbe.

"He said something that was very profound and very real: 'Remember, Mr. Zacks, if you want to change the world, you must first change yourself.

"'When you change, it's like dropping a pebble in a lake. There are ripples that go out from the point of contact, which influence all those around you. If you change and become connected to G-d in your soul, and as a consequence you behave in a manner that G-d would require of you, it will impact the people around you. And the power of that impact is the first and the most important step toward making the world a better place. So remember to focus on yourself first.'"[51]

In Dark Times

WHILE A SENSE OF purpose is always vital, it can be particularly potent for getting through hard times. It tells a person: There is a reason for you to fight. There is a reason for you to be resilient. There is a reason why you—yes, you—need to be here.

The following is a letter to a teenager who wrote of her despondency and unproductive lifestyle. It seems that she had lost all motivation and faith in herself, and consequently developed a pessimistic outlook on her future. The response begins by assuring her that, contrary to her present self-perception, she has a lot to contribute:

> Understandably, I do not agree at all with the foundations upon which you construct your views [of yourself] and your subsequent conclusions. By this I mean that I believe them to not be grounded in reality. Your current state of mind is only temporary, and the more effort you put in, the quicker it will change. It is absolutely clear that you have the power and also the talent to be of benefit not only to yourself but to others as well. Only, like all matters in this world, it is necessary to reveal and develop this potential into reality, which almost always takes effort. However, this is a degree of effort that is eminently attainable.
>
> When one considers that their relatively brief efforts will benefit themselves and others for many years to come, improving their and the community's welfare—spiritually, materially, or both—and that these improvements will likely have a ripple effect and reach even further, then one will easily appreciate that their efforts and exertions to achieve this end are well worthwhile.
>
> Without a doubt, in the vast majority of instances, it is impossible to radically change one's frame of mind instantaneously. However, this is not what is required. It will suffice that upon receiving my letter you will resolve to move in the right *direction*—to begin leading a productive life. Start by taking a first step

in this direction, and then, step by step in an accumulating progression, you will soon find yourself on the road to a life that brings you contentment and self-satisfaction.

If you wish to heed my advice, continue your studies next year, but in addition to studying, you should also involve yourself with providing education—it would be best to do so several times a week. My intent is that you organize groups of children and be their counselor, or even teach them subjects that can be understood on their level, holding Shabbat and festival get-togethers for them and similar activities.

Think to yourself: There is so much to accomplish in the world, there is so much potential in every single person, but because of the vast amount of work to be done we can't afford to give up on even one capability or talent. It is [therefore] the mission of every single person to activate *all* the potentials and talents they possess to improve their part of the world.

The beginning, as with everything, starts with learning the profession, acquiring necessary knowledge in general, and especially the knowledge that is necessary for using the individual's unique talents. When you think about this once and again, my hope is that you will start being active [in the above] right away and will not be fazed by the work and effort.

Shortly you will also see good fruits from your labor.⁵²

Ruth Benjamin was born to Christian parents and raised in South Africa. In her twenties, she converted to Judaism and later developed a relationship with the Rebbe. A clinical psychologist by profession, she consulted with the Rebbe on how to counsel patients who questioned the value of their lives. (She was an active member of the Jewish community, and a large number of her patients were Jewish.)

Benjamin recalled: "Regarding my Jewish patients, he said that I should tell them that following the Holocaust, with so many millions of our people murdered, those alive today have a double duty. They must live not only for themselves, but also for those who are not here. When they realize this, they will find that their own turmoil will be eased.

"Regarding my patients who aren't Jewish, the Rebbe said I must explain to them that they have obligations in this world. All human beings are mandated by the Torah to fulfill the Seven Laws of Noah [seven ethical principles given to all humankind to ensure a society of justice and kindness].

"I cited an example of a suicidal patient of mine (who wasn't Jewish), whom I managed to get to the hospital in time, saving his life. Afterward, he came to me and said, 'You are responsible for my being alive. Now give me something to live for.' I had not known how to answer him, and I asked the Rebbe what I should say to a patient like this.

"'Tell him that he is part of G-d's world,' the Rebbe responded. 'And that means, he has to answer to G-d.'"⁵³

RABBI MENACHEM M. SCHNEERSON
Lubavitch
770 Eastern Parkway
Brooklyn. N. Y. 11213
493-9250

מנחם מענדל שניאורסאהן
ליובאוויטש

770 איסטערן פארקוויי
ברוקלין, נ. י.

By the Grace of G-d
23rd of Shevat, 5744
Brooklyn, N. Y.

Dr.

New York, N. Y.

Blessing and Greeting:

This is in reply to your letter of Jan. 23, 1984, in which you write that you were born in a DP camp in Germany, a child of parents who survived the Holocaust, and you ask why G-d permitted the Holocaust to take place, etc.

No doubt you know that there is a substantial literature dealing with this terrible tragedy, and a letter is hardly the medium to deal adequately with the question.

However, since you have written to me, I must give you some answer. Hence, the following thoughts.

Jews - including you and me - are "believers, the children of believers," our Sages declare. Deep in one's heart every Jew believes there is a G-d Who is the Creator and Master of the world, and that the world has a purpose. Any thinking person who contemplates the Solar System, for example, the complexities of an atom, must come to the conclusion and conviction that our universe did not come about by some "freak accident." Wherever you turn, you see design and purpose.

It follows that a human being "also" has a purpose, certainly where millions of human beings are concerned.

Since the Creator created the world with a purpose, it is also logical to assume that He wished the purpose to be realized, and therefore would reveal to the (only) creature on earth who has an intelligence to understand such matters, namely, mankind, what this purpose is, and how to go about realizing it. This, indeed, is the ultimate purpose of every human being, namely, to do his or her share in the realization of the Divine design and purpose of Creation.

It is also common sense that without such Divine revelation, a human being would not, of his own accord, have known what exactly is that purpose and how to achieve it, any more than a minuscule part or component in a highly complex system could comprehend the whole system, much less the creator of the system.

The illustration often given in this connection is the case of an infant, whose lack of ability to understand an intricate theory of a mature scientist, would not surprise anyone, although both the infant and the scientist are created beings, and the difference between them is only relative, in terms of age and knowledge, etc. Indeed, it is possible that the infant may some day

CHAPTER 3

- 2 -

Dr.

surpass the scientist in knowledge and insight. Should it, then, be surprising that a created human being cannot understand the ways of the Creator?

It is also understandable that since every person has a G-d-given purpose in life, he or she is provided with the capacity to carry out that purpose fully.

A further important point to remember is that since G-d created everything with a purpose, there is nothing lacking nor superfluous in the world. This includes also the human capacity.

It follows that a person's capacity in terms of knowledge, time, energy, etc., must fully be applied to carrying out his, or her, purpose in life. If any of these resources is diverted to something that is extraneous to carrying out the Divine purpose, it would not only be misused and wasteful, but would detract to that extent from the real purpose.

In the Torah, called Toras Chaim ("instruction in living"), G-d has revealed what the purpose of Creation is, and provided all the knowledge necessary for a human being, particularly a Jew, to carry it out in life. Having designated the Jewish people as a "Kingdom of Kohanim (G-d's servants) and a holy nation," a Jew is required to live up to all the Divine Precepts (Mitzvoth) in the Torah. Gentiles are required to keep only the Seven Basic Moral Laws - the so-called Seven Noahite Laws with all their ramifications - which must be the basis of any and every human society, if it is to be human in accordance with the will and design of the Creator.

One of the basic elements of the Divine design, as revealed in the Torah, is that G-d desires it to be carried out by choice and not out of compulsion. Every human being has, therefore, the free will to live in accordance with G-d's Will, or in defiance of it.

With all the above in mind, let us return to your question, which is one that has been on the minds of many: Why did G-d permit the Holocaust?

The only answer we can give is: Only G-d knows.

However, the very fact that there is no answer to this question is, in itself, proof that one is not required to know the answer, or understand it, in order to fulfill one's purpose in life. Despite the lack of a satisfactory answer to the awesome and tremendous 'Why?" - one can, and must, carry on a meaningful and productive life, promote justice and kindness in one's surroundings, and, indeed, help create a world where there should be no room for any holocaust, or for any kind of man's inhumanity to man.

As a matter of fact, in the above there is an answer to an unspoken question: "What should my reaction be?" The answer to this question is certain: It must be seen as a challenge to every Jew - because Jews were the principal victims of the Holocaust - a challenge that should be met head-on, with all resolve and determination, namely, that regardless how long it will take the world to repent for the Holocaust and make the world a fitting place to live in for all human beings - I, for one, will not slacken in my determination to
*)=the not being given the answer" and at the same time being expected to serve Hashem etc. -

- 3 -

Dr.

carry out my purpose in life, which is to serve G-d, wholeheartedly and with joy, and make this world a fitting abode - not only for humans, but also for the <u>Shechina</u>, the Divine Presence Itself.

Of course, much more could be said on the subject, but why dwell on such a painful matter, when there is so much good to be done?

With blessing, M. Schneerson

P.S. Needless to say, the above may be accepted intellectually, and it may ease the mind, but it cannot assuage the pain and upheaval/of one who has /especially been directly victimized by the Holocaust.

Thus, in this day and age of rampant suspicion, etc., especially when one is not known personally, one may perhaps say - "Well, it is easy for one who is not emotionally involved to give an 'intellectual' explanation...."

So, I ought, perhaps, to add that I, too, lost in the Holocaust very close and dear relatives such as a grandmother, brother, cousins and others ה׳׳יד . But, life must go on, and the sign of life is in growth and creativity. (according to Mitzvath <u>Hashem</u>)

Takeaway

You were endowed with a special role, to uplift and sanctify your own mind and body, as well as a portion of this world that was set aside just for you. You were given everything you need to succeed at this task.

Consider your unique circumstances, that distinctive confluence of matters like: family, friends, community, occupation, schooling, neighborhood, and more.

Think about your talents, your knowledge, and your expertise. Together, these comprise the highly personalized tools, opportunities, and challenges that were assigned to you to fulfill your unique purpose on earth.

Reflect on your personal mission regularly, and follow up with mission-centered activity. This will help you stay focused and navigate life's many challenges with clarity and confidence.

So far, we explored three essential outlooks for a healthy self:

- Cultivate a giving mindset.
- Know that G-d is always with you.
- Embrace your special mission on earth.

The next two chapters (4-5) discuss practical lifestyle tools that form the bedrock of emotional wellness.

Chapter 4
Build Healthy Habits

REUVEN DONIN WAS A man who did things all the way.

Raised in the traditional Jewish environment of pre-independence Jerusalem, he left his studies as a teenager to go live on a kibbutz and work the land. A tough youngster, full of energy and uncompromising chutzpah (which earned him quite a reputation), he would compensate for his grueling days of labor with long nights of partying with fellow rebels and friends. "It was full-time life without pause," he later recalled.

However, during the long hours on his tractor, alone with nature, "I would think a lot about the world; I would ask questions and search for answers." Over time he was introduced to the teachings of Chasidut, and he began to study it seriously. Being the uncompromising character that he was, in 1958 he left his native country and went to the Rebbe's yeshiva in New York. There he dedicated all of his energy to immersive study and self-refinement, and he developed a close personal bond with the Rebbe.

One night, Donin entered the Rebbe's study for an audience in an emotionally charged state. He sat down and passionately exclaimed, "Rebbe, I can't take the struggles of life! I just want to stay here in this room forever…. I just can't anymore…."

The response was not what he was expecting.

"Did you eat properly today?" the Rebbe asked.

When Donin answered in the negative, the Rebbe instructed him to go eat immediately, and counseled him on the general importance of taking care of his body and the impact it would have on his emotions. He then gave him detailed guidance for what he should do daily to properly care for his bodily health.

Over the next few months, when the Rebbe would see Donin, he would often ask him whether and what he was eating, how long he was sleeping (reminding him of Maimonides' ruling that a person should sleep between six and eight hours a night[54]), and whether he was taking walks and getting fresh air between his hours of study. Of course, Donin began making it a point to do all of these things.

Donin later married, built a family, and, alongside the Chasidic lifestyle he had adopted, went back to working the land on his tractor. However, people—especially young people—gravitated to his fiery personality and would consult with him about their existential or emotional dilemmas. It was to them he would tell this story to impart the message that sometimes, under a heap of emotional turmoil, there might simply be a neglected body…[55]

CHAPTER 4

INTUITIVELY WE MIGHT ASSUME that toxic or depressive thoughts result from the emotional aspects of our lives. Family dynamics, childhood trauma, or social rejection are some of the factors we might consider, and for good reason. However, in our search for deeper insight, we may overlook the practical details of our daily lives.

A recurring theme in the Rebbe's counseling is that every person has basic mundane needs on which their mental health depends, and deprived of these necessities, their psyche suffers. Disturbing thoughts and emotions, even when they take a seemingly profound turn, can actually be symptoms of neglecting those simple needs that are the framework for stable mental health.

In this chapter we will explore four such needs. We've already touched on the topic of physical self-care (in Reuven Donin's story). The other three necessities are: an occupation, a schedule, and social engagement.

The Need for Bodily Self-Care

AT FIRST GLANCE IT might seem that the mind—the mental and emotional faculties—and the body run on two independent tracks. Biological ailments weaken the body, and emotional stressors disrupt the spirit. Nutrients and medicines heal the body, and social, emotional, or religious interventions soothe the spirit. They seem to be two distinct fields, with two different textbooks, in two different languages.

However, the mind and body are in fact deeply interconnected. Recent studies have shown that purely psychological trauma, say, from childhood verbal abuse, manifests in alterations in brain circuitry clearly observable in brain scans.[56] Conversely, studies have illustrated how positive changes in nutrition and exercise directly improve a person's emotional health in empirically measurable ways.[57]

This unity of body and spirit, which is discussed at length in early Chasidic teachings,[58] was a central idea in the Rebbe's counsel.

"To a remarkable degree," reads a letter to a 1955 medical conference,
> the wellness of body is dependent on the wellness of mind. If in ancient times the medical aphorism spoke of "a healthy spirit in a healthy body" [this may refer to the Latin phrase "mens sana in corpore sano"], in our time it has become clear to what extent a small disturbance in one's spirit causes a large disturbance in their body. Similarly, the healthier one's spirit, the greater its control on the body and the greater its ability to mend deficiencies in the body. Indeed, we observe that many physical treatments are significantly more effective in healing the body when accompanied by the patient's resilience, willpower, and inner strengths.[59]

The same is true in the reverse: the condition of our body has a direct impact on our mental and emotional state.

"It appears," reads a letter to a middle-aged man,
> that you are not properly taking care of your bodily health. Naturally, it is impossible that

this won't also affect your emotional health, as explained in the well-known teaching of the Maggid [Rabbi DovBer of Mezeritch (1704–1772), an early Chasidic master] to his son, that "a small hole in the body causes a big hole in the soul." Therefore, if you will take my advice, you should watch your health in the most literal sense—eating, drinking, sleeping, and so on—and this will be good for you spiritually as well.[60]

Moshe Levertov's adolescence in Russia was spent on the run from the Nazis, contending with hunger and illness. After being orphaned from his father, who was arrested by the Soviets and died in a Siberian gulag, he ultimately made it to the United States and developed a connection with the Rebbe. A serious and reflective individual, he would often consult with him about his inner state.

In a 1951 private audience, the Rebbe addressed the thoughts that were plaguing Levertov. The following is an excerpt from his journal:

[The Rebbe said to me:] "If you would look better physically, you would do better spiritually, too.... You should make sure to take care of your health. Your body should be rested. You should eat well. Don't indulge in food cravings, but you should eat enough. And you should make sure to get enough sleep."

After giving me guidance in other areas, the Rebbe concluded: "*Nu*, Reb Moshe, be well; it's going to be good." He then looked at me with a smile and continued: "In truth, it's already good, but it will be good in a way that you'll see it, too..."[61]

When counseling people to better tend to their physical health, the Rebbe would often invoke the Jewish teaching[62] that your body doesn't belong to you—it is rather entrusted to you to take care of properly. Thus, you shouldn't view it as something that is yours to destroy or abuse at will; rather, it is a divine artifact loaned to you to sensitively care for.

> "You should increase your vigor," reads a letter to a teenager, in watching your bodily health according to your doctor's guidance; for the body is G-d's possession given to you as a deposit, and therefore it is upon you—the one it has been entrusted to—to watch the deposit, that it should be whole and healthy in the literal and physical sense.[63]

The Need for Productive Occupation

THE VERSE IN JOB teaches, "Man is born to labor."[64]

The Rebbe understood this verse not only as a dictum for how man is ideally supposed to live, but also as an essential truth about human nature.

In the 1970s, many alternative movements were on the rise in the United States, captivating the minds and hearts of young Americans. Feeling stifled by the careerism, materialism, and raging consumerism of their parents' generation, these spirited youths gravitated to approaches that promised inner harmony and fulfillment rather than luxury and fame.

The Rebbe viewed these trends as the impassioned outbreak of uncompromising souls who refused to resign to a banal life centered around material success. He worked tirelessly to help these seekers find the divine, and frequently expressed his hope that they would not end their search in frustrated disappointment. However, in a wide-ranging address delivered in 1979, the Rebbe critiqued one misguided sentiment prevalent amongst them.

Some of the doctrines attracting young adherents advocated that to truly achieve inner peace one must free themselves of all work stresses, return to nature, and live in a state of meditative transcendence and undisturbed emotional quiet.

Addressing this phenomenon, the Rebbe began by noting that the Patriarchs chose to be shepherds in order to escape the noise of the city and connect with G-d,[65] indicating the value in an occasional retreat from city-bustle. Additionally, he emphasized that those in need of therapeutic healing can indeed significantly gain from such retreats, provided they are "kosher" and do not include vestiges of oriental idolatrous practices. However, as a way of life for all, he emphatically continued, this is decidedly not the path to lasting mental health:

> The verse teaches that "man is born to labor." For a person to remain mentally and emotionally healthy, they must labor and feel the sense of work and accomplishment. The Talmud tells us about the porters of [the Babylonian city of] Mechoza that when they were unable to do their work of carrying loads, they became ill.[66] The same is true of all of us: G-d created us in such a way that to be emotionally well, we must be engaged in productive activity.[67]

Productive activity—be it a job, a business, volunteer work, course of study, or raising a family—should not be viewed as mere capitulation to the practical demands of life.

It is not an obstacle to inner peace to shrug off as soon as circumstances allow, but rather a significant component of our psychological health.

This need is even more pronounced as one advances in age. Responding to a son who expressed disappointment that his mother needed to work in her golden years, the Rebbe wrote the following note:

> Of course not all occupations are the same, but in principle, it is important especially at this age to make an effort to be occupied in some form of work. This helps take the mind off various ailments, and we see clearly how work (compatible with one's physical strength) is one of the critical necessities for a person's wellbeing.[68]

Sometimes the solution to emotional problems might in fact lie in shoring up the occupational areas of life.

"Following the pleasure of our meeting," reads a letter to a Californian father and businessman,

> I wish to add here in writing some thoughts which, for obvious reasons, I did not wish to express in the presence of others, namely, in regard to your son....
>
> I believe that the best help that can be given your son, in general, is to get him to work.
>
> I should only add that in view of the fact that this would entail a change in your son's way of life for a period of time, it would be well if his job would, in the first stage at any rate... not impose on him too much responsibility, so that he will not be frightened or discouraged by it.

If it is the kind of work which he might consider beneath him, it might be explained to him that it is only a start, and temporary, and, indeed, the first step to advancement. It is well known that here in the U.S.A., people at the top often take pride in the fact that they worked their way up from the bottom of the ladder. After he adjusts himself to a part-time occupation of several hours a day, he could probably be induced to work half a day and in due course a full-time job.

Needless to say, the above is in addition to what we spoke about—the importance of his feeling that his parents and friends have the fullest confidence in him.[69]

The Need for Structure

"INTERNAL HARMONY IS DEPENDENT on living an ordered life externally too,"[70] explains a handwritten note. If we improvise every day—waking up, working, studying, or socializing with no rhythm at all—our thoughts and emotions unravel as well.

"Naturally (and this can't be changed)," reads a response to a man who wrote of his confused state of mind,

> for a person to be successful in what they do—and in general, to act correctly, to know what they truly want, to make good decisions, etc.—one must have as much peace of mind and body as possible. This requires living a properly organized life in the *literal sense* of the word.[71]

Living with a structure is also vital for inner satisfaction. When we create a schedule, we dedicate time to what's really important and commit ourselves to systematically pursuing it no matter our moods. (We don't usually include hours for binging on social media...) Otherwise, it's hard to escape the hollow feeling that much of what we do is motivated by fleeting impulses. In the Rebbe's handwritten words:

> For a person to feel that they are *truly* doing objective *good* (and not only satisfying their *momentary* desire)—self-discipline and a *structured* lifestyle are a *necessity*.[72]

"As to your request for actionable advice," concludes a letter to a young woman,

> based on how you described [your present habits], you should begin organizing your life in a manner that accustoms you to having a structured daily routine. Doing so will make it easier for you to embark on a stable course, practice self-discipline, and have your mind govern your emotions effectively...
>
> It appears that a primary contributor to your present mental state is the disarray and instability in your life's external facets—which then mirror themselves internally, [unsettling] your inner self, your emotions, and so on.
>
> Since it is difficult to adjust to an orderly lifestyle after a long period of scatteredness, one strategy to ease this transition is to create an external motivator—by this I mean to take a job (or a similar commitment) where you know

that you're accountable to others to accomplish consistent work during established hours.[73]

Reading between the lines of your letter, it appears that you assume your state of mind is the symptom of serious subconscious issues. However, in my opinion, the primary causes are the above-mentioned two points—conduct in accordance with the Torah, and living a structured life. When you mend the above (little by little, at least), your disposition will significantly improve, perhaps even becoming completely restored.[74]

Ironically, our schedule may sometimes appear to us like the very factor that's ruining our happiness ("If only I could live my day as I wish without these annoying commitments..."). However, such thoughts tend to backfire in the long run.

"My practical advice to you," concludes a long, philosophical letter to a young woman on her existential questions,

is to order your life in a way that would commit you to a useful routine, so as not to have to think and decide each day what to do with it.

You should also bear in mind that the *yetzer* [see chapter 9] will try to counteract this effort by causing a depressed mood and planting the thought that by breaking your discipline your mood will improve. The truth, however, is that even if momentarily there seems to be a relief, it is only a fleeting one, attained at the cost of an ordered and regulated life, which alone can assure success and contentment of a lasting nature.[75]

It was 1961, and Jack Hanoka—a twenty-six years old New Jersey native turned beatnik, sporting a goatee and studying physics at Penn State University—noticed a sign from the local campus Hillel. It displayed an evocative painting of dancing Chasidim and the words "Join Us for an Experience." He was intrigued.

Hanoka attended a Shabbat meal at Hillel that Friday night and was instantly captivated. A musician at heart, he was deeply moved by the Chasidic melodies they sang. Some tunes expressed the yearning of the soul, others expressed its ecstatic joy—all of them stirred him to the core.

In the following days, Hanoka couldn't concentrate on his studies. He approached the Hillel rabbi, who offered to arrange for a meeting with the Rebbe. On a rainy Thursday two weeks later, they drove together to Brooklyn.

"I had no idea what to expect," Hanoka recalled. "It wasn't the kind of thing your typical college student was prepared for. But the Rebbe made me feel comfortable. He let me talk for a while about my life and some of the issues I faced. I then told the Rebbe that the Hillel rabbi recommended that I study in yeshiva to quench my thirst for authentic Judaism. The Rebbe agreed that it was a good idea, but advised me to first finish the semester."

When the semester was over, Hanoka returned to New York to study in the Rebbe's yeshiva. The Rebbe frequently checked up on him to make sure he was comfortable and progressing well in his studies of Torah and Chasidut. Seeing him once wearing a suit that was large on him, the Rebbe asked him if he had lost weight, reminding him that "Chasidisim is not asceticism."

After a year of diligent study, the Rebbe encouraged Hanoka to return to university to complete his PhD in physics. He then shared with Hanoka an observation he had made in his own time in the University of Berlin in the 1920s. He had been taking a course with the renowned Nobel-prize winning chemist, Walther Nernst. However, he couldn't understand: why would such a respected professor be teaching an introductory course? It turned out, the Rebbe continued with a broad smile, that the teachers were paid based on the number of students attending their classes. Many more students took the introductory courses than the advanced ones...

"I think he said that just to lighten the mood a bit," Hanoka observed. But the conversation was serious, and Hanoka agreed that he should return to Penn. Before he left, the Rebbe imparted an important piece of advice to him.

"At that time, I had a lot of problems keeping an order to my day," Hanoka recalled. "When I was in graduate school, before I came to study near the Rebbe, I had a very irregular schedule. I used to work in the lab until eleven or twelve at night, then meet my friends for a beer, after which I would read for a few hours. Then I would sleep for the better part of the morning, waking up at ten or eleven o'clock. Then I would have lunch, or rather brunch, and would eat supper a few hours later.

"Before I returned to school, the Rebbe emphasized to me how important it is to have a regular schedule—to eat at the same time every day, to do everything at the same time. And then he added something special: 'I have found this to be very helpful in my own personal life.'"

"I don't think he would say that to most people," Hanoka reflected. "But I guess to make an American college student feel comfortable, he put a personal touch to his counsel."[76]

The Need for Social Interaction

MAIMONIDES, THE GREAT MEDIEVAL Jewish sage, writes in his *Guide for the Perplexed*, "Man is innately a social being. Unlike [some] other animals for whom banding together is not a necessity, it is human nature to seek out society."[77]

This is true of all of us. No matter how fiercely independent or introverted we might be, every human being needs other people.

"I have received your letter," begins a 1959 response to a young woman,

> where you describe your [negative] state of mind, etc.
>
> I believe I have already written to you several times that in my opinion—which I have also seen borne out in reality—every person, without exception, is "innately a social being," though of course not everyone to the same degree. When one tries to behave contrary to this nature, it understandably leads to [emotional] complications, etc.

Despite this inherent desire to connect with others, actually approaching people and talking to them can be difficult and uncomfortable. In today's day and age, we might find ourselves resorting to effortless digital simulations instead of pursuing real human interactions. However, our craving for the simple physical company of our peers cannot be placated by sophisticated stand-ins. We have an undying need to see and talk and bond with other living beings just like us. And there is only one way to do this. The letter continues:

CHAPTER 4

For those who, for one reason or another, have a difficult time mixing with other people—ultimately, there is no way other than the process of metaphorically "learning how to swim." It is impossible for a person to begin developing swimming skills before they enter the water. Even if they stand on the river's edge—it is insufficient. They must jump into the water, and then they'll naturally begin learning how to swim. And in the end, they'll finally master it. However, all the lengthy ruminations while still standing on the riverbank—about how they'll learn, and what it will entail, and in which particular manner—are futile. For it's impossible to learn how to swim anywhere else but in the water.

After asking your apologies, it is precisely the same in your situation. You articulate in your letters your arguments for and against taking on an occupation that would involve being in the presence and company of others. However, this entire thought process takes place while you're sitting in your own room or in your own personal space.

Of course, my intention is not to rebuke you; I am only trying again, with the hope that perhaps this time my words will finally have an effect, and you will "jump" into an endeavor that will force you (at least for the first few days) to be among other people outside your home.

I hope that within a short period of time, you will not need to force yourself, and you will

> see for yourself how much meaning and how much benefit there is to being in other people's company, [not only for you, but] also for them—for it is not to no purpose that human beings were created with a social nature.
>
> Indeed, how wondrous are the words of our Sages,[78] which are also intended as a practical lesson in our daily lives, that everything sacred must be done in a communal setting.

Our innate need for others is not a nuisance or a weakness, the Rebbe explains here. We each have our own unique virtues and life-experiences, and our social instinct was divinely designed to compel us to grow and learn from each other. While some might associate self-development with solitude, Jewish wisdom teaches that the exact opposite is true: not only is it *possible* to achieve great heights in unison with others—*it is the only way.*

The letter concludes:

> There is a well-known Chasidic saying, attributed to several of the great Chasidic masters, that "it is worse to be alone in Paradise than [in Hell] together with others."
>
> Finding ourselves at the end of the month of *Elul*, a month of infinite divine mercy—may it be G-d's will that you begin to make real positive movement in this direction, and that you are soon able to report good news.[79]

Of course, this move toward healthy social engagement might sometimes need to be in gradual steps. As another letter explains, to the teacher of a student going through an emotionally challenging period:

> It appears that an important component in his recovery is that he begin re-engaging with others.... It is self-understood that my intent is not that he should change suddenly from one extreme to another and begin interacting with others for many hours a day. Rather, he should do this step by step, and with the people with whom he finds it easiest to connect.
>
> However, he should do so with the intent and goal of progressing steadily until he is able to speak and mingle with others naturally and without strain.
>
> Together with the above, and this is of paramount importance, he should be strong in the knowledge (which is, in fact, true) that his current situation can be improved one hundred percent, though, as mentioned, it will require a step-by-step approach....
>
> Since you took care to communicate his predicament, certainly you will not neglect him [throughout this process], and, ultimately, he too will thank you for your efforts—even if he won't appreciate them initially.[80]

LET'S CONCLUDE WITH A touching example of the Rebbe encouraging someone away from seclusion and towards engagement with others.

Zelda Mishkovsky, a celebrated Israeli poet, was born in

Ukraine in 1907 to Shlomo and Rachel Schneersohn, their only child. When she was eleven years old, she moved with her parents to British-ruled Palestine. Soon after their arrival, her father became ill and died.

As Mishkovsky was entering adulthood, her mother fell ill as well. She abandoned her university studies to help care for her mother while working as an elementary school teacher.

The years went by. Her mother's illness gradually worsened while Mishkovsky remained at her side. At the age of thirty-five, she wrote to a friend, "It appears that the last fire of youth has flared up inside me before it fades entirely and goes silent; before it makes peace with the profane, with death, with illness, with falsehood. It cries out for love, for freedom, for beauty, for knowledge, for song, for the wonders of creation—for truth. And then again verses of poetry beat in my pitiful and lonely heart. Oh! How alone. How alone."

A year later, she met her future husband, Chaim. "In his presence," she wrote to the same friend, "I feel a certain serenity, an inner peace that I've never felt in another person's company... As if there is nothing superfluous in me or him. Or the world." After they married, they moved into her mother's home so she could continue to care for her.

Mishkovsky was first cousins with the Rebbe—her father and the Rebbe's father were brothers—and the families, while still in Ukraine, had enjoyed a close relationship. Throughout her life, she would write to the Rebbe about her experiences. One of the letters that she wrote during her mother's illness reads as follows:

> Suffering and pain fills my soul, seeing the
> agony of those near and dear to me while I
> am powerless to help them. It is so terrible to
> see the pain; it is so terrible to witness how

mortality conquers, day after day, the body and spirit of someone close to you.

From the depths of my consciousness arises a rebellion to suffering, as if I lifted my head and saw the eternal sky above, the fresh new grass growing between the ruins; but I am experiencing one blow after another. When I identify with someone's pain, I am entirely overtaken by their tragedy and nothing else exists in the world. Understandably, after this I become physically ill, so my health is not at all in a shining state. And sometimes, for some reason, what is happening [to another] doesn't affect me, and then I feel guilty, coldhearted. My soul yearns for happiness, inspiration, bonding, to connect myself with other people....

Your cousin,
Shaina Zelda, the daughter of Rachel

After her mother succumbed to her illness, she found solace in her marriage. She and her husband moved into a house of their own, and, though the couple never merited children, they built a warm Jewish home, founded in faith, modesty, and kindness. They would often study and read books together, and it was her husband who encouraged her to finally bring her poetry to the public. She later described their unique bond as they carried together the reality of childlessness:

Chaim and I have been created by G-d as one....
We have been expelled from the paradise of the righteous who are "planted beside streams of water, who bring forth their fruit in its season, and whose leaves do not wither."[81] We have been

> expelled from the paradise of "Your wife shall
> be like a fruitful vine within your house; your
> children, like olive saplings around your table."[82]
> We have been expelled, and we now live on top
> of a cloud, and the entrance to our home is the
> rainbow in the cloud....
>
> We both have a dim perception, a faint
> memory, of the connection that existed between
> us before we were born. We belong one to
> another and are inseparable.

However, after ten years of bliss, her husband developed a serious heart condition. For nine long years she watched him ebb away as she hoped for a miracle ("I prayed that his candle not go out, I vowed a thousand vows...") But alas, at the young age of sixty-four, Chaim passed on, leaving her entirely alone in the world.

We do not have her letters to the Rebbe from this period, but it appears from the Rebbe's letters to her that part of her felt like disengaging from people and retreating into solitude after all she had gone through.

"It is now some time since I received your letter," begins a response from the Rebbe,

> and for understandable reasons it was hard to
> reply, for it is difficult to find the right words and
> the appropriate ideas. But as yesterday was the
> *yahrtzeit* [anniversary of passing] of my father,
> of blessed memory, and in connection with
> my reflections on the *yahrtzeit*, the time and
> emotions are more ripe to respond to your letter
> and to share some glimmers of thought....
>
> One of the ideas here is that since we are

dealing with a dear one's soul ascending to Heaven, it is upon those who remain close to him to continue those activities that he was involved with throughout his time on earth.... These efforts bring pleasure and elevation to the soul of the departed, for, finding themselves in the World of Truth, they know all that is being done in their merit, as if by their emissaries.

From the above it is understood that there is no room for conclusions about solitude, etc., for, on the contrary, specifically such an occurrence must propel one to work with other people with increased vitality and on a larger scale. For, as is explained in sacred sources and is logically understood as well, there is no room to say that an illness of the body [even one resulting in death] can harm the soul, its life, or its eternity. The change was only in the soul's connection to its body, a connection that brought along also various limitations to the soul, limitations that are now abolished. Thus, such activities, wherever they may physically take place, are immediately known to the soul, for it is now not limited by time and space nor by the faculties of vision and hearing.

I conclude with my wish that you organize your life in such a way that will allow you to use the talents you were gifted with for the benefit of the [general] public, in addition to the benefit of the individual [self] or [specific] individuals, and [to do this] with vitality and vigor. And may

> G-d grant you long and happy years, filled with visible and tangible goodness.
> With blessings to share good news about all the above soon,
> M. Schneerson
>
> P.S. Certainly every detail in how you will settle from here and on interests me, including, and this is also important, with regards to financials. And certainly you will write about all this as it really is, rooted in our familial closeness, etc., especially considering that only a few survivors of our family remain.[83]

Mishkovsky went on to open her home to young women in need of room and board. She offered them sensitive care and dedicated mentorship, and "Zelda's girls," as they became known, adored her like a wise and loving grandmother. She continued to write poetry, publishing another five books to wide acclaim. Her works depicting her lonely struggles and redemptive insights continue to garner a devoted readership, and are included in many school curricula to this day.

By the Grace of G-d
3rd of Cheshvan, 5721
Brooklyn, N. Y.

Blessing and Greeting:

I received your letter of October 18th, with the enclosure.

In reply, I want to say at once that the situation seems to me much better than your brother-in-law described it, for the reasons for your younger daughter's condition are not at all complicated. The causes seem to lie in the fact that your daughter is subconsciously jealous of her older sister, and such a feeling manifests itself by a desire to not to be interested in those activities where the person is unable to compe successfully. Therefore, your younger daughter shows little inclination to engage in the activities in which her older sister is more successful than she. However, since such is the attitude of jealousy, creating a subconscious feeling of guilt, one is prone to compensate for it by an outward show of attachment. That is why she flies to the defense of her sister if anyone should say anything disparaging against her. All this confirms my general view of her conduct. I trust that her therapist fully agrees with this diagnosis, for he knows her even better than I.

At the same time, this diagnosis suggests also the method of therapy, namely, that every effort should be made to restore her confidence by offering her opportunities to engage in such activities where she can take a leading part and excel herself. Needless to say, this should be done in a gradual way, for, in her present state of mind she would be re luctant to undertake responsibilities all at once. But surely, both at school and in other cultural circles, there are opportunities for her to develop her artistic and other talents. It would be psychologically ben ficial to her if these activities would be of a kind in which her sister does not participate. The choice of such activities is fairly wide, and they could be cultural, charitable, or youth work among Jewish youth, an the like.

You do not mention anything about her physical health, especially in re- gard to puberty. It often happens that where these aspects can be regu- lated and normalized, there is an immediate improvement in the state of mind, for the emotional life is closely linked with the physical.

Finally, and this is just as essential, the physical and mental life of the Jew is directly linked also with their spiritual life. I trust, therefore, that your daughter will make every effort to live up to the

- 2 -   3rd of Cheshvan, 5721

Jewish way of life, in accordance with the Torah, which is called the Law of Life, and the Mitzvoth whereby Jews live, since these are the channels and vessels to receive G-d's blessings. Needless to say, the parents themselves have to show a living example.

I would suggest that you have the Mezuzoth of your home checked, to make sure that they are Kosher. No doubt you also know of the good custom of Jewish women to put aside a small coin for Tzedoko before lighting the candles.

Hoping to hear good news from you,

With blessing,

By

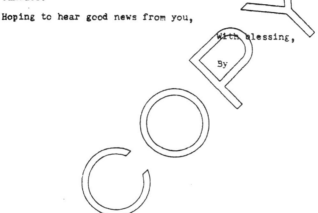

Takeaway

You are an integrated organism. The soulful you, the embodied you, the emotional you, the practical you, the inward-focused you, the social you—are all intertwined and deeply affect one another.

Therefore, to achieve optimal mental health, it is imperative to maintain a healthy body, a productive work ethic, an organized schedule, and a socially connected life.

Especially in times of inner turmoil when you might be tempted to slack off on your practical needs, remember that tending to your "external" self is a prerequisite to improving your "internal" state.

Just like there are physical habits that are necessary for a lifestyle that fosters emotional wellness—there are *spiritual* essentials as well.

Chapter 5
Be Spiritually Anchored

> *[Living a spiritually committed life] obviously does not mean that we must renounce all worldly pleasures and live a life full of suffering and pain; for, as Chasidic teachings emphasize, self-affliction is not the ideal nor the goal. However, it is necessary to know what is truly important and what is only secondary. A "golden calf" shouldn't be made of money or cinema and the like—surely you see for yourself that they are only of secondary value, or perhaps even entirely empty.*
>
> *When you hold onto the Torah's ways in your everyday life—particularly in your thought, speech and action—you "acquire your world."[84] And [not only a spiritual world, but] also this*

> *physical world, for your life is full of meaning and satisfaction... It is my prayer and hope that every one of you will walk on the path which our forefathers have paved for us, and you will each stride with confidence along your life's way, happy and fulfilled physically, because you will be happy and fulfilled spiritually.*[85]
>
> — To a group of teenage girls, 1954

THE REBBE HELD A firm conviction: a lifestyle anchored in G-dly ideals and spiritual practices is the most conducive to emotional stability. In the following chapter we will explore why this is and what it means.

The Iceberg

"IT HAS BEEN EXPLAINED in our Torah," reads a letter from 1965,
> and this has also been confirmed by modern science—that a surface layer may cover up an essential trait or quality. Or to use modern terminology, the subconscious may be overlaid by the conscious mind. In such a case, conflicts are inevitable, for man's essence is linked to the deep internal layers and not the superficial "cover," which is subject to change and is under the influence of external forces.[86]

Drawing on age-old Jewish teachings, the Rebbe maintained that our conscious thoughts are but the tip of the iceberg. Underneath them lies an infinitely vaster, more powerful world full of subconscious suprarational drives. Although we don't usually feel our subconscious, it nevertheless defines who we are, for a simple reason:

Our conscious selves are vulnerable to transient influences. As we all know from personal experience, our opinions and behaviors often change because of new circumstances and societal pressures. That malleable version of ourselves can hardly be called who we *really* are. But our inner, subconscious selves are different. They remain inherently unmoved by the outer world. They are beyond the news, beyond other people, beyond any fluctuation—they are our innate and consistent selves.

Therefore, when we succumb to the pressures of the outside world and drift away from our innermost desires, it naturally leaves us feeling unmoored and torn.

SCIENTIFIC RESEARCH AND MODERN psychology have largely affirmed the general notion of a subconscious self. However, in defining what actually lies beneath our surface, Jewish wisdom differs significantly from early modern theories, especially those of Sigmund Freud.

In a letter to a NASA scientist, the Rebbe pointed out how a teaching from Maimonides[87] in his magnum opus, *Mishneh Torah*, articulates what has become a mainstay of modern psychology—that human beings are composed of conscious and subconscious layers, and that society's demands often cause our conscious selves to behave in ways that conflict with our innate subconscious desires. He then explained:

> [However,] nothing in the above can be
> construed as confirmation of other aspects of
> the Freudian theory to the effect that man's
> psyche is primarily governed by libido, the sex

drive, etc. For these ideas are contrary to those of the Torah, whose view is that the human being is essentially good (as in the teaching of Maimonides, above). The only similarity is in the general idea that human nature is a composite of a substratum and various layers.[88]

Freud saw the human being through a materialistic, evolutionary lens. He presumed a person's most basic urges to be generally the same as an animal's—to avoid all pain and seek boundless pleasure. In Freud's conception, the tectonic clash between these insatiable drives and societal norms creates an inevitable tension at the center of the human experience that can only be managed, never reconciled.

The Rebbe believed something else entirely. Citing the works of Maimonides and the Chasidic masters, he taught that a human being's subconscious core is in fact their essential and eternal divine spark. No matter our conscious thoughts, no matter our overt behaviors, underneath them lies an unflinching soul that yearns for divine connection, that yearns to bond with others, that yearns to do what is just and to avoid all that is wrong.

Yes, life's many pressures sometimes cause us to suppress our subconscious divine urges and instead go down a hedonistic or immoral path, leading to painful inner friction. But we *can* effectively resolve this dissonance by allowing our conscious selves—our everyday thoughts and actions—to mirror and align with our deeper selves buried under all the rubble.

Therefore, the Rebbe saw a lifestyle imbued with spirituality as the only way to be true to ourselves and one with our essence. To achieve the feeling of wholeness we long for, we must allow our divine soul to have a tangible home in our daily lives. When we tie our fragile outer selves to our unchanging inner core, a serene sense of harmony can rest upon us.

NEWER TRENDS IN PSYCHOLOGY have inched closer to the outlook of the Jewish mystics championed by the Rebbe.

Changing Attitudes

"ON CLOSER SCRUTINY," a 1960 letter states about Freud, one will indeed find many loopholes in his theory, and, in fact, it is remarkable that many of his most prominent disciples drifted away from his theories and established their own. And although they may differ from one another, they all have one thing in common; namely, the denial of Freud's basic approach. Suffice it to mention only Jung, Adler, and, recently, Frankl.
It is especially interesting that Dr. Viktor Frankl, professor at the University of Vienna, makes purpose in life the cornerstone of his psychoanalytical system.[89]

Indeed, one of the major areas where Jung and Frankl broke with their teacher was in positing that spirituality and religion contribute profoundly to emotional wellbeing.

"I have treated many hundreds of patients," Jung wrote. "Among those in the second half of life—that is to say, over thirty-five—there has not been one whose problem in the last resort was not that of finding a religious outlook on life. It is safe to say that every one of them fell ill because he had lost that which the living religions of every age have given their followers, and none of them has really been healed who did not regain his religious outlook."[90]

Frankl responded similarly to an inquiry about his thoughts on religion:

"In contrast to Freud's system of psychoanalysis, logotherapy [Frankl's form of psychotherapy] sees man as a being dominated not by a drive for pleasure, and not by a will to power, but rather by a will to meaning. Therefore, logotherapy sees a person struggling for a life as meaningful as possible or being frustrated.

"And here is where religion comes in. Man, or a large essential part of the human population, goes one step beyond and strives also for an ultimate meaning. A religious individual is not satisfied only with finding a meaningful task to complete. He or she goes a step further to also include the awareness of a *task giver*—which is Divinity."[91]

The Rebbe lauded Frankl's views on the essence of man and the importance of spirituality in emotional wellbeing. He personally encouraged Frankl to not give up on his groundbreaking theories, despite the ridicule he was facing,[92] and would often urge other psychologists to acquaint themselves with Frankl's innovative writings.[93]

"I would like to take this opportunity," concludes a letter to Dr. Stern-Miraz, a mental health professional based in Haifa, Israel,

> to add another point, although this is in your field: the improving condition of [name omitted] illustrates (if evidence is necessary) the great power of faith—especially faith that is expressed in practical action, community work,

observance of *mitzvot*, etc.—to foster emotional tranquility in a person, to reduce and sometimes even eliminate their inner conflicts, as well as [to alleviate] complaints they may have about their surroundings, and so on.

I've taken particular interest in the writing of Dr. Frankl (from Vienna) in this matter. To my wonder, however, it appears that his approach has not yet been appropriately publicized and appreciated....

With respect and blessings that you succeed in your work to heal those who are ill, and to effectively lead them to a healthy life—a life worthy to be called "life."[94]

In the ensuing years, Frankl's approach has indeed gained widespread recognition. His seminal work, *Man's Search for Meaning*, was translated into over fifty languages, and was named by the Library of Congress as one of the ten most influential books in the United States.

WHILE THE REBBE THOUGHT spiritual practice was necessary for every human being's mental health, in letters counseling Jewish individuals he would explain how this need is particularly urgent in the case of a Jew.

The Psychology of Jewish Identity

BEYOND A CULTURAL AFFILIATION or a reason to be discriminated against, the Rebbe believed that Jewish identity is deeply rooted in the subconscious. Therefore, giving expression to this element of self by practicing Judaism has profound mental health benefits. And wittingly or unwittingly suppressing it—leaving it hidden somewhere deep inside—leads to inner tension and undesirable outcomes.

One letter[95] draws a comparison to a person with an intellectual bent whose time is spent entirely in hands-on occupations (say, in the construction industry). He or she might find their daily routine to be stress-free and even enjoyable. However, it is likely that something would be nagging at them. An essential part of them—their intellectual capacity—finds no expression in their conscious existence.

Similarly, when a Jewish person gives no expression to their Jewishness, it creates internal strain. Conversely, when they cultivate it by actively practicing Judaism, it fosters a sense of harmony between their innermost self and their everyday lives.

In November 1980, "The Major Conference for the Jewish Community on Issues and Needs of Jewish Retarded" (standard language at the time) convened in New York City. The Rebbe addressed the conference with a two-page letter. Here is an excerpt:

> With regard to Jewish retarded—parenthetically, I prefer some such term as "special" people...[96] the Jewish identity factor [for them] is even more important, not only per se but also for its therapeutic value.
>
> The actual practice of *mitzvot* in everyday life provides a tangible way by which these special people of all ages can, despite their handicap, identify with their families and with other fellow Jews in their surroundings, and generally keep

in touch with reality. Even if mentally they may not fully grasp the meaning of these rituals, subconsciously they are bound to feel at home in such an environment, and in many cases they can participate in such activities even on a conscious level.

To cite one striking example from actual experience during the Festival of Sukkot this year: As is well known, Lubavitch activists on this occasion reach out to many Jews with the *lulav* [a palm frond] and *etrog* [a citron], bringing them the spirit of the Season of Our Rejoicing [the taking of the "Four Species" is one of the special Sukkot *mitzvot*]. This year being a year of *hakhel* [every seventh year is a *hakhel* year, when Jews of ancient times would gather in the Temple], I urged my followers to expand this activity as much as possible, to include visits to nursing homes and senior citizens' hotels as well as other institutions. I was asked—what should the attitude and approach be to people who are senile or confused, etc.? I replied—all the more reason to reach out to them in this tangible way.

Well, the reports were profoundly gratifying. Doctors and nurses were astonished to see such a transformation: people who had spent countless days in silent immobility, deeply depressed and oblivious to everything around them, the moment they saw a young man walk in with a *lulav* and *etrog* in his hand, suddenly displayed a lively interest, and eagerly grasped the proffered *mitzvah* objects, some of them reciting the blessings from memory, without prompting. The joy in their hearts shone through their faces, which had not known a smile in all too long.

One need not look for a mystical explanation of this reaction. Understandably, the sight of something so tangible and clearly associated with the joy of Sukkot evidently touched and unlocked vivid recollections of experiences that had permeated them in earlier years.[97]

Needless to say, the benefits of practicing Judaism are equally applicable to Jews with ordinary cognitive abilities. The following letter explains this to a Jewish man who wrote that he lacks inner peace:

For a Jew to eliminate conflict, it is necessary for him to bring to the fore his inner essence, which is his deep-rooted faith in G-d. Failing this, he is bound to feel perturbed, even though the cause may be concealed from him. In other words, a Jew must live his daily life in accordance with the Torah and *mitzvot*—the Jewish way of life— for it is only in this way that he can attain true harmony and peace of mind.

It does, however, require an effort, oftentimes a strenuous effort, and much determination, including at times the sacrifice of certain conveniences, whatever they may be. But considering what is at stake—nothing less than the attainment of peace of mind and inner harmony, and even simple physical health (inasmuch as the physical and the spiritual are interrelated), every effort made in this direction is surely worthwhile and most rewarding. I would suggest that as a start you begin putting on *tefillin* every weekday morning and that in addition you say at least a short prayer.[98]

CONSIDERING THAT JEWS ARE the perennial minority, it is all the more important for Jewish people to be in touch with their inner selves. People of any minority, especially one that consistently faces prejudice and hostility, are prone to feeling small and inferior. This leads to simmering self-doubt about successfully fitting in with the dominant majority, and an underlying wish to find favor and be accepted.

The antidote to these toxic complexes lies in embracing one's Jewishness by proudly practicing Judaism. For when one is at peace with who they are, they are naturally at peace with the world around them.

"Jews have always been a minority among the nations," reads a 1974 letter,

and are of course a minority in the United States. Regardless of the democratic principles which are professed in this country... it is natural for a minority to develop an inferiority complex in relation to the majority.

Therefore, it is necessary to implant in the Jewish child from earliest youth a feeling of pride in the heritage and tradition of his parents and ancestors and a strong feeling of Jewish identity. Thus, instead of hiding their Jewishness, they will be able to be proud of it without any inhibitions, despite any derision by non-Jewish neighbors or any prejudiced individuals.

This calls for, above all else, instilling into the child a sense of true Jewish values—prioritizing the spiritual over the material, as well as inner peace and harmony over materialistic considerations of career.[99]

ELLIOT LASKY WAS A law student at SUNY during the early 1970's. Born soon after the war to Holocaust survivors in a displaced persons camp, he moved with his parents to the United States and was raised in a traditional Jewish environment. However, as he grew up, he drifted away from his Jewish upbringing, and by the time he got into college he no longer maintained an active connection to Judaism.

While in college, Lasky got involved in the raucous music scene of the time, and went on tour across the United States with the Rolling Stones band, working as a concert promoter. Things seemed to be going well for him, but in the months after his return from the tour, he found himself gripped by existential questions that wouldn't let up. When he approached a rabbi on campus, he suggested that the young man go see the Rebbe.

"It was a bitter cold day in January of 1973," Lasky recalled. "I was told that I'd be able to approach the Rebbe and speak with him briefly as he walked into 770 [the address of the Rebbe's synagogue in Brooklyn] before the afternoon *minchah* prayers. And so I waited in the cold, wearing my snakeskin boots, tight jeans, and a leather jacket. I suppose I was a sight with my shoulder-length hair and unconventional dress....

"As I was waiting, a car pulled up and the Rebbe emerged. Since Yiddish was my first language, I felt this was the appropriate way to address him, so I said, '*Antshuldig, bistu der Lubavitcher Rebbe?*—excuse me, are you the Lubavitcher Rebbe?'

"Our eyes locked. In my whole life I had never seen eyes like his. And suddenly, it felt to me like I had been transported to another dimension, like there was nothing around us and it was just the two of us in the whole world. This was an incredible spiritual experience for me.

"He said, 'What is your name, and where are you from?' I gave him my name, told him where I was from, and where my parents were from.

"'I have a question,' I said.

"'Ask,' he responded.

"'Where is G-d?'

"'Everywhere,' he answered me.

"I persisted, 'I know, but where?'

"'Everywhere. In everything. In every tree; in every stone...'

"But I found myself asking again, '*Ubber ah vu*?!—but where?!'

"To which the Rebbe responded: '*In dein hartz, oib dos iz vi du fregst*—He is in your heart, if that is how you are asking.'

"That answer completely stunned me. In all the years I had spent in Jewish institutions in my youth, I had never grasped that G-d was in my heart.

"At that point, I asked him if we could speak in English, because I could not ask in Yiddish all that I needed to know. He agreed. I said, 'When we say the *Shema*—"Listen, Israel, the L-rd is our G-d, the L-rd is One"—do we mean that there is one G-d for all people, be they Black or Indian or Jew?'

"He answered, 'The essence of the Black man is to be what

he is as a Black man, and the essence of the Indian is to be what he is as an Indian, and the essence of the Jew is tied to G-d through the Torah and its commandments.'

"These were very, very powerful words to me.

"Altogether, we spoke for approximately fifteen minutes on the steps of 770 on a freezing winter day and, at the end, he gave me two things to do. One was to learn the *Kitzur Shulchan Aruch* [the Abridged Code of Jewish Conduct] in English, and the other was to put on *tefillin* every day.

"He then explained to me that if I'd connect with the Torah it would be a source of blessing for me, and that lacking this connection 'will lead to being downtrodden.'

"All this time, he was looking into my eyes directly—our eyes were locked—and I was the one who broke eye contact first. The Rebbe went inside for the afternoon prayers, and I started crying.

"It took some time for his words to sink in. I'd say about three months. That's when I started putting on *tefillin*, something which I had not done for many years. From that day I have never missed it once.

"Today, I have four beautiful children, all of whom are Torah observant. And I do believe that everything has turned out like this because of that fateful meeting with the Rebbe on a cold winter afternoon. Because of him, my life was forever changed, as well as the lives of people I affected. All for good. All for blessing."[100]

FOR EVERY HUMAN BEING, of every identity, living in accordance with G-dly ideals profoundly enhances emotional wellness. This is particularly relevant in our times.

CHAPTER 5

Terra Firma

"PEACE OF MIND IS conditioned on inner security," reads a 1958 letter.[101]

We live in a fast-changing world: The stock markets rise and implode seemingly at whim. Cutthroat politics are the norm across governments. The ills plaguing society, and the grassroot movements they inspire, are constantly in flux. The cutting edge of science is rife with breakthrough discoveries, inevitably bringing in their wake revolutionary technologies. The sand is shifting under us all the time.

Some of these changes are promising developments that bode well for our world. The danger is in their effect on our *internal world*. When our deepest aspirations are tethered to such transient forces as the markets, the political climate, or technological innovation, we are left with a lingering anxiety. And when our psyche rests on shaky ground, our thoughts and emotions are more likely to become volatile.

This is why integrating spirituality into our daily lives significantly improves our mental health, especially today.

When we embed spiritual practice into our normal routines, it offers us a serene oasis from a stormy world. When we strive to align our behavior with the divine will, and make this central to how we negotiate our everyday decisions, it provides us with a secure anchor from which to approach the human experience.

The 1958 letter continues, comforting a father upset over his son's choice to lead a more spiritually committed life:
Not many years ago, "peace of mind" was
variously predicated on the attainment of certain goals:
To the materialistically inclined it meant

the amassing of wealth, which they felt would give them security. Others sought security in scientific progress, considering modern science to be the panacea for all human ills. Others sought security by identifying themselves with a certain movement or ideology, such as socialism, communism, fascism, etc....

In recent years, however, especially in the last decades, it was clearly demonstrated that wealth offered no security, for we have seen how economically "secure" families have been impoverished overnight. Political regimes and social movements and "isms" of all sorts have proved similarly disappointing. As a result, an overwhelming feeling of insecurity has taken root among growing youths and thinking adolescents, reflected in their vacillation from one extreme to the other, in emotional and mental disturbances....

It is, therefore, more vital than ever before that the young generation should feel terra firma under their feet. This solid basis can be provided only by finding religion. Consequently, when one's own child has happily found this security, it should be regarded as G-d's greatest blessing, for far from being a disturbing factor to their happiness, it is The Factor, the one and only, that will ensure their true happiness.[102]

CHAPTER 5

RABBI MENACHEM M. SCHNEERSON
 Lubavitch
770 Eastern Parkway
Brooklyn, N. Y. 11213
493-9250

מנחם מענדל שניאורסאהן
ליובאוויטש

770 איסטערן פארקוויי
ברוקלין, נ. י.

By the Grace of G-d
22 Av, 5739
Brooklyn, N. Y.

Mr. R. Wilkes, Asst. Program Director/
Chairman, Region II Council For Mental Retardation
Coney Island Hospital
2601 Ocean Parkway, Brooklyn, N. Y. 11235

Greeting and Blessing:

 This is in reply to your letter of Aug. 9, in which you ask for my views on "the care and education of Jewish retarded children," outlining some of the problems connected therewith and prevailing policies, etc.

 I must, first of all, make one essential observation, namely, that while the above heading places all the retarded in one group, it would be a gross fallacy to come up with any rules to be applied to all of them as a group. For if any child requires an individual evaluation and approach in order to achieve the utmost in his, or her, development, how much more so in the case of the handicapped.

 Since the above is so obvious, I assume that you have in mind the most general guidelines, with a wide range of flexibility allowing for the necessary individual approach in each case. All the more so, since, sad to say, our present society is poorly equipped in terms of manpower and financial resources to afford an adequate personal approach to each handicapped boy and girl. Even more regrettable is the fact that little attention (at any rate little in relation to the importance of the problem) is given to this situation, and consequently little is done to mobilize more adequate resources to deal with the problem.

 Now, with regard to general guidelines, I would suggest the following:

 (1) The social worker, or teacher, and anyone dealing with retarded individuals should start from the basic premise that the retardation is in each case only a t e m p o r a r y handicap, and that in due course in could certainly be improved, and even improved substantially. This approach should be taken regardless of the pronouncements or prognosis of specialists in the field. The reason for this approach is, first of all, that it is a precondition for greater success in dealing with the retarded. Besides, considering the enormous strides that have been made in medical science, human knowledge, methodology, and knowhow, there is no doubt that in this area, too, there will be far-reaching developments. Thus, the very confidence that such progress is in the realm of possibility will inspire greater enthusiasm in this work, and hopefully will also stimulate more intensive research.

 (2) Just as the said approach is important from the viewpoint of the

-2-

worker and educator, so it is important that the trainees themselves should be encouraged - both by word and the manner of their training - to feel confident that they are not, G-d forbid, "cases," much less unfortunate or hopeless cases, but that their difficulty is considered, as above, only temporary, and that with a concerted effort of instructor and trainee the desired improvement could be speeded and enhanced.

(3) Needless to say, care should be taken not to exaggerate expectations through far-fetched promises, for false hopes inevitably result in deep disenchantment, loss of credibility and other undesirable effects. However, a way can surely be found to avoid raising false hopes, yet giving guarded encouragement.

(4) As part of the above approach which, as far as I know has not been used before, is to involve some of the trainees in some form of leadership, such as captains of teams, group leaders, and the like, without arousing the jealousy of the others. The latter could be avoided by making such selecations on the basis of seniority, special achievement, exemplary conduct, etc.

(5) With regard to the efforts which have been made in recent years to create "group homes" for retarded individuals, which, as you say, has been a source of controversy - it is to be expected that,as in most things in our imperfect world, there are pros and cons. However, I believe that the approach should be the same as in the case of all pupils or students who spend part of their time in group environments - school, dormitory, summer camp, etc., and part of their time in the midst of their families, whether every day, or at weekends, etc. Only by individual approach and evaluation can it be determined which individual fits into which category.

(6) There is surely no need to emphasize at length that, as in all cases involving Jews, their specific Jewish needs must be taken into account. This is particularly true in the cases of retarded Jewish children, yet all too often disregarded. There is unfortunately a prevalent misconception that since you are dealing with retarded children, having more limited capabilities, they should not be "burdened" with Jewish education on top of their general education, so as not to overtax them. In my opinion this is a fallacious and detrimental attitude, especially in light of what has been said above about the need to avoid impressing the child with his handicap. Be it remembered that a child coming from a Jewish home probably has brothers and sisters, or cousins and friends, who receive a Jewish education and are exposed to Jewish observances. Even in the American society, where observant Jews are not in the majority, there is always some measure of Jewish experience, or Jewish angle, in the child's background. Now therefore, if the retarded child sees or feels that he has been singled out and removed from that experience, or when he will eventually find out that he is Jewish, yet deprived of his Jewish identity and heritage - it is very likely to cause irreparable damage to him.

On the other hand, if the child is involved is involved in Jewish education and activities - and not in some general and peripheral way, but in a regular

-3-

and tangible way, such as in the actual performance of Mitzvos, customs and traditions - it would give him a sense of belonging and attachment, and a firm anchorage to hold on to, whether consciously or subconsciously. Eventually even a subconscious feeling of inner security would pass into the conscious state, especially if the teacher will endeavor to cultivate and fortify this feeling.

I am, of course, aware of the arguments that may be put forth in regard to this idea, namely, that it would require additional funding, qualified personnel, etc., not readily available at present. To be sure, these are arguments that have a basis in fact as things now stand. However, the real problem is not so much the lack of resources as the prevailing attitude that considers the Jewish angle as of secondary importance, or less; consequently the effort to remedy the situation is commensurate, resulting in a self-fulfilling prophecy. The truth of the matter is that if the importance of it would be seen in its true light - that it is an essential factor in the development of the retarded Jewish child, in addition to our elementary obligation to all Jewish children without exception, the results would be quite different.

Perhaps all the aforesaid is not what you had in mind in soliciting my views on "group homes." Nevertheless, I was impelled to dwell on the subject at some length, not only because it had to be said, but also because it may serve as a basis for solving the controversy surrounding the creation of "group homes" for those children who are presently placed in an environment often quite distant from the individual's home and community - to paraphrase your statement.

Finally a concluding remark relating to your laudatory reference to the Lubavitch movement, "with its deep concern for <u>every</u> Jewish individual's welfare," etc.

Needless to say, such appreciation is very gratifying, but I must confess and emphasize that this is not an original Lubavitch idea, for it is basic to Torah Judaism. Thus, our Sages of old declared that <u>ve'ohavto lre'acho komocho</u> ("Love your fellow as yourself") is the Great Principle of our Torah, with the accent on "as yourself," since every person surely has a very special, personal approach to himself. To the credit of the Lubavitch emissaries it may be said, however, that they are doing all they can to implement and live by this Golden Rule of the Torah, and doing it untiringly and enthusiastically.

May the <u>Zechus Horabbim</u>, the merit of the many who benefit from your sincere efforts to help them in their need, especially in your capacity as Regional Chairman of the Council For Mental Retardation, stand you in good stead to succeed in the fullest measure and stimulate your dedication for even greater achievements.

With esteem and blessing,

Takeaway

Establish a spiritual foundation for your daily life. Doing so will provide a secure oasis amid a tempestous world, and will keep you in touch with your inner self.

Begin with something actionable.

Some ideas: Upon awakening, thank G-d for a new day. Give a few coins to charity. Dedicate a time for daily prayer, and reflect on how to better align your behavior with the Divine will. *If you are Jewish, some additional ideas*: Say the *Shema* prayer. Put on *tefillin* (men). Light Shabbat candles (women). Dedicate (more) time to studying Torah.

In addition to being intrinsically valuable, these practices will enhance your sense of peace with the world around you—and with your own self.

Part 2

Overcoming Darkness

A Brief Introduction

THE REBBE CONSISTENTLY EMPHASIZED the importance—and preference—of "preventive medicine." He critiqued approaches that focus exclusively on treating illness—"curative medicine"—rather than pouring equal resources into fortifying stable health, preventing maladies and suffering to begin with. Thus, a book on the Rebbe's guidance for emotional wellness must begin not with problems, but with the mindsets and habits that keep us strong in the first place. These are the core concepts we've explored until this point.

However, our discussion would be profoundly incomplete without also addressing some of the common ailments we experience. In the following chapters, we will explore a few specifics (discontent, worry, bad moods, and self-criticism), as well as general coping methods useful for all emotional struggles.

But before we begin, it is important to introduce a foundational principle that informs many of the ideas to come.

IN A LETTER FROM 1959, responding to the dilemmas of a young woman, the Rebbe wrote the following:

> Regarding your question about the role of your intellect and emotions:

You are correct in thinking that you should not suppress your emotions. Rather, as with all areas of a person, your emotions should be activated so you can reach your fullest potential.

However, the activity of your emotions should be under the guidance of your intellect. Put differently, in the words of our Sages, "The mind should rule the heart."[103] This teaching indicates two points: 1. The mind should rule. 2. The heart must indeed be active—but under the rulership of the mind.[104]

Our emotions can seem beyond our control. They react instinctively—*emotionally*—to stimuli around us and inside us. They make us upset, worried, or depressed, without quite waiting for our approval.

However, the Chasidic masters taught that "the mind rules the heart." We *can* redirect our heart—by redirecting our mind. This doesn't mean becoming extremely cerebral or forcefully suppressing our passions. That would be a gross neglect of the powerful and beautiful range of emotions we were purposefully imbued with. What it does mean is that we can utilize our mind's innate influence to steer our heart towards healthier, better, and deeper feelings.

This foundational Chasidic approach sets the tone for the next chapters. As we will see, the way the Rebbe counseled people to prevail over negative emotions often involved applying a different mindful perspective to them.

With this established, let's continue.

Chapter 6
Discontent

ONE OF THE PRIMAL characteristics we share as human beings is the quest for that special something we call happiness. Or contentment. Or serenity. And yet, for many of us, it can feel perpetually elusive.

We tell ourselves, when my situation falls into place (when I get promoted at work… when I have a family of my own… when my kids grow up…), *that's* when I'll finally experience happiness. But now? No. The present is just too broken for happiness to be possible.

Jewish wisdom, however, offers a different perspective.

Choose from the Mix

WHEN PEOPLE TURNED TO the Rebbe feeling down about the difficulties of their lives, he would often remind them of the Kabbalistic teaching that *everything* in this world is composed of both good and bad.[105] Our personal lives are no exception. That perfect life—an image of which might occupy our imagination and amplify all that we're missing—doesn't actually exist. As one letter puts it:

> Human life on this earth is unfortunately not free from various factors that bring about unhappiness, and this is universal, though the causes vary. In some cases, it is children; in others, health; in still others, livelihood; and so on. To go through life in complete happiness is not destined for man.[106]

Considering this reality, the true frontier to achieve lasting happiness is in the internal realms of our minds, not the circumstances of our lives. No matter how great our state of affairs, there will *always* be something to feel down about. The primary path to happiness is therefore to proactively train our minds to focus on the good.

"Despite the tone and content [of your letter]," reads a 1960 letter to a woman who wrote of her bleak feelings about life,

> I have not, G-d forbid, lost hope that eventually you will see the good in life—including the good in your own life, and, moreover, that you will feel it in your heart as well. This is especially so considering the Chasidic teaching that in our world everything is composed of both good and bad, and human beings must choose which aspects they will emphasize, contemplate, and pursue. In everyone's life there are two paths— to see the good or [to see the opposite]....
>
> Needless to say, my intention is not to imply that anyone deserves suffering, G-d forbid. My

point is simply to underscore the reality: the type of lives we live, whether full of satisfaction and meaning or the opposite, depends in large measure on our will, which dictates whether we focus on the positive or the negative.[107]

Good Deserves More Attention

FOCUSING ON THE POSITIVE is obviously sensible from a pragmatic perspective—the end result is a happier you. But Kabbalah explains that an objective assessment calls for it, too.

Yes, everything in the universe—including our personal lives—contains both good and bad. But these two forces are not equal. Good, Kabbalah teaches, is inherently real and thus unlimited and eternal. Bad, on the other hand, is distant from the essence of existence and is ultimately transient. Hence, in the objective scale of reality, what's truly good in our lives outweighs the bad by infinite proportions.

The 1960 letter continues:

> If this [imperative to focus on the good within life's mixture of good and bad] speaks to every individual, how much more so for a member of the Jewish people, who believe firmly in the eternity of the soul, which means the eternity of the spiritual, which means the complete triumph of good. For it is impossible that something fleeting and transient will not be overtaken entirely by the truly existing and

everlasting; why, there isn't even a comparison between them.[108]

Even when the negative components of our lives are searingly painful (say, a major career disappointment or the passing of a loved one), nevertheless, life's real treasures (say, our positive accomplishments or our meaningful relationships—including with the souls of our departed loved ones) are resilient and everlasting. The bad, distressing as it might be, will ultimately be outlived by the good.

The following letter, written in connection with Rosh Hashanah (the Jewish New Year), uses this principle to address the dejection that might set in when we measure the good we've accomplished against our failures and wasted opportunities. After noting that our minds tend to exaggerate our shortcomings and misdeeds (see chapter 9 for more on this), the Rebbe continued:

> It is possible, however, that even without exaggeration the "balance sheet" may reveal that the liabilities' side is quite substantial, perhaps even outweighing the assets' side.
>
> But even in such a case, there should be no room for despondency. For alongside the feelings of sincere *teshuvah* [repentance] and a firm resolution to change for the better—which must be the necessary outcome of such self-searching—there is an encouraging feature in the general conduct of man, which should be borne in mind at this time.
>
> It is that every positive and good action— positive and good in accordance with the definitions of our Torah, the Law of Life—is

indestructible and eternal, being connected with and stemming from the divine spark that is in man, the *neshamah* [soul], which is eternal; while any negative and destructive action, being connected with and stemming from the *nefesh habahamit* [animalistic soul] and *yetzer hara* [evil inclination] in man, which are essentially limited and transient, is likewise of a temporary and transient nature, and can and must be corrected and completely wiped out through sincere and adequate repentance.

Bearing this in mind, everyone, regardless of what their personal "balance sheet" reveals, will find encouragement and renewed hope in the future, knowing that their good deeds in the past year are eternal, as are the light and benefit which these deeds brought into their own life, as well as [the lives of] their family and of our entire people.[109]

Appreciating this principle allows us to see our past and present in a new light. This letter to a grandfather puts it succinctly:

Even by your own assessment, the positive aspects of your life are of incomparably greater importance than the matters that are temporarily not as they should be. And when a businessperson makes an evaluation, they do not appraise every item separately; rather, they evaluate the general balance of the inventory.[110]

Begin With Nothing

HUMILITY IS A PREREQUISITE for joy, the early Chasidic masters would emphasize.[111]

When we evaluate our lives, our most fundamental abilities—that we can hear or walk, for instance—are often overlooked. It is easy to perceive such immense blessings as inalienable rights we somehow deserve. A humbler, less entitled perspective allows us to begin counting our gifts from zero.

In Jewish tradition, every day starts with proclaiming eighteen blessings expressing gratitude for our most essential assets.[112] One blessing celebrates that we were able to open our eyes, another that we have clothes, another that our body moves, and so on.

"If you pay attention," reads a note to a young woman,
> to the simple meaning of the eighteen morning blessings with which you bless G-d at the beginning of *every day*, you will see that you have been blessed with *all of them*. In addition, you have been blessed with good health, good parents, good education, a good community, a good profession, livelihood, and more. If so, what is the justification for complaining?![113]

Joy as a Calling

WHEN STUDYING THE REBBE'S correspondences, one repeatedly finds the Rebbe reminding people of the Torah's dictum, "Serve G-d with joy."[114]

Just knowing that to be happy is a divine imperative can

have profound impact. Sometimes, it appears from the letters, it is specifically the *higher* calling of joy that can motivate a person to rise above their depressing thoughts and nevertheless choose happiness.

"First and foremost," concludes a letter to a young man deeply bothered by his spiritual state,

> you should live in a way of "serving G-d with joy." When you ask yourself, "How can I be happy knowing my [spiritual] state?" remember the teaching of the holy *Tanya* that states, "One should not temper the joy of the soul with the dejection of the body,"[115] and everything has its proper time. And when you persist, with a strong will, in the service of joy—you will find success.[116]

It can be easy to get caught in thinking that being down or bitter carries some kind of virtue. We might tell ourselves that being pessimistic is a sign of superior character. The Torah teaches a different outlook.

"Please express my surprise to [name omitted]," reads one letter,

> that it seems he has not yet abandoned his method of serving G-d specifically with melancholy. Why this method is out of the question needs no explanation, as the verse clearly teaches, "You shall serve G-d with joy." This should be especially clear to one who belongs to the Chasidic community, as the Baal Shem Tov [founder of the Chasidic movement,

1698–1760] taught us about serving G-d specifically with joy.[117]

Avraham Shlonsky was a writer, poet, and linguist, considered one of the fathers of modern Hebrew. Having grown up in interwar Europe, his first writings reflect the optimism of the early twentieth century, and his early poems are filled with evocative descriptions of new beginnings and revolutionary ideas. However, as he aged, his poetry assumed a darker tone.

During a yearlong stay in Paris, Shlonsky came to recognize the silent isolation spreading beneath the cacophony of modernity, and he was exposed to the horrors of the Holocaust on a later visit to postwar Europe. These experiences resulted in painful expressions of alienation, grief, and terror in his poetry. For example, one verse about Paris:

You will cry out—
And the screaming metropolis
Will silence your howl
With its encaging tumult.
Only a stranger's ear will notice
The cry from the prison.

One more:
Then at night I will make pilgrimage to you
O' tower of Eiffel/darkness
To pray by radio
To the master of the universe.

Much of his later work expresses questioning and doubt, and his final collections are imbued with a dismal, tragic note.

In honor of his seventieth birthday, all his writings and translations were collected in a celebratory ten-volume set. As it happens, the last volume included his translations of

Shakespeare's plays, the last of which ended with a character saying these words:
> The weight of this sad time we must obey,
> Speak what we feel, not what we ought to say.
> The oldest hath borne most; we that are young
> Shall never see so much nor live so long.

The play then instructs the actors and musicians to reflect the gloomy mood and "exit with a dead march." Shlonsky's translation of this instruction into Hebrew—*yotzim l'kol neginas eivel*—became the concluding line of his entire collected works.

Enjoying a long-standing relationship with the Rebbe—he had Chasidic roots and was profoundly influenced in his childhood by the Rebbe's father, who was his first cousin—he sent his books to the Rebbe as a gift. "With great delight," Shlonsky finished his letter to the Rebbe, "I am sending to you these ten volumes—the fruits of my spiritual labor in the field of song (original and translation)."

After congratulated him on this milestone and commenting on other parts of his works, the Rebbe concluded his response with the following:

> After requesting your apologies, it is regrettable that the [collection] concludes with [the words] *yotzim l'kol neginas eivel* ["they exit with a dead march"]. Although it is only a translation of another's works, nevertheless, it is unfortunate. For it is the role of every individual, and particularly a Jew, and especially one who has been fortunate enough to grow up in a Chasidic environment and to have a profound appreciation for it, to fulfill the directive of "you

shall serve G-d with joy" in all the particulars of his life.[118]

While we cannot know for certain, it would appear that this comment is more than a simple editorial remark. It seems the Rebbe was trying to impress upon Shlonsky that his life's work should end on a different note, that he shouldn't "exit with a dead march," that he should find within himself poetic inspiration in the spirit of joy. He should be able to see joy as a value, a Jewish and Chasidic one no less, that contains depth and beauty to write about and sing about. And, contrary to literary convention, he should see it as a powerful way to end a career.

A response to another poet, Zelda Mishkovsky (see chapter 4 for more about her), contains similar themes of encouragement. Mishkovsky was a humble person who, despite experiencing significant tragedy in her life, never resigned herself to despair. Alongside many poems expressing torment, her writing is filled with an unceasing love for life, other people, and G-d. For example, while the Second World War was wreaking havoc on everyone's lives and moods, she wrote:

> I see joy—particularly today, in this terrifying darkness—as the most precious thing, as the most moral thing. I very much desire to kindle in the hearts of my students, frightened by the fear of war, a joy that will guard them from despair.... If only I had enough love and patience and warmth! If only I could teach them the joy in the sight of a living person... who is molded with such strength and tenderness... then the joy of life would elevate them to the starry heavens, even in the depths of a dark cellar.[119]

However, considering Mishkovsky's life experiences, this wasn't always easy. Her struggle to maintain her spirit often spilled over in her writing. For example, in a poem published in the years following her husband's death in 1970, she wrote:

And I awoke and the house was lit
—But no one was with me in the house
And such sadness
And pain.
Isn't the sun's joy
A daily occurrence?
Aren't there mountains?
Isn't there fire?
Oh!
The beauty is like a knife
To the heart.

Responding to a letter of hers in 1977, the Rebbe began by noting the special timing of his writing. It was the Eve of the Shabbat of Song, commemorating the song the Jewish people sang at the Red Sea when G-d saved them from the Egyptians. Additionally, it was just after the 15th of *Shevat*, the Jewish New Year for Trees, and this date carries extra significance as "man is like a tree of the field."[120] Moreover, being just after the fifteenth of the lunar month, the moon had reached its full glory and completion. The Rebbe then went on to wish Mishkovsky that she find the strength to continue her literary celebration of life:

With blessings to publish (in the near future) additional books of poems/songs [the Hebrew word for both poems and songs is *shirim*], and may they be *songs* in spirit too [reflecting an uplifted, not dejected mood], and with blessings

for joy of life, which stems from the Source of
life and goodness—G-d almighty.[121]

A poem in her next book reads as follows:
In the kingdom of sunset
Even thorns glow bright.

Suddenly crowns dissolve
And thorns become thorns again
And mountains return to their nakedness
The attribute of judgment exposes itself
And the skeleton of existence emerges.

But we do not die from fear
For the kindness of night is coming
And the soul soars to a new appreciation
Of the Creator.

A model of the human capacity to take up the call of joy, no matter the circumstances, was the great medieval Jewish sage Rabbi Moshe ben Maimon (commonly known as the Rambam, or Maimonides, 1135–1204).

At the young age of thirteen, Maimonides was forced to flee his home in Spain and wander destitute from city to city for refusing to convert to Islam. After finally settling in Egypt, in a two-year period, his father, wife, and two of his sons died in a plague. Just a few years later, his younger brother David, with whom he was especially close and who was his financial benefactor, drowned in the Indian ocean on a business trip. Of this tragedy, Maimonides wrote, "On the day I received that terrible news I fell ill…. How should I console myself? He grew up on my knees, he was my brother, he was my student."[122]

And yet, despite it all, the works of Maimonides portray a persistently optimistic approach towards life and the world.

A letter to a man who had evidently experienced hardship combines this lesson from Maimonides' personal life with a teaching from the Talmudic sage, Rabbi Elazer HaKapor (2nd–3rd century CE), that, "Against your will you are born, against your will you live, and against your will you die."[123]

The letter begins by explaining how the statement "against your will you live" implies the inevitability of suffering:

> In general, among the list of things that are against our will, our Sages have also included the statement "against your will you live"— indicating that life is not a series of delights, nor peaceful experiences, nor even minor difficulties.
>
> However, we see clearly that to a large extent, the effect of our life experiences depends on how we react to them. Who is a better example of this than Maimonides, whose life externally was filled with misfortune, turbulence, suffering, and tragedy—may the Merciful One spare us— to a greater degree than the average person's. Nevertheless, internally he maintained a very positive—in today's vernacular, optimistic— view of life, as articulated in his work, *The Guide for the Perplexed*.[124] On the other hand, we see many people who, although apparently successful in their external life, nevertheless rarely feel any inner contentment....
>
> It is hard to say this to someone else knowing what they have gone through. My intent is only to guide you to some ideas in our Torah that can

alleviate the weight of your load and calm your spirit, at least in a small measure, until...G-d will shine His countenance upon you in all that you need.[125]

LET'S CONCLUDE WITH A letter to a young woman encouraging her to take charge of her mind and proactively pursue joy:

> Even a brief reflection will reveal that this change [from gloom to contentment] is less dependent on the world outside of a person than it is on the person themselves. Everyone can find examples of individuals around them who exemplify this for the good and for the better.
>
> This means that even those who until now have seen things through a dim lens have the ability—and therefore the responsibility and privilege—to put their mind in control, as the known dictum states, "The mind rules the heart," and as the Alter Rebbe [Rabbi Shneur Zalman of Liadi, 1745-1812] adds that "this is part of our nature, embedded from birth"[126]....
>
> This will change your own small world into one filled with joy and light, and, by extension, your surroundings and wherever you reach will be similarly transformed. And, in the words of the known dictum, the full ability is there—it is only dependent on the will.[127]

RABBI MENACHEM M. SCHNEERSON
Lubavitch
770 Eastern Parkway
Brooklyn, N. Y. 11213

Hyacinth 3-9250

מנחם מענדל שניאורסאהן
ליובאוויטש

770 איסטערן פּארקוויי
ברוקלין, נ. י.

By the Grace of G-d
4th of Cheshvan, 5733
Brooklyn, N. Y.

Blessing and Greeting:

I am in receipt of your letter of the 27th of Tishrei. Thank you very much for letting me know the good news about an improvement in the various matters about which you wrote in your letter. This surely strengthens the confidence that also the other matters will be improved and go from good to better.

With regard to the question of being cheerful, etc., surely when you will think deeply on the blessings which G-d had bestowed upon you and your husband, especially to have good children, enjoying good health, and so forth - surely this should arouse true joy in your heart.

In connection with your mentioning your forthcoming birthday, may G-d grant that your Mazel should be renewed in the forthcoming year, in addition to the blessing for a good and pleasant year received on Rosh Hashono.

With blessing,
M. Schneerson

Takeaway

Happiness (or a lack thereof) is not an inevitable consequence of your life's circumstances; it is a decision.

This world will always be composed of good and bad—positive developments and stressful setbacks. Life will never give you *only* reasons for happiness, so it is your focus that matters most.

Take a step back and look at the broader picture of your life—all those tremendous treasures and blessings hiding in plain sight. They are far more important and enduring than what's temporarily lacking. They *deserve* so much more of your attention.

Reflect on the higher calling to "serve G-d with joy." Don't wallow. Pull your mind and heart towards this achievable goal. When you resolve to take up this call, no matter your circumstances, you'll soon find that happiness is nearer than you thought.

However, even as we find contentment in our present life, it can be undermined by anxiety over the future.

Chapter 7
Worry

> "Do not allow worry into your heart, for worry has killed mighty men."
> —*Talmud Sanhedrin 100b*

> "Why worry what will be tomorrow as long as the bartender is willing to serve us on credit?"
> —*Nineteenth-century Chasidic song*

WE ALL WORRY. WE fret over the past ("I messed up that interview"), we're concerned about the future ("Those bills are coming!"), and we're anxious about our long-term prospects ("Will my skills be relevant in the years to come?").

Naturally, Jewish wisdom offers multiple methods to address this universal emotion.

One approach is to meditate on the transient and unknowable nature of everything. What is the point of worrying about a future you have no idea whether you'll participate in? It is wiser to just live in the present. In this spirit, the Talmudic sage Rabbi Yosef (3rd–4th century CE) would recommend: "Grieve not about tomorrow's trouble, because you know not what a day may bring; perhaps tomorrow you will no longer be, and you will have worried about a world that is not yours."[128]

However, we will focus here on a more basic idea. It is one of the foundational tenets of Jewish ethics and a central theme in the Rebbe's counseling: *bitachon*.[129]

Bitachon means trust (in G-d). Trust is different from a feeling of love or awe towards G-d; it is absolute reliance with peace of mind. This is how the medieval Jewish sage Rabbi Bachya Ibn Pakuda (1050–1120) defines it:

> The essence of *bitachon* is the emotional calm of the one who trusts. Their heart relies on the one they trust to do what is good and proper for them.[130]

Trust is synonymous with calm. Have you ever sat in a cab or in a friend's car and thought, "I just don't trust this driver"? The road might be clear, but your heart can't stop its uneasy thumping. You keep anxiously checking out the window. You know it won't help you. It doesn't matter. You're worried.

Compare that experience with the times you were convinced of your driver's responsibility and good judgment. When you trust the driver, you can sit at ease and let your mind wander. You may not know what the next turn will bring, but you're calm. You feel you're in good hands. That feeling is *bitachon*.

The internal thought process of *bitachon* can be broken down into three steps:

1. There is a higher power—G-d—who runs the world, including the events in my life.

2. He is the essence of goodness, and "the nature of goodness is to do good." He loves me and cares for me.

3. Therefore, though I may not know what the future might bring, I need not fear or be anxious. I am in the best of hands.

A letter to an elderly man reads,
> "Through reflecting on the idea that G-d watches over every man and woman, in their day-to-day lives, and even in such details that the world considers petty and insignificant—[it becomes clear that] there is no foundation for worry of any type. It is like the calm of a little child who finds himself near his father, though in the analogy the father is only all-powerful in the child's imagination, whereas our Father in Heaven is all-powerful in reality as well.[131]

Between Doing and Fretting

THIS DOESN'T MEAN YOU can lie back, do nothing, and rely on G-d to take care of it all. Jewish wisdom repeatedly references the verse "G-d will bless you in all that *you do*,"[132] indicating that proactive *doing* is absolutely vital to receiving the blessing of success.

The reason for this need to *do*, explain the Chasidic masters,[133] evolves from the mystical underpinnings of creation. G-d wills a world where His divine energy is not in conflict with the natural order, but rather flows and works through natural channels. Therefore, you must do your best to create a practical framework that most aligns with a positive outcome.

But once (and moreover, while) you're doing what you can, it should be carried out with a healthy calm. Imagine you work a desk job in a large corporation. Your only responsibility is to complete the task you were assigned. You don't need to, nor should you, lose sleep thinking of the corporate balance sheet. Similarly, our role is to do what we can within the natural order to create a vehicle for the best result. What happens in the end is not for us to fret over. It is in better hands than ours.

The following handwritten note to a woman, addressing her anxiety, drives this point home:
> By meditating "with a full heart" and "with intensity" (as you wrote is your manner of approaching everything) on the concept of G-d's providence, that it is *He* who conducts the world at all times—any basis for worry or strain is nullified. G-d indeed wants a person to *do* what is necessary in natural means, but *not* to worry in their mind.[134]

> "The way to ease stress," reads another letter, is, first of all, to strengthen [one's] *bitachon*—complete trust—in G-d, whose benevolent divine providence extends to everyone individually and in all particulars, as our G-dly Psalmist, King David, often reminds us, "G-d is my shepherd, I will lack nothing," and more in this vein. Hence, there is really no reason for anxiety. Needless to say, this is one of the basic tenets of the Torah.
>
> To be sure, G-d expects a Jew to *do* what is necessary in the natural order of things,

promising that "G-d, your G-d, will bless you in all that you *do*." So one *has* to go about doing what is necessary, but without worry; on the contrary, with confidence. It is also self-evident that when one views such pressures as a temporary test, and takes them in stride, calmly, with a clear head, it is much easier to find the right solutions and carry them out effectively.[135]

However, letting go of our worry is not always easy.

Actually Letting Go

THE MAGGID OF DUBNO (1741–1804), a preacher famous for his fables, explained the meaning of *bitachon* with the following tale:

A poor man trudged along the road carrying a heavy bundle on his shoulders. An expensive-looking carriage, drawn by two mighty horses, was passing him by when it came to a sudden halt. The owner of the carriage emerged and offered the traveler a ride. Weary, the poor man gladly accepted the offer.

The carriage was continuing along the road when the wealthy man noticed that his passenger was still carrying his load. He asked, "My good man, what in the world are you doing? Why don't you put your sack on the floor?"

The humble traveler replied, "Dear sir, you have been kind enough to me already. Your carriage has to bear the weight of my body. How can I burden you with my bundle as well?"

The host laughed and chided his guest, "Don't you see that

it's the same for me if you hold your load on your shoulder or put it down? I'm carrying it anyway!"[136]

Putting down our load and allowing G-d to carry it for us can be hard. Like the poor man in the story, we each have a burden we're used to carrying, and we can't always fathom letting it go. It takes reflection and practice, but the rewards are transformative.

"Man is the master of his lot only to a certain extent," reads a 1951 letter.

> For the most part, it depends on G-d. Thus, a person need not carry everything on their own shoulders, feeling an overwhelming responsibility for everything. And certainly, one need not be filled with despair about specific matters or specific situations.
>
> When a person connects with their inner fount of faith and *bitachon*, which without a doubt remains deeply rooted in them, it gives them inner calm, enables them to go through life in a healthy manner, and allows them to better fulfill the unique task every individual has in life.[137]

"WHEN I WAS ABOUT eighteen years old," Mr. B. recounted, "I had a psychotic episode and ended up in a psychiatric hospital for six weeks. I was subsequently diagnosed as manic depressive, which nowadays is referred to as bipolar.

"Over the years, the Rebbe encouraged me to seek out a

good psychiatrist and follow their directives. He constantly supported me along the way and offered me reassurance.

"One time, after I had a psychotic episode, I wrote to the Rebbe that I was very nervous. The Rebbe's secretary responded telling me that the Rebbe had advised me to do four things: 1) *hesech hadaat meihanal*—to take my mind off the fact that I had been nervous [see chapter 10 for more on this]; 2) to check my *tzitzit* to make sure that the garment was kosher; 3) to check my *tefillin* to make sure they were kosher;[138] and 4) to study *The Gate of Trust* by Rabbi Bachya Ibn Pakuda.

"I followed all these instructions. I checked my *tzitzit*, and even though I didn't find any problem with them, I bought new ones just to be sure. I had my *tefillin* checked, and, when an issue was found, I had it rectified. I also stopped focusing so much on how nervous I was. Instead, I began to study *The Gate of Trust*, which explains how one can live a life of total faith in G-d, free of worry. I recall feeling a tremendous sense of comfort and assurance when I did so. I learned that G-d runs every facet and detail of life, so when we trust in Him, we can deal with others calmly and with confidence.

"I felt like someone who had been parched in a desert and who was suddenly given a drink of cold, refreshing water. Slowly, my insecurities and worries melted away. I felt that I could navigate life and relationships in a secure and worry-free way.

"Ultimately, I found a job that suited me; I got married and started a family. And looking back, I can say that, thank G-d, my life has been very productive and happy."[139]

RELEASING THE LOAD IS the first, more passive, step of *bitachon*. But there is a second, active step often found in the Rebbe's counseling.

Cognitive Power

"THINK GOOD AND IT will be good," the Tzemach Tzedek (the third Lubavitcher Rebbe, 1789–1866) counseled a worried disciple.[140]

Drawing on this teaching, the Rebbe would often encourage people experiencing anxiety over the future to proactively cultivate a stance of positivity. Instead of indulging thoughts of doom and gloom ("This date is going to fail for sure!" "I know this job interview is hopeless!" "This illness will only get worse!"), you should consciously think that things will turn out well.[141]

Nosson Leiman, a successful Canadian business owner, was facing the possibility of financial ruin.

Born in Ukraine in 1903, he had escaped to Canada at age twenty to evade the Soviet draft. In Montreal, the young immigrant built up a clothing business and eventually came to enjoy a modest sense of financial stability.

However, in the early 1960s, this hard-earned security was shaken to its core. His son explains:

"My father owned an old building—his store was on the ground floor, and he rented out the upper floors to small manufacturers. One of these manufacturers found it more lucrative to start fires and collect insurance than to sell merchandise. So he did that a few times in my father's building until the insurance people got tired of paying out. They came to my father and said, 'You have a choice: Either you install a sprinkler system, or you tear down this old building and put up a new one. Until you do one of those things, your insurance is canceled.'"

Leimann was terrified of losing his insurance—his entire inventory was highly flammable menswear. Between the two options, it was more sensible to tear down the old building than to install an expensive sprinkler system through its fragile structure.

Leiman hired an architect to draw up plans for a new building, but funds ran out before he could complete the project. Now he had no cash and no insurance for his merchandise—a frightening situation for the conscientious business owner.

Feeling at a loss, Leiman became deeply depressed. In his desperation, he decided to travel to New York and go see the Rebbe, bringing along his two sons.

"When we came into the Rebbe's office," his son relates, "my father was quite despondent. He was totally bent over. He walked up to the Rebbe's desk and laid his hands flat on the desk surface, as if to support himself. He just embodied the picture of depression.

"The Rebbe looked at my father and said in a commanding voice, 'Reb Nosson, stand up straight!' My father took his hands off the desk and stood up straight.

"He then asked my father for the architectural plans and reviewed them in detail. ('Why make the basement ceiling so low?' 'Why create a foundation that forever limits the building to three floors?')

"When he finished, he smiled at my father and said, 'You have to be *b'simcha* [joyous]. Be like a soldier going into battle. The soldier doesn't know what's going to happen, but he has firm faith that he will win. This is how you have to go back to Montreal, this is how you have to go back to your bank manager and mortgage company—with full confidence that G-d is on your side and everything will turn out right.'

"My father walked out of there a different person. In those few minutes, the Rebbe transformed his anxiety into confidence.

"Upon returning to Montreal, my father was back to himself. With newfound optimism, he was able to proceed confidently and request things that he had been previously reluctant to ask for. He managed to secure a mortgage of six percent interest when the going rate was twelve percent. The new building went up, and thereafter his business prospered."[142]

OPTIMISM ISN'T SIMPLY A way to fend off needless anxiety. The saying "think good and *it will be* good" indicates that positive thought has the power to be a self-fulfilling prophecy. It can itself influence the future for the better.

This can be understood on both psychological and spiritual levels.

From a psychological perspective, when you replace angst with optimism, you tend to make better choices, resulting in better real-world outcomes.

"You should have every confidence that you will succeed," reads one letter.

> Such confidence, as is generally recognized, is a strong psychological factor in seeing things in their proper perspective and finding the best ways and means to obtain the objectives.[143]

Another letter, addressing a father who wrote about his

discontent and worry over his children's behavior, reads as follows:

> The expression of our Rebbes, "Think good and it will be good," applies to your children's behavior as well. This can also be understood logically, for when you view their behavior with a good eye, your behavior toward them will naturally shift accordingly—especially your speech. And it is self-understood that words of affection have a much greater effect than the opposite approach.[144]

"The [dejected] spirit of your letter is very puzzling," begins a letter to a veteran educator who wrote of the challenging dilemmas he was facing at the educational institution he directed,

> especially coming from an educator who for tens of years has observed how children turn into adults, and how those without comprehension transform into understanding people, without them even putting in effort....
>
> The very fact that G-d created the world in such a way that even without effort, when a person turns twelve or thirteen [the age of maturity and some liability in Jewish tradition], they are given [the gift of] understanding from Above—an understanding strong enough to differentiate between good and evil—clearly indicates that essentially good prevails in the world. Though a person, seeing only a small part [of the world] and being biased by various factors, isn't always able to see the situation

> as it is but instead evaluates it through their emotions....
>
> It is almost certain that after reading these lines the question will arise [in your mind] that in all of the above there isn't a solution for even one of the problems you have written about.
>
> The relevance of all the above to [the problems in] your letter is because the approach to resolving a dilemma depends on the general outlook of the person who needs to resolve it. If their outlook is that they are sure to eventually find a good resolution to the dilemma, then they will search with increased vitality, knowing with certainty that the treasure exists and [that finding it] only depends on their efforts. This is not the case, however, when they are in doubt whether there is even a solution to be found.[145]

Positive thinking has a real-world impact from a spiritual perspective as well.

Chasidic philosophy explains that the universe has a spiritual dimension which is mirrored in the material realm.[146] When you conjure up certain thoughts and images in your mind, you are, in effect, introducing and creating that scenario on a spiritual level. Thus, the way you envision the future influences how it actually turns out. When you imagine positive scenarios, you bring them closer to materializing, and the same is true with visions of doom.

"Clearly," reads a letter to a man who wrote of his gloomy predictions for his financial endeavors,

> I have not yet been successful at inspiring within you a spirit of optimism, despite having

told you on numerous occasions that according to Jewish teachings, one should refrain from introducing negative and melancholy ideas into the world, which is one way of averting their actualization.

This applies not only to speech.... Thought, too, has the power to materialize, as we see from the teaching of our Rebbes, "Think good and it will be good."[147]

LET'S CONCLUDE WITH A short story.

Josh (Yehoshua) Gordon was the energetic Chabad rabbi of California's San Fernando Valley for decades.

"On one occasion," he related, "my wife and I faced a very serious challenge in our lives. The particulars are not important for the story I want to tell, but suffice it to say, it was a debilitating time for us.

"I suggested that my wife write to the Rebbe about it, and she did—she sat down and wrote a ten-page letter detailing everything. The day her letter arrived in New York, I got a call from the Rebbe's secretary with his handwritten response:

> Time and again in your holy work, you have imagined that the situation you found yourselves in was the end of the world, but then you saw how the situation flipped over and became one of visible and revealed good.... You must follow the command of the Tzemach Tzedek to think optimistically, and things will turn out well.

"What an answer! I have this answer hanging on the wall of my office, and I have it on my dresser at home. This answer is a teaching I try to remember every day—that as bad as things may look, they looked bad last time, too, but everything turned out fine.

"With that encouragement, we decided to move forward and do what we had to do. And a couple of days later, the problem was solved."[148]

This story appears to illustrate a deeper meaning in "think good and it will be good." It's not a flowery, out-of-touch approach that predicts no hardships at all. It is, in fact, a profoundly *resilient* approach to life and its momentary setbacks. It teaches a person to stare down their current complications, resist despair and worry, and defy them with active faith that all will be good. Then it will.

RABBI MENACHEM M. SCHNEERSON
Lubavitch
770 Eastern Parkway
Brooklyn 13, N. Y.

HYacinth 3-9250

By the Grace of G-d
23rd of Av, 5720
Brooklyn, N. Y.

Blessing and Greeting:

I received your letter of the 16th of Menachem Av, in which you write about your general frame of mind and your anxieties. I also understand that your husband has been in a similar mood lately.

Needless to say, I am quite surprised at both you and your husband, in view of your background. For the matter of Bitochon is not an abstract thing, but a real feeling that should fill the mind and heart with the awareness of G-d's proximity and closeness at all time and under all circumstances, in every aspect of one's daily life. Surely you know the emphasis which Chassidus places on the idea of Divine Providence, which extends to everyone and everything individually, and that it is a benevolent Providence, inasmuch as G-d is the Essence of Goodness, and that, as a result, every Jew should and is able to serve G-d with joy and gladness of heart.

I trust that you will again reflect on the points mentioned above, which our Sages of blessed memory summarized in their well-known statement, "All that the Merciful One does, is for the good," and you will strengthen your faith and trust in G-d and rid yourself of the troubling thoughts and anxieties. And this very faith and trust will provide the additional channels and vessels to receive G-d's blessings in all your needs.

Hoping to hear good news from you about yourself, and about every one of your family, accompanied by inner joy and gladness of heart,

with blessing
M. Schneerson

Takeaway

Liberate yourself from the grip of anxiety by shifting your perspective:

Think about G-d's infinite care for all His creations. Recognize that He certainly wants what's best for you. And reflect on His benevolent providence over everything that happens to you.

In the end it's all up to G-d, and He can be trusted. So why be anxious? Let it go.

Furthermore, when you cultivate an optimistic outlook and have faith that things will go well, not only will you *feel* better, but the result will actually *be* better.

Let's turn to another struggle endemic to the human experience: bad moods.

Chapter 8
Bad Moods

EVERYBODY KNOWS THE EXPERIENCE of a bad mood. Sometimes it lasts only a few hours, and other times it lingers for weeks. Sometimes it's triggered by an external reason, and other times it just shows up unprompted. We will explore some tools that can make bad moods easier to handle. But first we need to understand the source of our mood swings through a quick Kabbalah crash course.

The World of Chaos

IN THE BEGINNING OF times, the Talmudic sage Rabbi Abahu [3rd–4th century CE] taught, "G-d built worlds and destroyed them, until He built the current one and said: 'This one pleases Me; those did not please Me.'"[149]

The meaning of this teaching was discussed and debated for centuries.[150] It wasn't until the work of the great Kabbalist

Rabbi Yitzchak Luria (1534–1572), popularly known as the Arizal, that an entirely new perspective was introduced.[151] The Arizal explained that prior to reality as we know it, there existed a spiritual world called Tohu—the world of chaos.

In Tohu, every *sefirah*—divine attribute—reigned alone and allowed room for no other. The *sefirah* of kindness, for example, demanded infinite kindness, leaving no room for judgment and discipline. Alternatively, the *sefirah* of judgment demanded absolute justice, leaving no room for forgiveness. And so with all the other divine attributes. Every component of the world of chaos was one-dimensional. And infinitely so.

Think of the emotional world of a child, explained the fifth Lubavitcher Rebbe, Rabbi Shalom DovBer Schneersohn (1860-1920). A child in the throes of an emotion knows no buts or whys. They are entirely overtaken by the emotion that grips them at the moment. When one emotion reigns there is no room for another to exist simultaneously. There is no nuance, context, or complexity. This was the spiritual reality of Tohu.[152]

That world didn't last. That world *couldn't* last. The pulling at the seams of every component led to a cosmic demise.

In its place, G-d created the world of Tikkun, the world of order. It was to be a world of intersectionality, in which every being was to include in itself diverse (and opposing) characteristics. This is the multidimensional world in which we human beings live.

Our Transient Nature

ZALMAN GOPIN WAS A young man of Russian-Jewish descent whose family escaped Soviet oppression in the crack that opened in the Iron Curtain after World War II. They ultimately made it to Israel, where Gopin became known to his friends as a diligent boy who engaged seriously with matters of spirituality. He would take account of his behavior in search of areas that needed improvement, immerse himself in soulful prayer, and meditate for hours on the sublime ideas of the Kabbalists and Chasidic masters.

In 1965, when Gopin was twenty years old, he came to spend a year in the Rebbe's presence and study his teachings firsthand. In a private audience upon his arrival, he brought up the various ills that afflicted him in his personal growth. One of them was his vulnerability to mood swings.

"Sometimes I get on a good streak for a while," he wrote in his note, "but it doesn't last because my mood changes for the worse and disrupts it all. Other times, I am in high and loose spirits, which leads to acting out."

Knowing of Gopin's immersion in Kabbalistic teachings, the Rebbe responded: "Every person is a changing being. Why, this is the difference between the world of Tohu and the world of Tikkun. In Tohu there was but one emotion—if it was the attribute of kindness, then it was only kindness, and if it was the attribute of strictness, then it was only strictness. But in our world, the world of Tikkun, it's sometimes like this and sometimes like that"—Gopin recounted that while saying these words, the Rebbe illustrated the fluctuation with hand motions—"sometimes a person feels down, and sometimes a person feels happy and joyful."

There is no need to feel anxious or self-critical about being susceptible to mood swings, the Rebbe appears to be saying. This is built into our nature as humans.

"Every one of us," reads a letter to a young woman demoralized by a recent decline in her mood and confidence, together with the whole of humanity, is not consistently in the same mood, which is why human beings are in a state of flux between ascent and descent. Who is greater than the truly righteous? And yet, even about them, the verse states, "Seven times the righteous person falls and [then] gets up,"[153] indicating that they, too, have ups and downs (though the downs are relative to their earlier level).

From the above it is understood that it is quite normal that your concentration and self-confidence, etc., are not always in the same state.[154]

"Every person," reads another letter,
> is a changing being and therefore also experiences changes in their state of mind. However, this shouldn't be perceived too severely, as your unpleasant state of mind is only a transient phenomenon....[155]

So here is a basic but important perspective to keep in mind when you experience a shift in mood, and you feel disappointed or even a little scared ("What's going on with me?"). There is nothing to worry about. We are multifaceted beings, and it is natural for us to experience various, sometimes negative, dispositions. Even when your current mood feels overwhelming and insurmountable, humans are dynamic, and there is good reason for optimism that your mood will change for the better.

CHAPTER 8

Harness the Mood

AFTER IMPARTING THIS POINT to Gopin, the Rebbe continued to advise him: "The key is to utilize each mood for divine service. When you feel bitter or melancholy, you should use that time for more diligent study and contemplative prayer. When you feel joyful, you should use that time to study and pray with a broad-minded approach, and to develop your love for your fellow."

Today, Gopin is a widely acclaimed teacher of Chasidic philosophy and a mentor to thousands. While recounting this event, he observed: "I was expecting the Rebbe to advise me on how I should *change* my somber disposition and impress on me the importance of maintaining a joyous spirit. But he didn't do that. Instead, he advised me on how to utilize each emotional state *as is*.

"And I took this as a broader lesson in life, not only for my particular issue of fluctuation in studies and personal growth: Life has ups and downs. Sometimes things go well and sometimes things get rough. But it's helpful to remember that every state we find ourselves in, even a challenging one, contains a special quality that can be utilized for a unique divine purpose."[156]

The [dejected] mood you write about—although of course it is painful (and rightfully so)—shouldn't be seen as more severe than it actually is. For it is the symptom of [your moving to] a new location and environment, which requires acclimation, compromises, and so on—especially since your parents don't live here, so now you need to carry the responsibility for things they usually decide. From the above it is also understood that your mood will improve as you become more comfortable and acclimated, if you only put in effort. Additionally—you should befriend the young women in your area....

It is understood that for various reasons, and especially to improve your mood, it would be beneficial for you to find a job (at least part-time), and it would be best if it is work that gives you satisfaction.

I will mention you in prayer in connection with the areas you wrote about. And the more you strengthen your *bitachon* in G-d (and, by extension, increase your happiness), the more you will receive G-d's blessings. May you be inscribed for a good year.

Takeaway

It is common to react to a shift in mood with disappointment or even despair. ("After successfully staying upbeat for so long, why am I suddenly feeling down?")

However, the experience can be a whole lot easier when approached from another perspective.

First, remember that human beings are dynamic, so it is entirely natural for your mood to fluctuate. By the same token, just as your sunnier mood might disappear for a time, it is certain to return again.

Second, when your somber self shows up, utilize its appearance for deeper reflection, more introspective prayer, and more immersive study. When approached this way, your mood change is hardly a system malfunction; it is a valuable and constructive opportunity.

The next chapter explores tools for another prevalent downer: our harsh inner critic.

CHAPTER 9

Chapter 9
Self-Criticism

WE ARE OUR OWN worst critics. ("What a lazy bum you are!" "What a selfish person!" "You're such a bad spouse/parent/child!") In this chapter we'll explore ways to soften the sting of such harsh self-critical thoughts. But first—a quick crash course in criminal law.

IN MEDIEVAL TIMES, CONFESSIONS were considered an indisputable reason to convict someone. If the prosecution extracted a confession from the defendant, the case was sealed. What more could possibly be needed? He admitted it himself!

As civilization progressed, it became clear that many innocent people were being forced to admit to entirely fabricated crimes. Beginning in the 1600s, the Western legal system adopted a law called corpus delicti ("body of the crime"). It stipulates that corroborating evidence of an actual crime having taken place is always needed for conviction. Confession alone is not enough.

However, even under corpus delicti, confession still plays a major role: Once police have confirmed that a crime has indeed taken place, confession can sometimes be the only evidence pointing to who the criminal is. In many legal systems today, self-incrimination is enough to determine a suspect's guilt, and no other evidence is required.

Jewish law takes a different position. Rava, the great chair of the Babylonian Talmudic academy at the turn of the second century CE, famously ruled: "A person is their own relative, and thus a person cannot be trusted to render themselves wicked."[157] Even if a crime has been confirmed, if there is no evidence indicating who the criminal is, one's own testimony is not relied upon to render them "wicked," i.e., guilty. The reason? "A person is their own relative."

What does that mean?

One interpretation[158] is that Rava's words point to a profound psychological truth: "A person is their own relative"—our minds are incapable of being objective about ourselves. Just as our minds can inflate our accomplishments and self-worth, they can similarly exaggerate the severity of our failures. Therefore, says Rava, even if you testify about your own guilt, your testimony is not sufficient evidence. Your subjective mind may see your actions in a far worse light than the objective reality merits.

WHEN PEOPLE WOULD BERATE themselves to the Rebbe, depicting their grim moral state or overall failed existence, he would often teach them Rava's ruling. He would explain that as human beings, we see things subjectively, and, being emotionally involved, it is easy for us to see our state as dramatically worse than it is. As he concluded a letter to a man who lamented his utter incompetence:

> May it be G-d's will that you recognize the truth in the saying of our Sages that "a person is their own relative" and therefore doesn't judge their own situation accurately, sometimes tilting their assessment to the right and sometimes to the left.[159]

Similarly, in response to a young man who asserted that despite a year of working to improve himself he remained the exact same flawed individual he was before, the Rebbe wrote the following:

> There is a well-known ruling of our Sages: "A person cannot be trusted to testify about themselves," since "a person is their own relative." And just as regarding legal matters one is trusted to testify neither in favor of their own innocence nor the opposite [i.e., their own guilt]—the same is true regarding matters of the heart…. Although it may be true that you had the ability to change more than you did, Heaven forbid to say that in the last twelve months you haven't changed at all! Indeed, the verse says,[160] "Distance yourself from falsehood."[161]

So the first point to remember when confronted by a self-critical thought is this: You are "your own relative." This taints your perspective, and makes you susceptible to exaggeration. Don't trust the dark picture your mind is painting. In all likelihood, it doesn't reflect reality.

JEWISH WISDOM TAKES THIS a step further: Overblown self-criticism is more than just a side effect of your subjective mind. It is also a symptom of a dark inner force that actively propels such destructive thoughts.

The Negative Inclination

THE TALMUD TEACHES THAT every person has two *yetzers*—two opposing inner forces.[162] One motivates you to do what is right, to grow, to be better; this is called the *yetzer tov*—the good inclination. The other seeks to hinder you and put you on the path of self-destruction; this is called the *yetzer hara*—the evil inclination.

The Chasidic masters would often[163] refer to the *yetzer hara* as *der klugenker* (Yiddish for "smart aleck"), explaining that this negative voice is quite clever with how it brings you down. It doesn't try to seduce you with obvious nonsense that's clearly out of line with your values ("Hey, why don't you rob that bank?"). Quite the contrary, it uses moralistic negative self-talk in the spirit of your dearest principles ("What a disgraceful hypocrite you are!") to shrewdly put your weaknesses on display and lead you to despair.

Nosson Gourary was an American teenager and yeshiva student in the 1960s. He had an ongoing correspondence and several personal meetings with the Rebbe about his studies and development. "One time," he related, "I complained to the Rebbe that everything I do is with ulterior motives.

"The Rebbe told me that being that this simply isn't true—there are times that you do things without ulterior motives—you should know that it is only your *yetzer hara* trying to bother you, and you should say to your *yetzer hara* that you don't have time to spend with him, since the issue is fundamentally false. Especially since the Talmud teaches that *mitoch shelo lishmah ba lishmah*[164]—one who acts out of ulterior motives will eventually come to act for the right reasons—a person must therefore continue to do Torah and *mitzvot* even with ulterior motives, and eventually his motives will be pure."[165]

Here we see the Rebbe take a common mode of self-critical thinking, one that teenagers are especially prone to ("Everything I do is to impress other people... to advance a personal agenda... in order to get attention. I'm a fraud!"), and expose it for what it really is—a devious tactic of the *yetzer hara* that will get you nowhere. Don't be convinced by this seemingly authentic self-censure. Dismiss the voice obsessing about motives and continue the good things you're doing.

In another instance, a young woman wrote to the Rebbe that she aspired to go into education and was currently enrolled in a course for teachers. However, she was experiencing a loss of concentration and self-confidence, leading her to doubt whether she was capable of being a good teacher.

"It is clear," begins the response,
> based on what I have heard and know about you, that divine providence has gifted you with a talent for education, with the ability to absorb knowledge well, and in general with those characteristics necessary to succeed as a teacher and educator....
>
> In addition to the above, one of the tactics of the *yetzer hara*, who wants to disturb a person from serving their Creator—which necessitates peace of mind; a confidence that everything the Creator does is for a good purpose; and thus a

confidence that alongside the talents gifted to you, you were also certainly provided the ability to actualize them purposefully—is to convince a person that a temporary and normal setback is in fact much more serious, by inflating and intensifying it in their eyes....[166]

Identifying highly self-critical thoughts as the voice of the *yetzer hara* can help you push back against that line of thinking. When you take a step back and see it for what it is—merely a tactic of your evil inclination—it loses its hold on your emotions and becomes easier to ignore.

ALL THIS LEADS US to an important question: Aren't some self-critical thoughts good? Don't some of them allow you to recognize your defects and growth opportunities? And if so, how can you know when the voice is constructive and when it's a tactic of the *yetzer hara*?

The Bottom Line

THERE IS A SIMPLE barometer from the Chasidic masters:[167] Ask yourself what the end result of these self-reproachful thoughts will be. Will they lead you to do good, to improve yourself, to be more productive? Or will they lead you to self-doubt, despair, and stagnation? If the answer is the latter, however profound and virtuous the thoughts seem, you can be sure they stem from the *yetzer hara*.

A response to a teacher who had written to the Rebbe that

he sometimes thinks to himself, "Who am I to teach others, knowing what I really am?" reads as follows:

> The barometer to discern from where such thoughts arise is already known: if they inhibit you from a good activity, it is certain that these thoughts stem from "the other side" [i.e., the side of *Kelipah*, or impurity], as the Rebbe Rashab taught. Be done with scatter-headedness and distracting thoughts of this sort, and may you share good news of your positive influence on your students.[168]

An American businessman once wrote to the Rebbe that he expected far more of himself than he was in the position to accomplish. These thoughts were plaguing him and he felt dejected. In the response, after noting that the sentiment to expect more of oneself every new day is usually a virtue, the Rebbe continued,

> Nevertheless, the important thing is that such calculations should bring an additional measure of energy and activity. But it should be remembered that energy and activity can come only from a state of vitality, which is the opposite of frustration. Therefore, if one's reflections have the result of bringing only frustration, then the thing to do is to dismiss such reflections from the mind in order to be able to carry on one's daily activities with joy.[169]

Tzvi Grunblatt was born in Argentina in 1954 to a father who had survived the concentration camps and a mother who had escaped Hitler's Germany. The community in Buenos Aires where he grew up was made up mostly of European immigrants and survivors seeking a safe haven from the ashes of Europe. Although they taught their children some nostalgic Jewish traditions, the vibrant spirit of Judaism was considered to be hopelessly lost, along with everything else of their old homes.

However, being a thirsty soul, young Grunblatt gravitated towards a Chasidic man who was active in the community. Something was different about him. His soulful prayers and his passion for life stirred something in Grunblatt.

"If you want to explore Judaism in depth," the man advised him, "go to New York and study in the Rebbe's yeshiva." Grunblatt took up his suggestion, traveled to Brooklyn, and eagerly ventured into the new world opening before him. He threw himself into the bottomless sea of the Talmud, the mystical universe of Chasidic teachings, the vigilant work of self-refinement, and the immersive experience of meditative prayer.

Nonetheless, despite his sincere efforts, he felt deeply inadequate. He would regularly criticize himself that he was failing in his pursuits and that he wasn't living up to the image of a true Chasidic yeshiva student. Vexed by these thoughts, he felt an urgent need to meet with the Rebbe to discuss his spiritual state. He beseeched the Rebbe's secretary to override the normal waiting time and squeeze him into the busy schedule. Finally, his request was granted.

Grunblatt later recalled: "The Rebbe said to me, 'Regarding what you write that you can't do this and can't do that, that you're not successful in this or that—our Sages have said that "if you put in effort *you will succeed*." This was said to me, and to you, and to other Jews. Thus, since you put in the effort, you certainly had success. Your critical thoughts that you're failing simply cannot be true.'

"The Rebbe then continued, 'Any type of thoughts that lead you to dejection [are certainly not virtuous, for they] only detract from your vigor in action, they only detract from *bitachon* [trust in G-d], and they only detract from your time and energy. Thus, any [denigrating] thoughts that deject you—you must throw them out!'"

Grunblatt took those words to heart. Two years later, as a newly-married man, he returned to Argentina with his wife, Shterna, and spearheaded one of the great Jewish revivals of modern times, building and overseeing what is today a network of over sixty synagogues, Jewish schools, and social service organizations across Argentina.

Recounting that meeting some forty years later, Grunblatt lingered for another moment: "Those were his words to me... 'You must throw them out!'"[170]

It Is Prohibited

THERE IS YET ANOTHER tool to disarm the *yetzer hara*'s weapon of self-denigration.

A central teaching in the Torah is the prohibition against engaging in *lashon hara*—derogatory speech.[171] Even if the content of the speech is accurate, one is prohibited from pointlessly speaking ill of someone, discussing their weaknesses, or recounting their misdeeds.

In his counseling, the Rebbe would often quote the Chasidic saying that "the prohibition against talking badly about someone *applies to talking badly about oneself, too.*" And this doesn't apply only in cases of exaggeration; such speech is prohibited even if it is entirely true. Bemoaning your flaws for no constructive reason is not only not a virtue—it is wrong.

"I just received your recent letter," begins a 1953 response, and I have also received your previous letter. I am dismayed by the [harsh] words you write about yourself. I have recounted multiple times in the past an anecdote that my saintly father-in-law [Rabbi Yosef Yitzchak Schneersohn, the previous Rebbe] repeated to me: An individual once visited him for a private audience and asked for a way to mend various things. While posing his query, he described himself and his spiritual state in dreadful terms. In response, my father-in-law told him that the severity of the prohibition against speaking badly about someone is well known—and this, he continued, includes also oneself.[172]

In a letter responding to a man who criticized himself sharply, the Rebbe explained the reasoning:
> The prohibition of *lashon hara* applies even to oneself. And this is true about every single person. Because each and every person has a divine soul that is "a part of G-d." And even at the time of failure, it remains connected to G-d.[173]

Pointlessly dwelling on our faults and mistakes is an affront to our essential divine soul, which remains untarnished. We are denigrating it by our self-depreciation, even if it is true. All the more so that it is often our subjective mind and evil inclination deceiving us.

LET'S CONCLUDE WITH A short story:

Mendel Lipskar was a Canadian teenager studying in Brooklyn in the mid-1960s. Gifted with an acute mind, he excelled in analyzing the cryptic dialogues of the Talmud. However, despite his academic success, he was running into difficulties with his study partner. "We were constantly at loggerheads with each other," Lipskar recalled. "Whatever he would say, I would contradict; whatever I would say, he would contradict." Lipskar began to harbor doubts about what this combativeness indicated about his character. Disturbed, he decided to bring it up in an audience with the Rebbe.

"I told the Rebbe that I thought there was something wrong with me that I was arguing with this guy all the time. But the Rebbe said to me simply, 'It would appear that you have a gift for *pilpul*.' By *pilpul*, he meant the ability to reach the core of a given idea through intense dialogue and debate. Suddenly, something that had seemed to be a problem, I now saw as something positive—we were arguing because we were dissatisfied with a shallow reading of the text; we wanted to find a deeper meaning. It wasn't a flaw to denigrate; it was instead a virtue to cultivate."[174]

RABBI MENACHEM M. SCHNEERSON
Lubavitch
770 EASTERN PARKWAY
BROOKLYN 13, N. Y.

HYacinth 3-9250

מנחם מענדל שניאורסאהן
ליובאוויטש

770 איסטערן פּארקוויי
ברוקלין נ. י.

By the Grace of G-d
15th of Shevat, 5714
Brooklyn, N. Y.

Mr.

Greeting and Blessing:

I received your letter of the 4th of Shevat. Because of the intervening 10th of Shevat, yahrzeit of my Father-in-law of saintly memory, I was unable to reply to you sooner. And now, too, there is an accumulation of work which prevents me from writing more than a few lines.

I was pleased to see that you have taken the trouble to write to me in detail, and I hope that you will continue to do so in the future.

With regard to the question of introspection and self-searching, my Father-in-law of saintly memory used to emphasize that one should not indulge in this continually. There are certain times which have been set aside for self-examination and thoughts of self-improvement, such as the month of Elul and the Ten Days of Repentance, etc. And, although every day one has to practice "turn away from evil and do good," reviewing the past and the like should not preoccupy one's mind all the time, since that would interfere with and weaken the proper discharge of our religious duties in our daily life.

In your case, I see that although you feel much better, there is still a lot of room for improvement. Your first thought should be to get well physically, following the instructions of the physician, remembering what Maimonides ruled (Hilechoth Deoth, beginning Chapter 4) to the effect that taking care of ones health is also one of the ways of serving G-d.

May G-d bless you with good health that you and your wife bring up your children to a life of Torah, Chupah and good deeds.

With blessing,

Takeaway

Self-critical thoughts are confusing. They speak in the name of character development, but they often don't feel quite right. Are they the voice of your moral compass? Or are they something else to be ignored?

Use this simple tool to dispel the confusion: Look ahead to the results. Does this line of thinking lead you to actionable growth? Or does it bring down your spirit and lead you to despair? If indeed the latter is the case—as it so often is—know that these thoughts are certainly the voice of your *yetzer hara* (evil inclination) trying to derail you. Treat this critic as the conniving enemy that it is.

It also helps to remember the following: "a person is their own closest relative" and you inevitably have a subjective perception of your own shortcomings. Furthemore, regardless of the objective reality, such futile self-denigration is morally wrong, as it disparages your beautiful, G-d-given soul.

However, once you have identified these thoughts as something you want to rid yourself of, they won't necessarily leave. Our minds are in fact populated by thoughts we prefer not to engage with. So what now?

This leads us to a broader cognitive tool found in the Rebbe's counseling.

Chapter 10
Don't Battle; Pivot

"Do not answer a fool according to his foolishness, lest you become like him."
—*Proverbs, 24:6*

"If you wrestle with a filthy opponent you are bound to become dirty yourself."
—*Tanya, Chapter 28*

RARE IS THE PERSON who hasn't experienced the hurt of a loved one's piercing words and the accompanying impulse to respond. The insult tugs at our hearts, lingers in our minds, and goads us to retort forcefully. Nevertheless, it's often wiser to resist this impulse and avoid making an issue of it by steering the discussion elsewhere. This allows the relationship to heal instead of falling down a rabbit hole of mutual resentment.

Just like in the fraught world of relationships, this approach is equally effective in our own inner world.

When people struggling with various negative thoughts consulted with the Rebbe, he frequently recommended an approach of *hesech hadaat*—to give the negative thoughts as little attention as possible. The goal is to disengage from the negativity entirely: not to think about it—and not to think about not thinking about it. In the Rebbe's words: "Diverting attention doesn't mean battling the thought, for even battling a thought is the opposite of stopping to think about it."[175]

When we give attention to an undesirable thought—through indulging it, picking it apart, or even vigorously attempting to shove it out of our minds—its hold on us only grows. When we give it less mental space, however, it is deprived of a platform, and is left to fade away.

"The analogy," a letter explains,
> would be in the behavior of a physical muscle, which, when not used, eventually becomes atrophied. Similarly, when the mind is trained to reject a certain thought or problem, it can be freed from it eventually.[176]

The less we are preoccupied with negative thoughts, the more our innate constructive energies can restore us to a healthy state. This letter to a professional who sought advice on how to help her patients (the exact clinical condition she specialized in is unclear) explains:
> It is difficult to offer counsel from afar, as the specifics of the country, the family, and so on, have a direct bearing in such situations...
> However, since you have already written to me, and everything is by divine providence,

I wish to stress a method—which to my amazement is not utilized, at least not as much as it should—that I have found to be helpful and effective in most similar cases. And that is the method of *hesech hadaat*. The more the patient succeeds in stopping to dwell upon their condition and treatment, the greater the ability of their body's *natural* healing and curative powers to function with increased vitality and bring about healing.[177]

Change the Topic

NO DOUBT, IT IS difficult to pivot away from thoughts and feelings that preoccupy us. Our minds flow with all sorts of notions whether or not we want them to. Thus, it's not enough to simply command the mind to stop thinking about something—we need to proactively change the topic to something else entirely.

"It is not an easy thing," reads a letter to a young man,
> to dismiss a problem from the mind, especially one that involves one's own self. This would be almost impossible unless one can engage one's thought and attention in a completely unrelated subject. For man's process of thinking is constantly in a state of flux, and has a tendency, consciously or subconsciously, to revert to the subject matter which one wishes to dismiss from the mind. Therefore, when resolving to dismiss the matter from one's mind,

it is necessary immediately to find some other subject, unrelated to the first, in which to engage one's attention.[178]

"To divert attention," explains another letter, means to *think about entirely unrelated matters*. When the troubling thought arises in the mind, do not give it any heed; do not delve into the thought or do battle with it. Rather, push it aside by thinking about something else.[179]

We don't have control of the flotsam that comes down the river of our mind. What *is* up to us is what we do once a bothersome thought arrives. When we have the presence of mind to use the *hesech hadaat* tool, we can tell ourselves: Just don't touch it. Think about something else. Keep doing what you're doing. If you don't engage with it, it'll ultimately pass.

(In my experience, I've found that the tool builds strength over time. In the beginning it's hard to practice. You fail a lot. You try to disengage and move your mind elsewhere, only to find yourself engaging again a minute later. And you try again. Again you fail. It can be demoralizing. But with time, persistence, and practice, you get better at it. And it in turn becomes more effective. Importantly, you become less worried when negative thoughts arise. You know you won't go into a tailspin. You can give it the *hesech hadaat* treatment. That will help it pass. Like water under a bridge.)

HERE WE MUST ASK: Should the *hesech hadaat* tool be applied to all human struggles? What if we have a problem that requires remedial action (say, a marriage on the rocks or a deteriorating health issue)? Should we try to use *hesech hadaat* even then? Why, simply diverting our minds from it won't fix it!

Let's unpack this a little.

A letter from 1956 outlines three types of problems in relation to the human mind:

> There are many issues whose existence lies outside the person; other issues that at least have existence within the individual's inner self; and finally, there are those issues whose entire existence consists of the person's thinking about them....[180]

This letter appears to delineate three types of distressing issues that can occupy our minds:

Some negative thoughts are stimulated by practical issues that exist entirely outside our psyche. For example, if we're having financial or health problems, and our minds become consumed with them.

Then there are thoughts whose subject matter are indeed real, substantive issues, but are nevertheless rooted inside our own inner world. For example, if we're disturbed about our challenges with anger or addiction.

Finally, there are negative thoughts whose *entire existence begin and end with themselves*. For example, if we're torturing ourselves about having made a minor, unfixable mistake, or if we're wrapped in the drama of one of those unfounded stories we tell ourselves, or if we're obsessing over what other people think of us. These are, of course, stressful thoughts that can genuinely overtake us. But they have no independent grounding. The letter continues:

Clearly, the thoughts that you are now experiencing are of the third type. This type of negativity is easier to nullify; and it often even dissipates on its own through mere *hesech hadaat*—either a diversion stimulated by an external catalyst, or even through your own resolve to divert your mind from it. Certainly, the above is known to you as well, but sometimes when things are expressed verbally or in writing and come from someone else, they become clearer. I hope it will be so with this as well.[181]

When a disturbing thought of this third type surfaces, you can tell yourself: Look, there isn't *really* anything here. There isn't really anything that's getting between you and freedom, between you and happiness, between you and whatever you should be doing now. So let it go. Sure, at the moment the thought feels like an elephant that's impossible to ignore. But if you divert your mind from it, and look back days or months later—you will realize that it was just a paper tiger. There was nothing there at all.

The following handwritten note puts it succinctly:

Since its entire existence is only in the world of thought and only [comes to life] through your "digging" into it, therefore, the more you refrain from thinking about it, the easier it will become [to tolerate], and these thoughts will begin to weaken until they will be entirely gone.[182]

HOWEVER, IT DOESN'T END there. While *hesech hadaat* is especially useful for problems that reside solely in our minds (the third type referenced in the letter), it has a far wider scope, too.

Even when experiencing real-world obstacles (the first and second type in the letter)—whether they are medical, psychological, financial, etc.—the distressed and nervous thoughts *around the issue* are counterproductive. Thus, returning to our earlier question, the *hesech hadaat* tool *is* indeed useful in such situations. For, alongside dealing with the problem by whatever means necessary, diverting our minds from constantly focusing on it significantly aids the healing process.

This notion—that instead of mentally or emotionally battling an issue one should try to approach it pragmatically, without the anxiety born of obsession—can be found in the Rebbe's counseling on a wide variety of challenges. Following are some diverse examples.

A HUSBAND WROTE TO the Rebbe that his wife was diagnosed by a doctor with agoraphobia (a fear of crowds). From the husband's letter it seems that he and his wife were terrified that this fear might continue for an extended period of time. The Rebbe's handwritten response begins:

> She should approach her condition [in an] "easy" [manner]. Meaning:
>
> 1. "She should know that there are *many* people who suffer from this condition and [nevertheless] live with calm and tranquility, etc.
>
> 2. When she needs to enter a hall, if she can go in *easily*, she should do so. However, if she cannot, she should not fight with herself nor force herself to do this *at all*... and a big deal should not be made about this.[183]

A WORRIED FATHER WROTE a letter to the Rebbe, explaining that his son had been training in the laws of kosher slaughter but had developed anxiety attacks. The attacks caused his hand to sporadically become weak and lose its grip on the knife. This had disrupted the son's training, putting his employment plans in limbo, and causing him much distress.

The Rebbe met personally with the son and subsequently wrote a letter to the father sharing the advice he had offered at the meeting, as well as his understanding of the son's issue. Here is an excerpt:

> In general one of the areas where the darkness of exile is evident is in the fact that although it is explained in various sources that "a person does not know [in advance] through what means they will support themselves,"[184]...nevertheless, [in today's society] from a relatively young age, a material plan [for a source of income] must be found, and toward this end all things that are necessary for a person's true happiness are disrupted....
>
> Unfortunately, this is what happened to your son. It appears that at some point within the last few years, for whatever reason, he became concerned with how he would support himself in the future. This anxiety has burrowed deep into his psyche and has left him with an inner "tightness." Because of this overwhelming anxiety (though it is possible that he doesn't realize *intellectually* how worried he is) he now looks at his current craft as the thing upon which his entire future is dependent.

This buried angst is what brought about the phenomenon [of his hand shaking].

It is understood that in one conversation one cannot change someone else's outlook entirely, especially given that this has already been entrenched deeply in his heart for a few years....

Thus, I did not explain the above to him for various reasons, and I made a few practical suggestions instead:

1. He should immediately begin to prepare another source of income. This way, even to his own mind, he will have reason to think he can support himself in this other way, so his future is not dependent exclusively on his current craft....

2. If the weakness in his hand appears again, he shouldn't fight against it to try and overcome it at precisely that moment; rather, he shouldn't give it any prominence—which includes not fighting with it either. [It's fine] if he won't sharpen the knife at that moment or even that day—he can sharpen it the next day or the day after....

3. To take him out of a narrow mental space of fears and concerns and needing to know how he will support himself and instead bring him to a broader mental space, it is necessary that he have a daily time to study the teachings of Chasidut—the soul of the Torah, the tree of life...[185]

A YOUNG MAN ONCE wrote to the Rebbe about his struggles with stuttering. After advising him to consult a specialist, the Rebbe added:
> A practical piece of advice: When you feel that the word you are about to speak is difficult for you to verbalize, do not force yourself to say that word immediately; go back a word or two, or speak about something else. When you alleviate yourself of the tension, the situation will naturally improve.[186]

A TECHNIQUE SOMETIMES FOUND in the letters for releasing the tense thoughts and feelings around an issue is to envision how life can be okay *alongside the struggle*; to consider that even if the problem remains, it won't necessarily be the end of the world. Paradoxically, the fact that you feel less anxious about the problem makes it easier to actually overcome it.

The following is part of a response to a woman who had developed a fear of travel (it's not clear, but it may have been specifically a fear of planes):
> Diverting your attention to the extent possible from your fear will weaken the fear. Of the considerations that will make it easier to not focus on your fear: consider that travel is not *at all* of central importance in a person's life. *Millions* of people today, and more in past generations, don't travel because they have no need or interest in it. For the Jewish people, Shabbat and festivals (which epitomize days of

pleasure and yet travel is prohibited on them) demonstrate this point.[187]

A MIDDLE-AGED MAN ONCE wrote to the Rebbe about his problem with obesity, his anxiety about it, and his struggles (and failure) to reduce the quantity of his eating. Following is part of the response:

> In my opinion, 1. The doctors exaggerate in their assessment of the damage caused by a person's larger size (additional weight).
>
> 2. Distraction, or at least not *constantly* thinking about it, will make your struggle with excessive eating easier. This will also increase your peace of mind, which will automatically strengthen your metabolism, reducing extra fat. In addition, and this too is central, you will be able to serve G-d with joy.[188]

SOMETIMES TAKING A TEMPORARY break is advised.

In 1986, a woman wrote to the Rebbe about her unsettled state of mind and her complex ruminations on her life and relationships. Here is part of the Rebbe's response:

> It would be most beneficial that for about a year you entirely cease making an accounting of your life: how others treat you, your relationship to the world, etc.... When soul-searching thoughts surface in your mind, tell yourself *decisively* and without debating it *at all*, that I refuse to think about these matters before the year 5748 [the Jewish year beginning in fall of 1987], and that presently my task is to ensure that my home and life be conducted with *simplicity, sincerity,* and joy.[189]

A WOMAN ONCE WROTE to the Rebbe about her inner confusion. (She seems to have been overtaken by thoughts in the spirit of, "Who am I really?" to the point of profound angst and befuddlement.) The Rebbe responded with a handwritten note. Here is part of it:

> There are periods in a person's life when they are unable to clearly identify how they feel, due to their frame of mind and similar reasons.... In such periods, it is advisable (and possible) to live a quiet life, without deep introspection.... Enjoying this quiet for (around) a half a year will [give you] peace of mind, and then you can begin to think about how to move forward.[190]

A BUSINESSMAN ONCE WROTE to the Rebbe about his contentious relationship with his competitors and asked for advice on how to handle it. The Rebbe responded:

> One point of advice is to divert your attention from them; and—in the spirit of the verse, "Just as water reflects [back] the face [presented to it], so does the heart of man respond to the heart of his fellow man"[191]—ultimately, this will cause that they, too, will move their attention away from you and your endeavors.[192]

A COUPLE ONCE WROTE to the Rebbe about the difficulties they were experiencing in their relationship (the details are unclear, but it seems to have been less about conflict and more about emotional stagnation). In a handwritten response, the Rebbe wrote the following:

> In the "Torah of *truth*," our Sages have *extolled* the greatness of marriage and [the value of] maintaining one.[193]

> In matters connected with the *subconscious*, it sometimes happens that without intention and without *identifiable* action something changes and an internal [emotional] blockage breaks open *naturally*.
>
> Therefore, you should continue putting in effort in the direction where you've seen benefit and success in the past (at least for a period)—seeing a psychologist, visiting the Holy Land during your vacations, etc.; and, importantly, to *minimize* worrying about this and to divert your attention from all this to the extent possible. And may G-d grant you success, and you should be able to share good news.[194]

Practical Tips

THERE ARE TWO PRACTICAL tips that can make *hesech hadaat* easier.

One is to prepare concepts or texts to which you can redirect your mind when unwanted thoughts appear.

"It would be well," reads a 1952 letter,
> that you should memorize a few chapters of *Mishnah* [the founding text of the oral Torah] and a few chapters of *Tanya*. Needless to say, this memorizing should be in a manner that does not cause you stress. When you feel that you are getting agitated, or unwanted thoughts intrude, you should then think over a few passages of *Mishnah* and a few lines of *Tanya*.[195]

A second practice that can make *hesech hadaat* easier is to occupy yourself in a hands-on, productive activity. This provides a helpful external distraction.

> "It appears," begins a note to a young woman,
> that the primary reason for your [negative
> health] condition lies in the fact that you
> are ruminating about it *constantly*. The more
> you *divert* your mind from it—the more your
> condition will improve, and the more effective
> will be the medical treatments you are pursuing.
> To make diverting your mind from it easier,
> *occupy* yourself with something completely
> different, whatever it may be (a job, studies,
> assisting other girls in their Judaism, *and so
> on*). If you divert your mind from it *completely*—
> within a short period of time, you will heal.[196]

Before concluding, there is an important point to underscore:

The Power of Light

WHILE THE MAIN CONSIDERATION in *hesech hadaat* is to divert your mind to whatever is most effective in keeping your attention away from the unwanted thoughts—replacing them with "thoughts of light" provides an added potency, because the nature of light is to automatically dispel darkness.

When you light a candle in a dark room, the candle's light causes the darkness to fade without even battling it. The same is true in the metaphysical sphere: "thoughts of light" have an increased power to dissipate dark and disturbing thoughts.

For this reason, the Rebbe would often counsel his students to try to redirect their minds to thoughts of Torah and Chasidut. The serene world of G-d's wisdom, and especially Jewish mysticism's teachings on the world, the soul, and the Divine—exert a magnetic pull in the direction of light. They illuminate the mind and expedite its liberation from the unwanted and dark thoughts.

"Since the human mind constantly flows," reads a letter to a young man,

> the way to dispel an undesirable thought is through [thinking] a desirable thought. And it would be best if it would be in a thought of light from the Torah of Light,[197] for "even a little light dispels a lot of darkness."[198] [199]

LET'S CONCLUDE WITH A short story that illustrates the power of a little light to peacefully soothe internal darkness. It was the early 1980s, and Raizel Wolvovsky, a young mother in her late twenties, had a lot going on.

She was busy transforming a budding preschool into a flourishing educational institution. She was an active community leader, looking after the sick and caring for the immediate needs of families that had lost loved ones. And, above all, she was an attentive mother to her five children under the age of seven.

Naturally, the many responsibilities weighed on her and she decided to ask for the Rebbe's counsel on how to better cope with the pressure.

The Rebbe's handwritten response was brief. "[Light] Shabbat candles without stress," it read.

She took this advice to heart, and it became a guiding principle throughout the rest of her productive life. Her son recalled:

"In addition to her eleven children, my mother always hosted many guests for Friday night Shabbat meals. So there was good reason for her to feel pressure right before Shabbat. However—and I remember this vividly—as the sun was coming down, and the time for lighting the Shabbat candles arrived, a serene cloud came to rest on my mother and everything around her—something otherworldly. If I had anything I needed to wrap up before Shabbat, instinctively I would move somewhere else to do it—my mother never told me a word. The calm spirit she radiated simply didn't allow for rushed energy nearby."

Reflecting on the Rebbe's response, another of her sons observed:

"The Rebbe didn't advise her to lessen her activity. He didn't counsel her to combat her feelings of stress. And he also didn't say it wasn't an issue. Instead, he recommended creating a serene space of light, an oasis in time at the culmination of one week and the cusp of the next.

"I heard from my mother how this helped her maintain her emotional equilibrium, and I personally witnessed its effect. These sanctified minutes hovered over her week and life. Despite keeping a busy and productive schedule until her last days, internally, she was a woman at peace.

"We were privy to watch," he concluded, "how transporting oneself to a place of light, literally and metaphorically, melts away darkness. And without a fight."

RABBI MENACHEM M. SCHNEERSON
Lubavitch
770 Eastern Parkway
Brooklyn 13, N. Y.

HYacinth 3-9250

מנחם מענדל שניאורסאהן
ליובאוויטש

770 איסטערן פארקוויי
ברוקלין, נ. י.

By the Grace of G-d
20th of Tammuz, 5725
Brooklyn, N. Y.

Greeting and Blessing:

After not hearing from you for a very long time, I received your letter of July 3rd, which reached me with some delay.

With regard to the thought which you express in your letter, I believe I have already written to you before, or spoken to you, that there are many problems and states of mind which are best dealt with by dismissing them from the mind completely, at any rate for a period of time. It is then possible to return to those problems with a fresh mind, and in a more objective state, so as to evaluate the problems in their true perspective and reality, and it is then easier to find the proper solution. In the vast majority of such cases the individual himself can decide how long this period of dismissal from attention should be, judging by the degree of objectivity which he can attain as time goes on.

Needless to say, also, that it is not an easy thing to dismiss a problem from the mind, especially one that involves one's own self. This would be almost impossible unless one can engage one's thought and attention in a completely unrelated subject. For, man's process of thinking is constantly in a state of flux, and has a tendency, consciously or subconsciously, to revert to the subject matter which one wishes to dismiss from the mind. Therefore, when resolving to dismiss the matter from one's mind, it is necessary immediately to find some other subject, unrelated to the first, in which to engage one's attention.

Another point which is also almost universally true is that it is not easy for the person involved to find the proper subject in which to engage one's mind. But here it is possible to receive help from friends who would know you and your psychological make-up. Undoubtedly you have such friends within reach.

With reference to sins, etc., generally there is the teaching of our Sages that "Nothing stands in the way of repentance." Here too the principle enunciated above may be applied, namely, that although it is necessary to end the sin immediately, whether it is a sin of commission or omission, it is also often necessary to end immediately any self recrimination, or brooding, etc., in regard to the sins of the past.

One of the obvious reasons for this is that brooding over past failures is bound to be depressing and discouraging, and would undermine one's confidence in the future, and even one's confidence in the efficacy of Teshuvo. Therefore it is advisable to dismiss such thoughts for the time being, and leave them for more propitious times.

May G-d grant that you should have good news to report in regard to all above.

Finally, I want to make one further observation, which is one of those things which although they go without saying, are better said. I want to say that there is no need for you to be embarrassed in expressing your attitude towards me, whether you have any trust or lack of trust, etc. Such feelings are best to be expressed openly, rather than concealed, when there is a danger of developing a distorted relationship altogether.

I trust that you know of the history and significance of the 12-13th of Tammuz which we have just observed, and that the inspiration of these days will be with you throughout the year. The essential message is, of course, that when a Jew does not permit himself to be discouraged by any obstacles, but resolves to go along the way of the Torah, he can even single handedly overcome all difficulties, and accomplish extraordinary and wonderful things. And while none of us can compare to my father-in-law of saintly memory, we must also remember that the obstacles and difficulties we may be facing are almost quite insignificant by comparison with those which he faced. Furthermore, he has already trodden out the path of Mesiras Nefesh for us, which makes it easier for all who wish to follow in his footsteps, all the more so since his Zechus stands everyone in good stead.

With blessing M. Schneerson

RABBI MENACHEM M. SCHNEERSON
Lubavitch
770 EASTERN PARKWAY
BROOKLYN 13, N. Y.

Personal

Takeaway

When an anxious, stressful, or depressing thought enters your mind, you might feel compelled to indulge it, pick it apart, or argue with it.

However, giving negative thoughts attention only makes them stronger. Try to not make an issue of them. Don't think about them, and don't think about not thinking about them. Instead, change the topic to something else entirely.

Constantly thinking about a problem only gets in the way of overcoming it. Take all necessary steps to solve it. But use the above method to divert your mind from it. This will crown your actions with greater success.

We've seen that diverting your focus from angst about a problem can help resolve the problem itself. But there is another important step to easing this agitation.

CHAPTER 11

Chapter 11
Transcend Isolation

AN ANCIENT JEWISH PROVERB says, "A trouble shared is half consoled."[200]

Personal struggles are made exponentially worse when we think that we're suffering alone. We become anxious and panicky, scared that something is awfully wrong with us ("Only warped people get addicted to this stuff"). We feel isolated and lonely, distant from the people around us who don't seem to share our issue ("My friends vacation every year, while I struggle with rent"). We experience gnawing despair, wondering if we'll ever be "normal" again ("Can a marriage recover after a fight like that?").

When people opened up to the Rebbe about their challenges, he would often preface (or conclude) his advice with this message: Know that you're not the only one struggling with this. Many others are going through the same thing.

Of course, it is unfortunate that more people are suffering. But the comfort in knowing that others share our issue is not simply a symptom of selfishness, or our inability (as Yiddish-speaking grandmothers would say) to *fargin*—to graciously accept that others are doing better than us. Instead, discovering that many others can relate gives us a sense of belonging in a time of alienation. Importantly, it *normalizes the issue*. Nothing is inherently wrong with us—this is a natural, familiar human experience.

"This happens to *many* people," begins a response to a young man frightened by his gripping doubts in the course of dating. "Doubts about life arise (including doubts about marriage). Don't take this out of proportion or frighten yourself because of it."[201]

THIS WAS A RECURRING theme in the Rebbe's counseling on a wide variety of issues.[202] For example, in a handwritten response to a woman suffering from obsessive-compulsive disorder (OCD), before encouraging her to consult her doctor and offering other practical advice, the Rebbe wrote:

> Your doctor has surely informed you that *many* individuals find themselves in a similar situation to the one you describe (i.e., it seems to them they did something imperfectly, they believe their hands are not clean and they must rewash them, et al).[203]

Similarly concludes a letter to a young man going through a particular (unspecified) challenge that led him to live in isolation for several months and doubt his ability to build a home of his own:

> Upon inquiring you will discover that others experience [difficult] occurrences like the ones

you describe and nevertheless weather them. Furthermore, not all that long afterward, they even establish themselves successfully in life, and help other individuals who struggle—which, especially in such instances, is the greatest satisfaction of all. May G-d grant you success that all this comes to be sooner than you imagine.[204]

This awareness can be particularly important in those turbulent years of self-discovery, when the security of childhood is lost and the level-headedness of adulthood has yet to set in. A handwritten response to a teenager who opened up to the Rebbe about her inner turmoil, and added that to do so was in itself scary, begins as follows:

> There is no reason *at all* to be afraid of writing to me; I endeavor to assist to the best of my abilities, not to make things more difficult nor to criticize, Heaven forbid.
>
> During *transitional* times in a person's life (from childhood to adolescence, from adolescence to adulthood, etc.), one is generally more sensitive and less stable. It is therefore *normal* during such a time for new questions or doubts to arise. Although now these conundrums might seem insurmountable, when this stage passes you will be able to resolve them on your own, and without torment. However, in these transitional periods these dilemmas can seem very complicated. Through talking it over with someone else, they can explain to you how it can be resolved simply, etc.

> What is occurring with you is happening to *many others* as well, and will pass with time.[205]

Similarly concludes a long letter to an American college student who described herself as a loner who doesn't feel close to anyone, and wrote of her doubts and confusion:

> In conclusion, I would again like to volunteer an observation, though this time in a different vein, that you should not be so downhearted, since it is not unusual for young people of your age to feel a sense of confusion, or even frustration. One needs only to feel for those who refuse to accept a helping hand from near and dear ones, including parents. I do not mean to say that one must readily submit to parental dictatorship, but neither does this mean that one should always reject parental advice and help in the hope that eventually things will straighten out themselves.[206]

Which leads us to our next point.

Talk to Others

"IF THERE IS WORRY in [your] heart," says the Talmud, "tell it to others."[207]

Don't keep all your angst pent up inside, the Sages advise. Let someone else know about the anxious thoughts unsettling your mind and alarming your heart. This alone can ease your burden.

"Since one is only human," concludes a letter to a young woman,

> it is not unusual to lapse occasionally into a mood of discouragement. But…if you do find yourself in such a frame of mind, you should not try to conceal it…. For our Sages have said that when a person has an anxiety they should tell it to others, for getting something off one's chest is in itself already a relief.[208]

The Rebbe constantly encouraged people to leave the nerve-wracking solitude of their minds and discuss their dilemmas with caring and trustworthy individuals—wise mentors, impartial family members, and "knowledgeable friends" [i.e. those who are experienced in your area of struggle and know you personally[209]]. He would explain how others pull you out of your subjective ruminations and—with their cumulated life experience, calming words, and practical advice—help you understand that such challenges are normal, people have been here before, and there are tried and true ways to navigate this safely. You need only take the first vulnerable step of reaching out.

It was the late 1950s, and Bessie Garelik was pregnant with her first child. She was in her early twenties, and, in addition to the physical pain, her first pregnancy generated in her a storm of emotional turmoil. She had just moved with her husband to Milan, Italy, to serve the local Jewish community, and she felt forlorn and secluded. Having previously met and corresponded with the Rebbe, she wrote a letter to him describing all she was going through.

At around the same time, her older sister, Kenny, took a trip from Pennsylvania to New York to join an annual Chasidic women's convention in Brooklyn. On the second night of the convention, after the group visited the Rebbe, she wrote the following letter to her sister in Milan.

> Dear Bess,
> It's only 2:30 a.m....
> Now we'll start not with the beginning, but with the most important. We came to 770 last night at about 8 p.m. to go in to the Rebbe... The Rebbe's room was packed, and we filled the little balcony and half the steps. They closed the door to the outside hall so that we could all hear what the Rebbe said clearly. But it was disappointing not to see him.
>
> [After the address,] there was still a group of women inside who were each speaking privately [to the Rebbe], and the secretary told me to wait until they were finished and see if the Rebbe would call me over. After three-quarters of an hour, the last women left and, sure enough, the Rebbe turned that delightful smile my way. The secretary closed the door and I had a private audience with the Rebbe—about you...

"In the next letter I'll write what he said..." she teased her sister, and then continued:

> Seriously, the Rebbe wanted me to write and explain to you that the discomforts that you feel now are normal and are a result of your pregnancy. This is so, Bess. I felt that way too. One expects the physical changes, but the

mental [changes] or whatever you're bothered with are as much a part of your pregnancy (especially and most times only during the first three or four months), and they will disappear as soon as you're feeling better. So you see, you're really just having a normal pregnancy.

The Rebbe advised that you should speak about these things to one of the women [to whom] you feel close, and you'll find that in discussing them they will get lighter, and soon, G-d willing, disappear."[210]

IN ADDITION TO THE psychological benefits of opening up to another, there is a spiritual perk as well.

Spiritual Math

AS WE HAVE SEEN (in chapter 6), Kabbalah teaches that everything in our imperfect world, including human beings, are composed of both good and bad.[211]

But there is a fundamental difference between these two forces.[212] The bad is sourced in a world of division and discord. Being egotistical and narcissistic, it seeks only to grow its own dominance, and thus views other people as hostile competitors for attention, success, and power. The good, on the other hand, feels itself part of a greater divine whole and thus always seeks to bond with others.

The Chasidic master Rabbi Dovber Shneuri (the second Rebbe of Chabad, 1773–1827) taught that this notion gives us a glimpse into what happens spiritually when two friends have a heart-to-heart conversation:

The negative sides within each of the two friends are too egotistical to combine forces. Only the good sides within them unite as one. So each of their negative sides now face a two-to-one ratio—both of their good sides are effectively teamed up against their disjointed negative sides. Thus, just by talking, the two friends each find themselves in a far stronger position to overcome their personal struggles. As Rabbi Dovber phrased it, "It is now two divine souls against one animalistic soul."[213]

This letter to a young man sums it up:
In addition to the fact that you certainly already consult with the elders of the community, you should have a true friend, meaning one before whom you can reveal what is pressing on your heart. There is a known teaching of the Sages that, "If there is worry in [your] heart, tell it to others." Regarding this teaching, the Mitteler Rebbe [the "Middle Rebbe," as Rabbi Dovber is commonly referred to] explained that this way there are two divine souls competing against one animalistic soul. And the benefits of this are clearly evident.[214]

Be There for Others

WHEN STUDYING THIS THEME in both the Rebbe's private counseling and public teachings, one senses an escalating insistency, even urgency, as the years go by. Again and again, he would emphasize, with growing emotion, how vital it is that we talk to one another, how much we will gain in the process, and how much stronger we will all become as a result.

It appears as though the Rebbe was addressing an increasingly fragmented society, where individuals presume they must guess their way through life's unnerving complexities wholly on their own. His words seem to ask, almost beseech: Why should you carry all that weight yourself? Why should you navigate this winding path without a guide? Reach out to a mentor you respect. Listen to their caring advice. Consult with a friend who knows. Be humble enough to let them help you. There are such treasures of wisdom, of empathy, of shared life experience in us and around us—if only we open our hearts to each other.

Indeed, along with the Rebbe's encouragement to consult with others, he also emphatically urged people to make themselves available *to* others, both practically and emotionally. For one, he said, advising others will enlighten you as well, as the Sages taught, "More than from my teachers and friends— I've learned from my students."[215] But far more importantly, being there for others is the natural outgrowth of the Torah's foundational commandment, "Love your fellow as yourself."[216]

A handwritten note to community activists under financial strain and struggling to raise funds reads as follows:

Consult with knowledgeable friends. [As] friends [they] will *certainly* take interest in your situation in all its details. For "love your fellow as yourself" is 1) a principle 2) foundational 3) to the Torah. I will mention this [in prayer] at my father-in-law's resting place.[217]

The Rebbe invokes here the teaching of the Talmudic sage Rabbi Akiva (1st-2nd century CE)—that loving your fellow as yourself is a "foundational principle in the Torah"[218]—and illustrates how each of Rabbi Akvia's words vests new significance into this mandate. For it's not just another dictum, but a principle. And not just any principle, but a foundational principle, over and above all other principles. And it's not a foundational principle of just anything—it is a foundational principle of the sacred Torah, the eternal book of life. Thus, the Rebbe assures these individuals in the midst of a financial nightmare that they can feel completely confident reaching out to experienced friends. Considering the towering importance of being there for others, there's no doubt that their friends will be happy to give abundantly of their time and expertise to help them through their difficult situation.

A different world is envisioned here. If only we take up the Torah's directive to "love your fellow as yourself," if only we heed Chassidism's calling to unconditionally bond with others remembering our shared divine soul—then there will be no more need for costly measures to heal all the painful ailments that festered in isolation. The Chasidic love and generosity of spirit will fortify us to begin with. In the words of Isaiah that the Rebbe often quoted: "Each person helps his fellow and to his brother he says, 'Take courage!'"[219]

ON THIS NOTE, a short story.

Yitzchak Gansburg, or "Itchke" as he was commonly called, was an impassioned Chasidic man. Born in Soviet Russia to a Chasidic family in 1928, Gansburg felt an intimate bond with the Rebbe and wished to see him in person. However, even after he immigrated to Israel, for many years this remained impossible due to visa complications and financial constraints. Finally, for the High Holiday season of 1957, his dream came to fruition. Throughout his month-long stay in New York he wrote detailed letters to his family describing his cathartic experiences of spiritual ecstasy.

Unbeknownst to him, Leib Levin, his old-time friend from their shared youth in Russia, had also made the trip to New York to see the Rebbe. In years gone by, they had often spent evenings together discussing their inner struggles, and encouraging each other to remain strong in spirit and resilient in action in the face of hardship and failure. However, many years back, Levin moved to France, and the two friends had not been able to see each other since then.

In one letter home, Gansburg described the following moment:

> It was 7:15 p.m. and evening prayers were about to begin. Suddenly, my friend Leib Levin from Paris materialized before me.
>
> I cannot describe to you my inner joy upon seeing this dear and beloved friend. Tears appeared in my eyes and we heartily embraced.
>
> At that very moment, the door of the Rebbe's study opened and he entered the sanctuary. We immediately stood still—but it turns out that the Rebbe had already glimpsed our embrace. He looked at us and a soft smile spread over his saintly face. He went [back] to his study for a short moment and immediately returned for evening prayers.
>
> Later, I heard that the Rebbe had remarked: "This is the meaning of Chasidic love."[220]

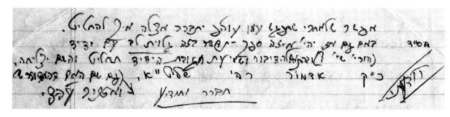

To a young woman in doubt while dating someone for marriage:

It is possible that after you meet with him again a decision will become clear to you. If you still have doubts—discuss them *open-heartedly* with a friend (your parents?). Make your decision according to how [you feel after] you talk and hear your friend's reaction, and may G-d grant you success. I will mention you in prayer at the resting place of my father-in-law.

(What is the mother's name of the young man [you're meeting, so I can pray for him as well?])

Takeaway

If you are struggling in a particular area in your life (say, work pressure, parenting, addiction, depression, or anything else), remember the following:

It may not appear this way, but many people—perhaps even in your immediate surroundings—deal with issues similar to yours. There is no reason to berate yourself or panic; you are going through a perfectly normal human experience.

On a practical level, you don't need to go it alone. There are caring and competent individuals to consult with. Reach out to someone with insight in this area. Open up to a trustworthy friend.

This will ease your emotional isolation, provide you with fresh perspective, and strengthen your fortitude to successfully navigate life's challenges.

So far we've explored essential outlooks for a healthy self: to be a giver, to know you're not alone, to recognize your special purpose.

We've surveyed lifestyle habits necessary for solid emotional health: to ensure your body has what it needs, to have a productive occupation, to maintain structure in your day, to remain socially engaged, to routinely practice *mitzvot*—G-dly acts.

We've discussed ways to cope with common emotional challenges, such as discontent, worry, mood swings, or self-criticism.

We've gained tools for easing the mental and emotional tension around struggles: to not indulge or battle those anxious thoughts but instead change the topic, to know you're normal and not alone, to open up and consult with a knowledgeable friend.

However, *everything* in this book hinges on one underlying foundation, without which no growth is possible: *the courage to change.*

Coda
The Courage to Change

DR. REUVEN FEUERSTEIN (1921–2014) was a globally acclaimed cognitive psychologist.

Born into a Jewish family in Romania, he narrowly escaped the Nazis in his early twenties and eventually settled in Mandatory Palestine. There he observed immigrant children, many of whom were either Holocaust survivors or refugees from North African countries, struggling in their studies, and he realized that their difficulties extended beyond language and cultural barriers. He came to the conclusion that these children, having grown up in tumultuous environments, had missed out on crucial stages of cognitive development—but that these deficiencies could be corrected with proper psychological support.

His observations propelled him to challenge the era's

prevailing belief that a person's intelligence is innate and unchangeable. During studies in the 1950s in Switzerland, under teachers including Carl Jung, Karl Jaspers, and Jean Piaget, he began formulating a method—today called the Feuerstein Method—to develop cognitive abilities in children considered intellectually challenged and hopeless.

As his theories were germinating, Feuerstein said, "I started getting referrals from the Rebbe. Wherever I came, wherever I visited for work in my field, people came over to me saying, 'The Rebbe wants you to see our child.' Sometimes I would myself receive a letter or message from the Rebbe concerning a particular case."

Seeing the types of children the Rebbe insisted were capable of considerable growth broadened Feuerstein's horizons and emboldened him. "My belief that even people with genetic or chromosomal disorders can be turned into normal functioning individuals—I got that very much from the Rebbe. At the time it was very daring. People didn't believe it was possible. They would ask me, 'Where did you find the courage to say this child will be able to speak, will be able to read, will be able to finish school?' Much of this belief, I must say, came from my interactions with the Rebbe."

One such referral Feuerstein recalled vividly. It was the hardest case of his fifty-year career. "This boy was falsely diagnosed as mentally defective in the country of his birth and was placed in a school for 'deficient' children. There he lived among troubled adolescents and began to imitate their behavior. Consequently, he became a real problem, and nobody believed he could ever function as a normal, independent human being.

"At some point, his father went to see the Rebbe, and the Rebbe told him to bring his son to me, which is what he did.

Thank G-d, all went very well, and we felt we had been successful.

"But after he left us, he returned to his old friends and slipped back into reckless habits. He went to a place from which few people return. They were involved with drugs, crime, and promiscuity, and there was no transgression they didn't commit.

"When I heard what had happened, I contacted the Rebbe, who said, 'Don't let him out of your hands. Send somebody to find him, bring him back and continue.' I didn't believe a rescue effort would succeed, but the Rebbe had instructed me to try, so I did. I sent somebody to take this young man away from these people, and we successfully coached him back to a healthy and moral lifestyle. He was lost but he came back, and today he is the father of four children."

Recounting this episode years later, Feuerstein reflected:

"As a psychologist, I would never have believed that such a turnaround was possible. Usually, in such cases, we just raise our hands and give up. But the Rebbe did not give up.

"Psychology is very limited in its understanding of the other. It is very much affected by, and related to, our understanding of ourselves. But the way the Rebbe saw the individual, the reason he suggested and felt empowered to say, 'Yes, do it,' stemmed from an entirely different way of seeing a person: not as a reflection of the self, but as a spirit that comes from Above."[221]

THE REBBE DEVOTED MUCH time and effort to lifting people out of entrenched despair. He showed them there is reason to be hopeful—because change is eminently possible.

Higher Than Angels

THE GREAT JEWISH PROPHET Zechariah (4th century BCE) received a prophetic vision with an ambiguous message about the potential of human beings: "I will give you [the ability] to walk among those [angels] standing here."[222]

Classically,[223] the verse is understood to be describing just how high a person can climb spiritually. Angels embody the ultimate level of perfection, while human beings are inherently flawed. The greatest spiritual level the verse can ascribe to a person is the ability to attain angel-like status—to walk among the angels.

However, the Rebbe often pointed to a different interpretation of this verse,[224] wherein human beings are considered *far greater* than angels: "I will give you [the ability] to *walk,* among those [who *only* have the ability of] *standing.*"

Angels are static beings. Sure, they are immensely spiritual, but within the realm of spirit they are stationary. They don't struggle and stumble, and therefore quantum leaps are simply not possible. *They stand still.* Human beings are entirely different. Yes, we make mistakes, but we have the unique capacity to completely transform ourselves—*the capacity to walk forward and reach entirely new places.*

For the Rebbe, this wasn't merely an interesting interpretation; it was a call to action. He believed in the ability of every individual to transcend their status quo, to move beyond the present—to stop standing and start walking.

"Even if you are correct with your assessment," reads a letter to a young woman dejected over her perceived spiritual decline,
> the solution is not to feel dispirited, inadequate, or inferior. On the contrary, this ought to evoke

within you the determination to bring your inner
powers to the fore to overcome this decline and
grow even greater than before.

A person is charged to go from strength to
strength and to "walk forward" their entire life.
And since this is the duty of man, the Creator of
man certainly gives a person all of the strength
necessary to fulfill this role.[225]

A letter to a woman who recently lost her job reads similarly:

Human life does not always proceed in a straight
line. Being that a person has the ability and
aspiration to ascend—this itself also presents
the possibility for descent. Thus, one should not
be fazed and dispirited, Heaven forbid, when
one encounters some level of descent....

On the contrary, a decline should awaken
within you deeper powers of faith, which
manifest in courage and equanimity in the face
of an unpleasant phenomenon, especially one
that [in your case] will last only for a very short
time.[226]

ONE OF THE IDEAS that can give us the courage to make the shift from resigned "standing" to determined "walking" is that renewal is built into the very fabric of existence.

New Beginnings

THE BAAL SHEM TOV, the founder of the Chasidic movement (1698–1760), would educate his students through pithy teachings that conveyed a new paradigm of the world, the self, and the Divine. The meaning of his teachings, and their application to the human experience, have been unpacked by generations of Chasidic masters.

One of these foundational teachings was that the world is divinely created anew at every moment of time.[227] The world of a second ago does not naturally spill over into the present moment. It is actively brought into existence again and again.

Think of a rock that is thrown into the air, explained the fifth Lubavitcher Rebbe.[228] It won't continue to fly forever—rather, considering that an object flying goes against the laws of gravity, the rock must be actively pushed forward by someone or something. When the energy that thrust the rock into the air runs out, the rock drops. Similarly, considering the profound novelty of the universe's existence—being something in the place of nothing—the world and everything within it must continuously be "pushed" into reality by a constant infusion of divine energy. If that divine energy would cease, the world would simply return to its natural state: not being.

Internalizing this, the Rebbe taught,[229] can help us break free from the shackles of the past. Every day we are renewed and given a clean slate on which to draw our lives. Our choices yesterday do not determine our choices tomorrow. Yes, the past teaches us, impacts us, and may even scar us, but it does not define us.

This is the reason human beings were designed with the need for sleep.[230] On the surface, sleep seems like a pointless waste of time. We would be so much more productive without it! But without intervals of sleep, life would be one long chain linking our past selves to our present selves in a seamless continuation. Going to sleep and waking up reminds us of the above truth: Every day is truly a *new* day, the past gone and slept away. A new present—imbued with new divine vitality and new personal opportunity—dawns.

This is also reflected in the natural flow of seasons. Winter is a time of gloomy stagnation for trees, vegetables, and plants. For long months they remain naked and dormant. Yet, despite this long hiatus, spring comes and a remarkable metamorphosis takes place. Fruits ripen, flowers blossom, green leaves grow, and the smell of revival is everywhere.

> "Applying this idea to the human element," reads a 1951 letter, there can be a state of winter—of apparent unproductivity—in the life of a person.
> But no individual should consider themselves—and certainly should not be considered by others—as having terminated their usefulness, even though a long time of fruitlessness has elapsed. Given the proper inspiration and stimulus, the state of winter can easily and suddenly be changed into spring and blossom time, which eventually will ripen into good fruits for G-d and man.[231]

This is true also of those who feel the bloom of their life has passed and only an unproductive winter awaits.

Jerry Grafstein, a businessman and longtime member of the Canadian Senate, was once in New York on a diplomatic trip. He scheduled an audience to consult with the Rebbe about his public affairs.

"The Rebbe listened to me with visible interest," Grafstein said, "and gave me some practical advice on my activities.

However, he saw that something was pressing on my heart. When we finished discussing the questions I had brought up, the Rebbe asked me what was bothering me.

"I told him that I was no longer young and I was starting to think about what I had managed to do in my life and what I still had time to accomplish.

"Upon hearing this, the Rebbe asked me if I knew how old Moses was when he *began* his career. I did not. The Rebbe banged on the table and passionately said: 'He was eighty years old![232] And you are very far from that age!'

"From then on, whenever such thoughts trouble us, my wife and I think of these words from the Rebbe."[233]

Despair's Seductive Attraction

HOWEVER, THERE IS A certain allure to thinking we *don't* have the possibility of change, personally or communally. In surrendering to our present condition, we relieve ourselves of the work that is required to progress. Despair can thus be relaxing, excusing us from the effort growth demands.

The Rebbe cautioned many people about precisely this pitfall. As one response explains:

> For then [i.e., when a person has resigned] what can be demanded of him and for what reason should he try? Why, he has already declared (to others as well as to himself) that he has given up all hope, Heaven forbid.[234]

Moreover, in the face of hardships, we can sometimes start feeling sorry for ourselves, falling into self-pity. Here, too, we must ask ourselves if we're choosing the easy way out, embracing our perceived helplessness instead of considering what can be done to better the situation. As another response puts it:

> It is understood from *Tanya*[235] that self-pity is one of the most successful enticements of the *yetzer hara*. A person says to themselves, "Seeing as G-d created me in this manner—this is my situation—and seeing as I am to be pitied more than any other human being, there is therefore nothing that can be done and I'm relieved of all obligations."
>
> The underlying point in all of the above is [as the Sages taught]: "If one says, 'I have tried but I haven't succeeded,' do not believe them."[236] This applies to all matters in life, in all their details.[237]

No matter how ensnared in a negative cycle someone may have been, no matter how hopeless and pitiful they felt, the Rebbe tried to instill in them a firm confidence in their own potential to transcend their current situation. As one letter to a respected Israeli writer explains:

> One who has faith in man and in the unlimited powers of his soul... also has faith that in a short time every individual can reach great heights, no matter their condition a moment earlier.[238]

It was the 1980s, and Avraham Krishevsky was living happily in Beitar Illit, Israel, with his wife and children, when he received a distressing phone call from New York City.

"On the other line was a family member of an old friend of mine," Krishevsky recalled. "Last I knew, he was in business, and married with kids. His relative informed me that my friend had recently fallen into serious substance abuse, as well as other lowly activities, and he was hitting rock bottom.

All sorts of interventions had already been tried, to no avail. The family heard we had a relationship, and they were wondering if I could help.

"I packed my bags and took a flight to New York.

"When I arrived, I went to visit my friend. He was in a truly wretched condition. He was lodging in some forsaken basement—his family couldn't stand living with him anymore. I sat with him for many hours, but I wasn't making progress. I realized that I could not help him alone.

"On one visit, I coaxed him to write a letter to the Rebbe with me.

"For the entire night, we sat together working on the letter. I told him, 'To the Rebbe you bare everything, there are no games.' He detailed all he had gone through—everything that had led him to hit this point in life. But he made one condition with me. He didn't want the letter to be delivered through the secretariat. He was concerned someone there would read it, and he felt ashamed. I gave him my word that I would deliver it personally.

"When he finished writing, I made my way to the Rebbe's home to deliver the letter. I also added a letter of my own. I wrote to the Rebbe that I had left behind my wife and children to come help this friend of mine, and I couldn't return home and abandon him like this. I wrote, 'You are like a father to me, and I want a blessing and advice on how to save my friend.'

"It was 7:00 a.m. when I knocked on the door. The housekeeper opened it and I explained that I had letters for the Rebbe. She got upset. 'This is not the way to do this,' she said. 'Drop it off at the secretariat like everyone else!' Then she closed the door. I knocked again. When she opened it, I simply placed the letters in her hand. Begrudgingly, she took them inside. I hoped they would reach the Rebbe.

"After dropping off the letters, I walked to 770 and waited near the Rebbe's study. When the Rebbe came into the building, he saw me. He looked at me with deeply penetrating eyes and then entered his study. About a half hour later, I was given the Rebbe's answer to our letters.

"He wrote a warm but pointed response, of which I will quote only the ending. My friend had written in his letter that 'my struggle with drugs began in the last six months.' The Rebbe added a star near those words and wrote in the margins:

> This means that until six months ago everything was okay with you, [despite] not using drugs. How, then, can you tell *yourself* that it is not in your ability now to abstain from them [and you can't live without them]? You have the ability to overcome these habits, and [it can happen] with much more ease than you imagine.

"I went back to my friend. We sat together and read the Rebbe's response. He started to break down, he started to cry. It touched him to the very depths of his soul. He began to come back to himself.

"Not too long after, he returned to his family, regained a healthy lifestyle, and put this whole period behind him—as if it never was."[239]

The Atomic Power Inside Us

"OUR SAGES ASSURE US," explains a letter to an American businessman who was considering making a difficult life change, that "nothing stands in the way of the will."[240] This is understandable, since every human being is endowed with immense potential powers. If material things have tremendous atomic powers, how much greater is the "atomic" power of the soul, which, as the Torah defines it, is "truly a part of G-dliness Above."[241] It is only necessary to actualize it; and this is a matter of the individual's own will and determination.[242]

It was the winter of 1971, and Tzvi Hersh Weinreb, a young father in his early thirties, had recently received a PhD in psychology and was beginning to work as a clinical psychologist in Silver Spring, Maryland.

"I suppose I was too young for a midlife crisis," Weinreb later recalled, "or maybe I arrived at it earlier than most—but around this time, I was deeply torn with pressing questions.

"I was highly uncertain about my career. Should I even continue in psychology? And if so, should I make a career in private practice or accept an offer from the county's social services?

"I was at a crossroads in my relationship with my wife. How could I do better? How could we get closer? We'd been married for six or seven years now—but how could I make it a bond that would last for sixty or seventy?

"I was confused about the right way to raise my children. What type of attitude should I take as a father? To which schools should I send them?

"I also had my own share of doubts on faith. The age-old question of why bad things happen to good people plagued me. Not in a philosophical way, but in a deeply personal way.

"I was confused to the point of depression."

Weinreb turned to his close friends for advice on navigating this crisis, and one of them encouraged him to consult the Rebbe. He was initially skeptical, but feeling increasingly desperate, he figured he had nothing to lose. And so, one day, Weinreb found himself calling the Rebbe's office.

"The Rebbe's secretary answered the phone in English, with a simple, 'Hello, who's this?'

"As I was talking to the secretary, in the background I heard the Rebbe asking in Yiddish, 'Who's calling?'

"'A Jew from Maryland,' I replied.

"I told the secretary that I had many questions I would like to discuss with the Rebbe—questions about what direction my life should take, questions regarding my career, questions of faith.... I explained that I was at a very uncertain stage in my life and I didn't know where to turn.

"And then I heard the Rebbe say in the background, in Yiddish: 'Tell him that there is a Jew who lives in Maryland that he can speak to—his name is Weinreb.'

"The secretary asked me, 'Did you hear what the Rebbe said?'

"I couldn't believe my ears. I knew for sure I had not given the secretary my name, but the Rebbe had just said my name! I was taken aback and I wanted to hear it again. So when the secretary asked whether I had heard, I said no.

"The secretary repeated the Rebbe's words: 'Tell him that there is a Jew who lives in Maryland that he can speak to—his name is Weinreb.'

"So I replied, 'But *my* name is Weinreb!'

"And then I heard the Rebbe say, 'If that's the case, he should know that sometimes one needs to speak to himself.'"

With that, the call ended.

Weinreb went on to become a respected psychologist, an esteemed scholar, and a prominent leader in North American

Jewry (amongst other roles, he served as the president of the Orthodox Union—a leading Orthodox Jewish organization in North America).

Recounting this phone call forty years later, he said:

"I think about this phone call a few times a week, if not every day. If I could put words in the Rebbe's mouth, I think he was saying, 'You're looking for answers outside yourself. You're not a kid anymore; you're a man. You are thirty years old; you are a father; you are a teacher. With all your problems—philosophical, career, family—the answer is within you. You must be courageous. You must overcome false modesty. Don't become arrogant, but never put yourself down. Realize that you can do it. And you can do it today.'"

RABBI MENACHEM M. SCHNEERSON
Office Address:
Lubavitch, 770 Eastern Parkway
Brooklyn 13, N.Y.

HYacinth 3-9250

16 Iyar 5711
Brooklyn, N.Y.

Blessing and Greeting:

I was pleased with the opportunity to exchange a few words with you. As you connected your visit with the day of Pesach-sheni which we observed on the day before yesterday, I want to make it the subject of this letter.

One of the significant lessons of Pesach-sheni is never to despair even when one has not attained the spiritual heights of others. Thus, while all the people are celebrating the Passover at its proper time, and one finds himself "far away," or otherwise unfit to enter the Sanctuary, he is told: Do not despair; begin your way towards the Sanctuary; come closer and closer; for you have a special chance and opportunity to celebrate the Second Passover, if you try hard enough.

Please convey my regards and best wishes to your circle.

Cordially,

M Schneerson

Encl.

Endnotes

Guide to the Endnotes

> *The Rebbe would send patients to me. But I would also send patients to the Rebbe. I saw the psychological impact he had on people. Whether he specifically studied psychology—I don't know. But he clearly had knowledge in human psychology. Perhaps he got it all from the Torah, the ultimate source.*
>
> *—Dr. A.J. Twerski*

THE REBBE DEEPLY BELIEVED in G-d and the wisdom He conveyed to humanity on Mount Sinai. His innovative thinking was anchored in thousands of years of Jewish thought passed on from generation to generation. The teachings of the Talmudic sages and the spirit of the Chasidic masters were the ground on which he rooted his timely guidance. It was from this fertile soil that he drew his steadfast faith in the individual, the resilient divine soul, and the unique, indispensable role each one of us has.

A primary goal of the endnotes is to highlight the times the Rebbe revealed the roots for his advice in the Torah—to give you some background on that Biblical, Talmudic, Kabbalistic, or Chasidic source, and to allow you to follow the fascinating evolution from an age-old quotation to the Rebbe's modern-day application.

Another goal of the endnotes is to enable you to further explore a given counseling point throughout the wide corpus of the Rebbe's letters. While in the chapters themselves the overriding consideration was clarity and concision, in the endnotes the goal was the opposite: to provide an array of examples for a given idea so you can journey beyond the scope of this book independently.

The final goal is to include the themes, letters, and stories that didn't make it into the book, but are nevertheless integral to the subject at hand.

In summary, while the guiding principle in composing the chapters was "when in doubt—take out," in the endnotes that principle was flipped. Thus, some notes have a research bent with many references in succession, while others include poignant lessons and stories. Some notes trace how the Rebbe derived his outlook from an esoteric discussion in the Talmud or Kabbalah, while others address our everyday human experience.

I hope this gives you some orientation for the windy section ahead. Browse as you wish; enjoy as you like. Safe travels.

ENDNOTES

1. *To Know and To Care* (SIE), Vol. 1, chapter 1; accessible at chabad.org/78391. The Rebbe conveyed a similar lesson learned from the sun and black holes to Prof. Velvl Greene, a scientist for NASA. See his interview in the JEM documentary *The Honest Truth*.
2. For what follows, see *Zohar*, Vol. I, p. 33b; *Siddur Im Dach* 97:c; *Maamar Az Yashir Yisrael* 5666; *Sichah of Purim Katan* 5746.
3. See, for example, *Torat Menachem 5750*, Vol. 2, p. 172; *Michtav Klali* dated 6 Tishrei, 5738. For another practical application of both the sun and the moon in a person's life—the sun representing stability and the moon representing change—see *Michtav Klali* dated 6 Tishrei, 5744 (included in *Likkutei Sichot*, Vol. 24, p. 633).

    A 1956 letter (*Igrot Kodesh*, Vol. 13, p. 234 (chabad.org/4994397)), to a certain Dr. Elkana—who seems to have had socialist leanings—explains how, in the Rebbe's vision, the ultimate utopian society lies not in an erasure of all differences between people, but in a harmonic interplay of giver and receiver. The letter states that G-d Himself is also both a receiver and giver. Following is an excerpt:

    "You conclude your letter by stating that redemption cannot be complete until 'there will be no poor man in the land' [Deuteronomy 15:11] and all people will work in joint labor and shared responsibility with no divisions of poor and rich.

    "I beg to differ. It is human nature that a sense of true happiness and fulfillment comes with the capacity to help another. And this is possible only when one is 'rich' and the other 'poor.'

    "However, in no way does this contradict your justified revolt against the injustice found in the very existence of such divisions [between rich and poor]. Chasidic teachings explain that every creation, if only their behavior aligns with their created design, functions as both a receiver and a giver. Put differently, if they are 'poor' in one area, they are to be 'rich' in another.

    "It is wondrous that even in regards to G-d, the Creator of the universe and its conductor, the Torah says that He too is sometimes a 'receiver.' As Chasidic teachings [*Yahel Ohr, Miluim* 132:5] deduce from the verse, 'You yearn for the work of your hands' [Job 14:15]. [Similarly,] our Sages taught that service [of man fills] a divine need' [*Shelah, Shaar Hagadol,* 29b]."

4. English letter, dated Elul 5721, accessible at chabad.org/2308526.

5. This theme recurs in many letters. The following are a few specifics:

For a boost in self-confidence—see *Igrot Kodesh,* Vol. 15, p. 184 (chabad.org/5054354): "It might be worthwhile to mention to the doctor that, based on his evaluation of your son's disposition, it would be very beneficial if your son would be given opportunities to help others... as this would increase his belief in himself." *Igrot Kodesh,* Vol. 18, p. 407 (chabad.org/5100639); Vol. 19, p. 373 (chabad.org/5287796); Vol. 26, p. 158. See also *Igrot Kodesh,* Vol. 11, p. 344 (chabad.org/4929204).

To ease loneliness—see *Igrot Kodesh,* Vol. 17, p. 9 (chabad.org/5099896). The letter adds that, on a deeper level, when you invest effort to help another you gradually begin to feel your inherent spiritual interconnectivity with other people, thereby diminishing subtler loneliness, too. See also *Igrot Kodesh,* Vol. 27, p. 99, on loneliness connected to grief. In another response to a woman whose grown daughter died tragically, leaving little children, the Rebbe advised to focus her energy on how to "sweeten the life of the widower and the lives of the orphans" as a way to help her cope with her own grief and find some comfort.

To ease dejection and melancholy—see *Igrot Kodesh,* Vol. 10, p. 42 (chabad.org/4872091), and Vol. 27, p. 527.

To add warmth and positivity—see *Igrot Kodesh,* Vol. 18, p. 138 (chabad.org/5100390): "Increasing your efforts to help others—aside from fulfilling the commandment to 'love your fellow as yourself' [Leviticus 19:18]—will also grant you inner satisfaction when you see the fruits of your labor. This will, directly and indirectly, improve your health and your perspective on everything that happens within you and around you." See also *Here's My Story* (JEM), Jan. 14, 2015, accessible at chabad.org/2842569: "If you want to have a warm home, see to it that you make it warm for the other, and then it will naturally be warm for you."

To increase feelings of gratitude and contentment—see *Petakim,* Vol. 2, p. 120: "As it appears that you need an additional measure of proper *Bitachon*—that not only is G-d the conductor of the world in general, but also of each and every one of us individually, including your life and the lives of your family members—for you will then appreciate even more the revealed blessings with which you were blessed (your children that give you such *nachat* [satisfaction]), and you will lessen your angst about the non-positive things that happened to you, thus:

"It would be advisable for you to begin every weekday (*bli neder)...* with placing a couple of coins into a charity box. This will remind you that there are many people who are in a position where they need *your help,* and G-d chose you as *His emissary* to make help available to them...."

6. Leviticus 19:18. The Rebbe would often note that Rabbi Akiva said that this commandment is a fundamental principle of the Torah (*Sifra* and *Rashi* on the verse; Jerusalem Talmud, *Nedarim* 9:3).

On a related note, in a private audience in the 1970s, the Rebbe asked his interlocutor:

"Why is it that the heart rests toward the body's left? In Jewish tradition, good is usually associated with the right side. For example, *mitzvot* are supposed to be done specifically with the right hand *[Shulchan Aruch, Orach Chaim* 183:4, and *Taz* ad loc.; *Mishnah Berurah* 206:18]. So why is it that such a vital organ as the heart leans towards the left?"

The Rebbe went on to answer: *"Because it's the right side of the person across from you;* for your heart beats not for you but for the other, for the fellow whom you must love as yourself" (*Here's My Story* (JEM), "It's Their Right," accessible at chabad.org/3779581).

7. chabad.org/2757 and lubavitch.com/the-rebbes-advice-for-life.
8. *Igrot Kodesh,* Vol. 26, p. 497.
9. English letter, 5721, accessible at chabad.org/2308526.

10. A photocopy of his transcript with the Rebbe's edits is available in *Techayenu*, no. 5, p. 76. The background story is recorded ibid. no. 3, p. 78. The translation is adapted from *A Chassidisher Derher*, no. 150.
11. *Igrot Kodesh*, Vol. 27, p. 99.
12. *Petakim*, Vol. 2, p. 130.
13. English letter, dated 23 Sivan, 5712.
14. *N'shei Chabad Newsletter*, Shvat 2022, p. 5.
15. Chanukah Day #2 | The Rebbe's Advice for Anxiety—YouTube.
16. he.chabad.org/395252.

    On the topic of the Rebbe's advice to Eini, that he write a book of his experience in captivity to help other prisoners of war—I heard firsthand of a (perhaps) similar directive to an individual who, in his early teens, witnessed his classmate drown to death. The Rebbe advised that he and a friend who was also there learn how to be lifeguards.
17. *Igrot Kodesh*, Vol. 19, p. 439 (chabad.org/5287861).
18. *Igrot Kodesh*, Vol. 4, p. 248 (chabad.org/4754442).
19. *Igrot Kodesh Admor Mehorayatz*, Vol. 13, p. 273. Their conclusion was included by the Rebbe in *Hayom Yom*, entry for 22 Iyar.
20. *Igrot Kodesh*, Vol. 23, p. 359 (chabad.org/5413720).
21. See, for example, *Shabbat* 100b; *Sukkah* 5a.

    In a 1977 talk (*Sichot Kodesh 5737* Vol. 1, p. 452) the Rebbe explained why he specifically references the Talmudic term "within ten *tefachim*" to express G-d's presence in our reality.

    The expression is rooted, he explained, in the halachic ruling (*Shulchan Aruch, Orach Chaim* 345) that the public domain (*reshut harabim*) on Shabbat extends only within ten *tefachim* of the ground. Above that height is considered an exempt area (*makom patur*), or sometimes a private domain (*reshut hayachid*).

    Now, Kabbalah teaches (*Tikkunei Zohar, tikkun* 24; *Tanya*, ch. 33) that, mystically, the public domain symbolizes an arena of division and discord. The private domain, by contrast, represents a unified reality brought together by the oneness of G-d.

    Thus, the term "within ten *tefachim*" implies that G-d's

presence can also be felt in our messy, disparate, and divided reality—in our "public domain." Not only "above ten *tefachim*," the transcendent, already redeemed, spaces of divine unity.

22. *Igrot Kodesh,* Vol. 19, p. 439 (chabad.org/5287861).
23. See *Igrot Kodesh,* Vol. 1, pp. 168-175 (chabad.org/4646055) for the Rebbe's extensive treatise, replete with sources, on the Baal Shem Tov's innovation on this topic.
24. These ideas appear in numerous letters. The following are a few examples:

    As an uplifting source of joy—see *Igrot Kodesh,* Vol. 4, p. 165 (chabad.org/4754371); Vol. 10, p. 376 (chabad.org/4872422); ibid., p. 389 (chabad.org/4872436); Vol. 17, p. 2 (chabad.org/5099887); Vol. 18, p. 98 (chabad.org/5100351).

    To overcome laziness—see English letter, dated 13 Teves, 5726, accessible at chabad.org/1878120. See also *Otzar Hamelech,* Vol. 1, p. 75 (in the latter response the Rebbe also recommends regularly meditating on the idea that wasted time is a "loss that cannot be recovered.")

    To let go of the past and begin anew—see *Igrot Kodesh,* Vol. 17, p. 320.

    To cope with anger—see *Igrot Kodesh,* Vol. 18, p. 169. (The letter offers an additional piece of advice—to make sure to *always* fulfill the Torah's directive (*Yoma* 87a; *Shulchan Aruch, Orach Chaim* 606:1) to ask forgiveness. Being that asking forgiveness is uncomfortable, she will think twice before unleashing her anger on someone, knowing she will later need to ask for their forgiveness.) See also *Igrot Kodesh,* Vol. 24, p. 124.

    To prevail over indecision—see *Igrot Kodesh,* Vol. 18, p. 408: "The Almighty G-d, Who created and directs the world, watches over every individual, not only in the major aspects of their life but also in the smallest details. This enables us to understand the principle of trust in G-d Who conducts the world and is the essence of goodness. Accordingly, everything is also for the good, plainly and simply....

    "The first direct result of this trust is that there is no worry and confusion. For even when a person is weighing in their mind what to decide and how to act, at that time, too, G-d is watching over them and helping them, helping all those who desire what is good and upright...."

To soothe night terrors—see *Igrot Kodesh*, Vol. 12, p. 64.

As a counterbalance to despair and hopelessness—see *Igrot Kodesh*, Vol. 16, p. 295; *Petakim*, Vol. 1, p. 116. See also the letter quoted in *Here's My Story* (JEM), titled "Special Delivery": "As for your mentioning the fact that no one seems to be interested in your work, etc., surely you will admit that G-d, Whose knowledge and providence extends to everyone individually, knows and is interested in what you are doing.... And I need hardly mention that I, too, am interested in your work." Accessible at chabad.org/2981604.

As an antidote to fear of nuclear war—see the 1965 Hebrew letter printed in *Vaad Hanachot B'lahak, Vayikra* 5780. (The letter adds that in almost every generation there was an invention that caused people to fear the world's end was near—gunpowder in the Middle Ages, the airplane bomber in the World War I era, and so on. Yet, the world still stands.)

To soldiers on the frontlines—see *Igrot Kodesh*, Vol. 1, p. 219. Drawing on the Torah's words, "For G-d, your G-d, goes along in the midst of your camp, to rescue you and to deliver your enemies before you; [therefore,] your camp shall be holy" (Deuteronomy 23:15), the Rebbe wrote to American soldiers fighting the Nazis in World War II: "Wherever you are, G-d Almighty finds Himself near you and with you, and He watches over you always and looks at all your deeds. Thus, there is no place for fear. Be strong in your spirit and confident in victory against the evil enemy.... With wishes that you soon return home intact after a complete victory...."

To incarcerated individuals—see *Heichal Menachem*, Vol. 3, p. 60: "The Almighty G-d, the Creator of the universe and its Conductor, the Creator of man, looks after each and every person with an individual providence; and 'there is no place bereft of Him' [*Tikkunei Zohar* 91b]; in the words of our Sages, 'not even the *sneh*' [*Shemot Rabbah*, 2:5, which states: 'A man asked Rabbi Yehoshua why, out of all places, did G-d reveal Himself to Moses in the *sneh*—a thorny bush? Rabbi Yehoshua answered that G-d wanted to teach us that He is present in 'thorny bushes' as well]. And may He fulfill each of your heart's wishes and help you go spiritually 'from the straits... to a vast expanse' [Psalms 118:5], which will lead you to physically leaving 'the straits' as well. And our Sages have assured us that 'one who wants to purify (himself and others) is assisted from Above' [*Yoma* 38b]."

As a general source of confidence to end procrastination and self-examination—see *Igrot Kodesh,* Vol. 10, p. 118.

To help control base instincts and temptations—see *Igrot Kodesh,* Vol. 22, pp. 28, 64.

*

The Rebbe would often point to the opening paragraph of *Shulchan Aruch* (the Code of Jewish conduct) to Illustrate the centrality of appreciating G-d's presence in Judaism. There, the Rama (Rabbi Moshe Isserles, 1530-1572) comments:

"'I place G-d before me always' (Psalms 16:8): this is a major principle in the Torah and amongst the virtues of the righteous who walk before G-d. For a person's way of sitting, his movements, and his dealings while he is alone in his house are not like his way of sitting, his movements, and his dealings when he is before a great king...."

See, for example, the following English letter (dated 6 Teves, 5737):

"It is well to remember the first directive of the *Shulchan Aruch*.... The very first paragraph contains the rule that, upon waking up in the morning, a Jew should remember the words that King David expressed on behalf of all Jews in his holy book of *Tehillim*: 'I place G-d before me always.' The explanation follows that a person who finds himself in the presence of a human king behaves and speaks quite differently than when he is in the company of his family and friends....

"Needless to say, the *Shulchan Aruch*, being a codex of laws, does not engage in nice phrases and euphemisms for their own sake, but every word is chosen and significant and of practical importance. So too in regard to the above quotation... It calls for a few moments of reflection when getting up in the morning, and from time to time during the day, that one is always in the presence of G-d, and this is a very effective method of being able to control one's daily behavior in every good way.

"The above is also the answer to the matter of *atzvut* ['dejection'], which you mention in your letter. Such a feeling is often the result of thinking oneself unimportant and therefore it is of no consequence how one acts or behaves, leading one to become apathetic and discouraged.

"But realizing that one is in the presence and company of the King of kings, whom the King has honored and privileged with very important tasks, this emphasizes the importance of every individual. In your case the emphasis is even greater, inasmuch as you have the ability and opportunity to influence many other persons directly as well as indirectly by showing a living example, which also gives you a special *zechut* [merit] if you will realize all your potentials in this way...."

To integrate this concept into one's thinking, the Rebbe occasionally advised individuals to memorize the Alter Rebbe's explanation of this *halachah* in his *Shulchan Aruch* (*Orach Chaim, Mahadura Tinyana* 1:5), and to regularly review it in their minds.

Similarly, as a source of motivation and empowerment, the Rebbe advised people to memorize the following two lines of *Tanya* (ch. 41): "Behold, G-d stands over you, and the whole earth is full of His glory, and he [nevertheless] looks at you, and searches your mind and heart [to see] if you are serving Him as is fitting." See, for example, *Igrot Kodesh*, Vol. 9, p. 150, and Vol. 15, p. 352. See also *Here's My Story* (JEM), "Very Old Wisdom for a Very Young Man" (accessible at chabad.org/3872620).

To some he recommended that they keep this passage available in their pocket in order to read it at moments of struggle. For example, he wrote to Rabbi Aharon Eliezer Tzeitlin, "Keep it in your pocket, and, most importantly, in the pocket of your heart...." For a similar letter, see *Petakim*, Vol. 2, p. 91. The Rebbe also included these words from the *Tanya* in the twelve foundational verses and teachings of the Sages that he encouraged children to learn and memorize.

25. This was often told over by Rabbi Elimelech (Meilach) Zwiebel,

of blessed memory. See also *Sichah* of 22 Elul, 5750 (*Sefer HaSichot 5750*, Vol. 2, p. 689).

On a related note, in a poem about G-d and his relationship with man, Hebrew poet Zvi Yair wrote the following verse, "Before creation, You were lonely, with no brother, no friend, no lover."

When he gave the Rebbe a draft of his upcoming book of poetry, the Rebbe (who rarely intervened) crossed out, "You were lonely" (*hayita [kivayachol] boded*), and changed it to, "You were one and only" (*echad umiyuchad hayita*). The verse now read, "Before creation, You were one and only, with no brother, no friend, no lover."

(A photocopy of this edit is available in *Kovetz Tishrei 5782*, no. 3. The final poem can be found under the title "*Pesukei D'zimra*" in Zvi Yair's volume of poetry, *Miknaf Eretz*.)

26. The phrase *teva hatov l'haitiv* ("it is the nature of the good to do good") is used in many letters to illustrate this point.

This expression can be found in *Tanya, Shaar Hayichud Veha'emunah*, ch. 4. However, in his notes on a Chasidic discourse of the Mitteler Rebbe (*Atah Echad, 5587*), the Rebbe found roots for this term in the works of earlier Kabbalists. The Kabbalist Rabbi Naftali Hertz Bacharach mentions it in *Emek Hamelech* (printed posthumously in Amsterdam in the year 1648), ch. 1. Similarly, the Kabbalist Rabbi Yosef Ergas (1685-1730) mentions it in *Shomer Emunim, Vikuach* 2, *se'if* 13-14. ("Because the infinite G-d is the ultimate good, and goodness is part of His essence, thus He created the world to do good to another.... He created the world because it is the nature of the good to do good.")

Many letters also reference the teaching of Rabbi Akiva (*Berachot* 60b), "*Kol mah de'avid Rachmana letav avid*" ("Everything G-d does is for the good"). Some letters add, "for the good of the individual He is watching over." See, for example, *Igrot Kodesh*, Vol. 16, p. 295, and Vol. 17, p. 100.

Interestingly, a 1965 English letter points to an earlier source for the fact that everything G-d does is for the good— the verse in Genesis (1:31), "And G-d saw all that He had done, and behold, it was very good." The Rebbe wrote: "One of the foundations of our faith and way of life is the firm conviction that G‑d's providence extends to everyone individually, and that He is the essence of goodness, and does only good, as the Torah states, 'And G‑d saw all that He had done, and behold, it was very good.'"

27. From Joseph Telushkin, *Rebbe*, p. 50. See also *Igrot Kodesh*, Vol. 15, p. 414, and Vol. 32, p. 254.
28. See, for example, *Likkutei Sichot*, Vol. 1, p. 278, and Vol. 17, p. 368. To a teacher who wrote that her students hurl insults at each other, the Rebbe responded (*Igrot Kodesh*, Vol. 20, p. 142) that teaching them to have an awareness of G‑d's presence would help diminish the issue. When the students feel they are in the presence of the Father of all the children, and He listens to what is being said about His children, they will naturally practice more restraint. The Rebbe also recommended hanging up a sign on the wall of her classroom with a motto that captures this theme.
29. *Sefer Hasichot 5687*, p. 194.
30. *Igrot Kodesh*, Vol. 32, p. 257.
31. See Rashi on the verse.

    A 1955 letter (*Igrot Kodesh*, Vol. 10, p. 133) reads as follows: "King David, finding himself in a dismal situation, said 'I will fear no evil—for You are with me,' and because of this [attitude], David triumphed over all the adverse circumstances.

    "This story was included in the Torah—the word "Torah" coming from the word *horaah* [i.e., a life lesson; see *Zohar* III, 53b]—because it serves as a teaching for every Jew, wherever they may find themselves, that if only they hold onto the steadfast idea that 'You are with me,' it will lead to the conclusion of the verse that 'only goodness and kindness will follow me all the days of my life.'"
32. *Igrot Kodesh*, Vol. 25, p. 256.

    See also *Igrot Kodesh*, Vol. 22, p. 81, for another letter that advises the recipient to study and reflect on Chapter 23 of Psalms as an antidote to fear. See *Igrot Kodesh*, Vol. 25, p. 136, for a letter that recommends verbalizing the chapter. See also *Igrot Kodesh*, Vol. 5, p. 242.

    Many letters on this theme also point to another verse from

Psalms: "G-d is with me; I shall not fear—what can a man do to me?" (Psalms 118:6). See, for example, *Igrot Kodesh,* Vol. 15, p. 353; Vol. 22, p. 141; Vol. 28, p. 347. See also *Igrot Kodesh,* Vol. 19, p. 297: "When it will be ingrained in your mind that G-d stands near you, and that He is the essence of goodness, and that He wants to make it good for His creations, and that He looks out with an individual providence [for] each and every person, as is explained in the teachings of Chasidut—this will diminish and weaken your feelings of lack of confidence and fear of other people. As the verse explains, 'G-d is with me; I shall not fear.'"

For other letters that counsel meditating on G-d's presence to diminish fear of other people and what they might think, see *Igrot Kodesh,* Vol. 15, p. 96, and Vol. 19, p. 161. To help ease fear about neighbors, see *Igrot Kodesh,* Vol. 6, p. 274. For a letter to a woman fearful that someone in India could hurt her with demonic powers, see *Petakim,* Vol. 2, pp. 134-135. On fear of public speaking, see *Igrot Kodesh,* Vol. 31, p. 339.

33. *Pnimiyut* is a central value in the tradition of Chabad Chasidut. It calls one to transcend superficiality and instead work to integrate what they study into their intellect, emotions, and behavior, to the point where their learning becomes part of who they are.

    On this note, see *Igrot Kodesh,* Vol. 3, p. 246, for a letter of encouragement written a month after the Previous Rebbe's passing, in 1950: "This was the call of the Chabad Rebbes to their followers: that they be Chasidim. Meaning, they shouldn't be only a man or a woman in whom the light of Chasidut shines, but more than that, they should bond so deeply with its teachings and emotions to the point that they become one and the same with it [hence the term 'Chasid'—that the person themselves *is* Chasidut]."

    The Tzemach Tzedek taught (included in the *Hayom Yom* entry for 24 Tammuz) that, "A *pnimi* is one for whom the very notion of asking for a blessing to succeed in his internal spiritual work is considered empty talk. He understands that the approach should be to 'let the work fall heavily on the people'

[Exodus 5:9]." See *Igrot Kodesh,* Vol. 9, p. 219, for an explanation of this teaching.

34. English letter dated 12 Cheshvan, 5722.

See also the English letter dated 24 Nissan, 5723: "It is also clear that success and attainment, whatever the goal in life, depends on inner peace and harmony. A thinking person will have peace of mind only if he has the feeling that his life is worthy and purposeful, and only then will he be able to forge ahead, unmoved by external distractions and unhindered by his own temporary moods or setbacks."

Similarly, see the English letter dated 10 Tammuz, 5739, responding to a Jewish man who felt his life was meaningless: "The purpose of life on this earth is to make it a fitting abode for the divine presence, which requires that it should be a world where justice, decency, and benevolence reign supreme. And everyone is expected to work for the realization of these ideals to the maximum degree—first and foremost in one's personal life, and through influencing the environment in this direction. For a Jew, the purpose of life is clearly spelled out in the Torah and is realized through everyday life and conduct in accordance with the *Shulchan Aruch.* And such a life is meaningful, worthy, good, secure and harmonious."

35. *Zohar,* Vol. I, p. 4a. *Tanya,* chapter 36.

The Rebbe would often point to the words in Genesis (2:3): "And G-d blessed the seventh day and He hallowed it, for thereon He abstained from all His work that G-d created to do." The final words, "that G-d created to do," seem out of place. What does it mean that G-d created the world "to do"? Rashi, elucidating the commentary of *Bereishit Rabbah* (11:6), explains that "to do" means "to repair." The following letter (*Igrot Kodesh,* Vol. 13, p. 240) explains:

"At the summation of the world's creation, the Torah says, as explained by our Sages, that 'G-d created it to do—to repair.' This means that the world was created in a way that man should contribute of his own accord not only improvements but also corrections. So long as there exists even one person in the universe, that is in itself evidence that the world still needs repair. And repairing the outside world goes in tandem with repairing one's internal world..." See also, for example, *Torat Menachem 5716*, Vol. 1, p. 189 (chabad.org/2987683); *Torat Menachem 5744*, p. 452; *Torat Menachem 5746*, p. 411; *Torat Menachem 5749*, p. 33 (chabad.org/4543686).

Another concept the Rebbe would often reference, found in *Tanya*, ch. 33, is that our task is to transform the world from a *reshut harabim* into a *reshut hayachid*, from a domain of multitude and separation into a domain for the singular divine unity. See, for example, *Torat Menachem 5712*, Vol. 2, p. 62 (chabad.org/4280217); *Torat Menachem 5719*, Vol., 1 p. 94 (chabad.org/2987768).

36. *Eitz Chaim* 26:1; *Tanya*, ch. 37.

Drawing on these sources, the Rebbe would often speak of the divine mission every individual has to "illuminate their body, their animalistic soul, and their part of the world" with the light of the divine soul—"The soul of man is the candle of G-d" (Proverbs 20:26)—and the light of Torah and mitzvot—"The *mitzvah* is a lamp and Torah is light" (Proverbs 6:23). See, for example, *Torat Menachem 5713*, Vol. 1, p. 245 (chabad.org/2987869). *Torat Menachem 5717*, Vol. 1, p. 25 (chabad.org/2988252); *Torat Menachem 5725*, p. 109 (chabad.org/4313283).

37. See, for example, *Hayom Yom*, entry for 3 Elul: "A person who believes in Divine Providence knows that 'the steps of a man are directed by G-d' (Psalms 37:23). [A person goes to] a particular place because his soul must refine and perfect something there."

See also *Hayom Yom*, entry for 18 Elul, for a similar teaching of the Baal Shem Tov on the verse "And you shall go to the place that the L-rd your G-d chooses to make His Name dwell there" (Deuteronomy 26:2).

The Rebbe also pointed to the words Joseph used to comfort his brothers when they unexpectedly met him in Egypt after selling him into slavery years earlier: "Be not grieved, nor angry with yourselves, that you sold me here, for G-d did send me before you to preserve life…. And G-d sent me before you to preserve you a remnant in the earth, and to save your lives by a great deliverance. So now it was not you that sent me here, but

G-d...." (Genesis 45:5-8). This, the Rebbe said, as everything in Torah, teaches an eternally relevant lesson: even when we find ourselves in places or situations that seem profoundly negative and dark, there is a divine mission for us to fulfill there. See *Torat Menachem 5747*, Vol. 2, pp. 170-172.

38. This analogy is given in *Likkutei Sichot,* Vol. 30, p. 150. For other iterations of this analogy, see *Torat Menachem 5744,* Vol. 4, p. 2646; *Torat Menachem 5745,* Vol. 4, p. 2088.

    Alongside the logical reasoning that G-d's actions are always intentional, the Rebbe would also point to the Talmud's teaching (*Shabbat* 77b): "Rav Yehuda said that Rav said: [Of] everything that the Holy One, Blessed be He, created in His world, He did not create [even] one thing for naught."

    This perspective lends new meaning to the time and talents given to us by G-d. They are gifts meant to be purposefully used—never wasted. As this handwritten response counsels a young woman (*Petakim,* Vol. 1, p. 192):

    "Since 'G-d didn't create [even] one thing for naught' [*Shabbat* 77b], and you were given a talent for mentoring and educating, you should utilize the summer for putting this talent to use. This would mean going to camp.... This way your talent will be activated for the entire summer, for the benefit of the public—and no doubt it will be to your benefit as well—both physically and spiritually."

    Similarly, a 1952 letter (*Igrot Kodesh,* Vol. 6, p. 252) responding to someone who wrote of his criticisms of the way other people were doing their job (the details are unclear), reads as follows:

    "[The verse says,] 'Days were formed, and there is not one amongst them' [Psalms 139:16]. Chasidut interprets this [see *Torat Chaim, Shemot,* p. 600] to mean that a person's days are measured so that they can fulfill their mission in this world ['days were formed'], and there isn't even one day or moment that is extra and unnecessary for the mission ['there is not one [superfluous] amongst them']. It is therefore understood that any amount of time—be it even very little—spent on insignificant matters detracts from the fulfillment of the mission.

    "Based on the above, it's a pity on the time you are spending questioning others—asking why they are doing it this way and not that way. That's a matter for them. What is most proper and necessary for every individual, with the exception of those with communal responsibilities, is to devote their time, energy, and talents to fulfilling their personal mission."

Similarly reads an English letter from 1970: "Our Sages tell us that G-d has not created anything in His world for no purpose. They also tell us that every person has been allotted a certain number of days and years. This means that every Jew, as well as every person in general, has been given certain capacities, as well as a certain allotted period of time, in order to fulfill his particular task or mission in the world. There is no excess of capacity, or time, because that would contradict the statement above. At the same time there is no deficiency, G-d-forbid, in capacity and time, since it would be quite illogical to impose a certain task without providing the means necessary to fulfill it...."

39. *Young Scholar's Daily Calendar & Encyclopedia* (Merkos L'inyonei Chinuch, 1943).
40. See, for example, Rabbi Lord Jonathan Sacks' account of his meeting with the Rebbe when he was a university student. A video of him telling the story is accessible at chabad.org/1690783.

See *Igrot Kodesh,* Vol. 22, p. 387, for a letter to a young man in intensive military training who lamented the nuisances of his circumstances. The Rebbe explained to him how, despite its hardships, the setting of military training has unique virtues that can be utilized for a special *shlichut* (mission).

The following is an excerpt of a long 1974 letter (*Heichal Menachem,* Vol. 3, p. 59) responding to individuals incarcerated in Israeli prisons. The Rebbe explained how, despite the tremendous pain of being in such a setting, prison provides a unique opportunity that isn't available in the rush of normal life:

"In light of the Baal Shem Tov's teaching (*Hayom Yom*, entry for 9 Iyar) that from everything a person sees or hears they can take a lesson for their divine service, one can meditate based on what is explained in Chassidic teachings, in *Tanya* [ch. 31] etc., that there are various angles through which to view life. One of them is that the soul of man finds itself in the 'prison' of the body. For the soul is a part of G-d above [*Tanya*, ch. 2], and the body is mere flesh and blood, and 'comes from dust and will end in dust' [*Unetaneh Tokef* prayer].

"This prompts the well-known question: Why did G-d, the Creator of man, do this? Why did He place 'the soul that You gave me [that] is pure, You created it, You formed it, You blew it into me' [*Elokai Neshamah* prayer]—into a body of flesh and blood, in this physical and materialistic world?

"And the explanation is given [see *Tanya*, ch. 31; *Torah Ohr*, p. 5a] that this descent is for the sake of [an even greater] ascent. For when a person reflects on his purpose in this world—to fulfill the will of his Creator despite being in a world filled with hurdles and distractions—this empowers him to transform these obstacles into a springboard for reaching even greater heights, like the beauty of "light [that comes specifically] from within darkness" [Ecclesiastes 2:13].

"These ideas are present, on a certain level, also in regards to prison in the literal sense. Its purpose is not punishment for the sake of punishment, Heaven forbid, but rather to provide an opportunity for the individual who finds themselves in prison to meditate on what they have gone through in life, and to reflect on their unique conditions of living—which also have a redeeming factor, for no bad can survive without having some good spark as well that keeps it alive [see the *maamar* entitled *Padah Beshalom* 5675]. One of those [positive] sparks is that being removed from the noise of the street, a person has the chance to reflect more deeply and without as many disturbances....

"And great is the power of the luminary in Torah, the 'Torah of light' [Proverbs 6:23], to illuminate a person's path in life, wherever one finds themselves, whether it be a physical prison or a spiritual prison, to ultimately fulfill their *shlichut;* in the words of the known dictum, to 'transform from darkness to light, and from bitterness to sweetness' [*Zohar*, Vol. 1, p. 4a]."

41. See, for example, *Igrot Kodesh,* Vol. 18, p. 414. See also *Igrot Kodesh,* Vol. 13, p. 458. For an articulate overview of the Rebbe's

approach to this, see Rabbi Mendel Kalmanson, *Positivity Bias* chapter 16, "On Youth and Rebellion."

In a 1956 talk (*Torat Menachem 5717,* Vol. 1, p. 63 (chabad.org/2988199)) exhorting the youth to recognize and utilize their unique strengths, the Rebbe pointed to the seemingly dismal Talmudic prediction (*Sotah* 49a) that in the pre-messianic era "the youth will shame the face of elders... a daughter will rise up against her mother, a daughter-in-law against her mother-in-law." Drawing on a Chasidic teaching from the Alter Rebbe (*Likkutei Torah, Parshat Bechukotai,* p. 48a) that the "curses" in the Torah carry profound blessing— so profound that they cannot be stated explicitly and must therefore be disguised in negativity—the Rebbe explained that this "negative" prediction about the audacity of youth in fact carries tremendous blessings. Young people are bestowed with a powerful revolutionary force, which they can and must maximize for the good.

A "New Year Message for Jewish Youth" from 1950 reads similarly:

"Time is like a vessel which must be filled to capacity and overflowing. Every second of time granted to us must likewise be crammed with productive and creative action, not only on behalf of ourselves, but also for the good of others, which is an integral part of our overall purpose in life. I particularly want to emphasize the feeling of responsibility which must imbue every Jew and Jewess towards one another, and towards one's environment in general. It is the obligation to spread the light of G-d all around us.

"This feeling of responsibility must be especially strong with the youth, because it is the young people who have been most generously blessed by G-d with the choice qualities of energy, courage, and enthusiasm. In the light of what has been said above, namely, that everything created by G-d must be utilized to its fullest capacity, youth has added responsibilities and duties, and a time limit to fulfill them.

Thus we have here at this moment, three important aspects converging together: the element of time in general, the present pre-Rosh Hashanah time in particular, and the element of youth with its special potentialities and responsibilities.

"I trust, therefore, that you will earnestly consider these circumstances, and resolve to fully utilize your vast potential resources in fulfilling your obligations, both to better yourselves, and at the same time also to influence your families, friends, and environment at large...."

See also chabad.org/392193.

42. See, for example, the account of Meir Zeiler, *Here's My Story* (JEM), "Jobs Jobs Jobs!", accessible at chabad.org/4103225. See also the recollections of Lukes Van Deer Walde of his audience, *Here's My Story* (JEM), "My Audience 43 Years Ago," accessible at chabad.org/2916031.

43. See, for example, *Petakim*, Vol. 1, p. 128. See also *Igrot Kodesh*, Vol. 27, p. 529.

44. See, for example, *Igrot Kodesh*, Vol. 27, p. 293; English letter dated 10 Iyar, 5732; English letter dated 12 Kislev, 5743 (to a Jewish community leader):

"There is surely no need to emphasize to you at length that retiring—withdrawing oneself from active service—can only apply in such matters as business, employment, and the like. It cannot apply, of course, to a lifetime service which is related to G-d. This *shlichut* [mission] is, in the words of our Sages (*Kiddushin* 82a), "I was created to serve my creator." Of course, the extent and form of the actual performance of this *shlichut* varies in the course of a lifetime, as, for example, it is not the same before bar mitzvah as after bar mitzvah, and thereafter much depends on the capacities and opportunities which Divine Providence bestows upon each individual.

"One of the Jewish characteristics is a sense of innovation and, especially, being 'different.' If ordinary retirement actually involves complete or partial withdrawal and a slowdown of physical and mental activity (though in my opinion this is a wrong and regrettable attitude even from the viewpoint of physical health)—it has this redeeming feature for a Jew, that it provides an opportunity to redouble his efforts in serving his Creator, now that he can divert much of his energy and attention to this most gratifying outlet. For now he has more time for Torah study, for daily prayer with *kavanah* [intention], and for all other daily *mitzvot* and *gemilut chasadim* [acts of lovingkindness]—in other words, the three pillars upon which the world rests [*Avot* 1:2], both the big world and the "small world" which is the human individual [*Tanchuma, Pekudei* 3]...."

For a more detailed account of the Rebbe's approach to aging and retirement, see S. Jacobson, *Towards a Meaningful Life*, chapter 13.

45. *Here's My Story* (JEM), "Not Just a Job.'"
46. In addition to what I heard firsthand, I gathered some additional details (including a peek at the page from his notebook) from his grandchildren, an obituary (chabad.org/5251382), and a memento from a grandchild's wedding (*Teshurah Karlinshtein*, 5783).

On the subject of art, see also the English letter dated 5 Kislev, 5728 (accessible at chabad.org/393257): "Those who have been divinely gifted in art, whether sculpture or painting and the like, have the privilege of being able to convert an inanimate thing, such as a brush, paint and canvas, or wood and stone, etc., into living form.

"In a deeper sense, it is the ability to transform to a certain extent the material into spiritual, even where the creation is in still life, and certainly where the artistic work has to do with living creatures and humans. How much more so if the art medium is used to advance ideas, especially [those] reflecting Torah and *mitzvot*, which would raise the artistic skill to its highest level."

47. *Here's My Story* (JEM), "Making Waves," accessible at chabad.org/4240461.
48. English letter dated 23 Tammuz, 5727.
49. *Heichal Menachem,* Vol. 3, p. 44.

See also *Igrot Kodesh,* Vol. 10, p. 352: "It doesn't mean accomplishments that boggle the mind, like a High Priest with eight garments of gold, etc.; the true [divine] purpose lies for each of us in our daily lives, and specifically in those aspects that are labeled by the world as 'gray,' that people 'tread over' [*Avodah Zarah* 18a]. To a member of the group of teachers in [location omitted] this means simply the small details in the daily [teaching] routine. For from these minute details, if done properly, an 'upright and blessed generation' [Psalms 112:2] will be built, a generation of redemption..."

See also *Igrot Kodesh,* Vol. 10, pp. 21, 116.
50. *Igrot Kodesh,* Vol. 8, p. 233. See also *Igrot Kodesh,* Vol. 9, p. 306.
51. *Here's My Story* (JEM), "A Pebble in a Lake."
52. *Igrot Kodesh,* Vol. 13, p. 487.

See also *Igrot Kodesh,* Vol. 14, p. 400 (to a man who wrote about his lack of inner peace):

"A universal point in all ways [of addressing these feelings] is to reflect on the fact that every one of us is a part of our society and surroundings. Therefore, one needs to not only be a receiver but also a contributor, or, more precisely, primarily a contributor and only secondarily a receiver.

"Since a person's essence is their soul and spirit, not their body and physicality, it is understood that their contribution should primarily be towards the spirit of their surroundings; to infuse it with the living spirit of our Torah, the Torah of life, which is simultaneously the ultimate spirituality but also vivifies the physical, even to its most mundane levels. As our Sages famously taught (*Shabbat* 88b), the Torah was given specifically to those who have an evil inclination, and spent time in Egypt, dubbed 'the earth's nakedness' [see Genesis 42:9, *Kohelet Rabbah* 1:4], and it was not given to the heavenly angels.

"Since this is the primary task of a person, they are assured that they will succeed with proper effort, so long as they don't retreat when encountering hardships. And if they don't entirely succeed the first time, or even the second or third time—ultimately success will come.

"When you will 'firmly fix your thought' (as the Alter Rebbe phrases it [*Tanya,* ch. 3]) into fulfilling this task—wide horizons of exalted accomplishments will be revealed to you; your inner satisfaction will increase manyfold when you see such a lofty goal in your life on earth; deeper meaning will be found in your family members personal matters, and even your own, for only through the harmony of all these together will there be success in fulfilling your primary task and seeing reward in your work—to strengthen the form over the matter, the spiritual over the physical, the soul over the body, and the divine spark inside you over everything around you.

"There is much to elaborate on all the above, especially in applying it to everyone's individual surroundings, talents, how they were raised, and so on. But the above [points] are universal to everyone. My hope is that what was written will serve as a [starting] point that you will develop in accordance with your [particular] surroundings and endeavors. I await good news."

53. *Here's My Story* (JEM), "The Power of the Pen."
54. See *Mishneh Torah, Hilchot Deot* 4:4, and in the commentaries of *Maase Rokeach* and *Avodat Hamelech* ad loc. See also *Siddur Yaavetz, Cheshbon Meah Brachot, se'if 7*.
55. See *Hatraktorist Shel Harabi*, p. 99-101.
56. Vermetten, E., and Bremner, J.D. (2002). Circuits and systems in stress. I. Preclinical studies. *Depress. Anxiety*, 15: 126-147. https://doi.org/10.1002/da.10016.
57. Sin, N.L., Wen, J., Klaiber, P., Buxton, O.M., & Almeida, D.M. (2020). Sleep duration and affective reactivity to stressors and positive events in daily life. *Health Psychology: Official Journal of the Division of Health Psychology, American Psychological Association*.
58. In addition to the teaching of the Maggid quoted in this chapter, the Rebbe would often point to a teaching of the Baal Shem Tov, the founder of the Chasidic movement.

    The verse says, "If you see the donkey of your enemy lying under its burden, would you refrain from helping him? You shall surely help along with him." (Exodus 23:5).

    The Baal Shem Tov interpreted this verse (*Hayom Yom*, entry for 28 Shevat) as referring to the struggle of body and soul: the Hebrew word for donkey, *chamor*, can also be read as *chomer*, i.e., the material body. Thus, the verse can be read: "When you see the donkey of your enemy lying under its burden"—when you see your body as an enemy that inhibits you, "and would refrain from helping it"—you might want to refrain from taking care of your body and instead let it weaken, "you must nevertheless raise it with him"—you must work *with* your body [specifically in divine service].

A 1950 talk (*Likkutei Sichot*, Vol. 1, p. 31) connects this teaching of the Baal Shem Tov with an earlier Kabalistic source. The *Zohar* (Vol. I, p. 122b) teaches that, mystically, "Abraham" alludes to the soul while "Sarah" alludes to the body. In light of this Zoharic interpretation, the Rebbe explained, the verse where G-d tells Abraham that "whatever Sarah tells you, do as she says" (Genesis 21:12) conveys, in essence, the important role of the body, and thus the spiritual mandate to keep it in good health.

On a more basic level, the Rebbe saw this approach as a natural derivative of the broader Chasidic outlook that the physical world is not in conflict with the Divine. Many letters point to a teaching in *Tanya* on the verse "one nation on earth" (Samuel II 7:23), which the Alter Rebbe interpreted as referring to the Jewish approach of bringing G-dly "oneness" even into "earthly" matters.

The following letter (*Igrot Kodesh*, Vol. 13, p. 234) elucidates this theme:

"Regarding what you write, that the feeling of happiness is a result of hormonal secretions of certain glands transported via the circulatory system to the brain. Allow me to point out that since the body and soul are truly integrated and united as a single whole, therefore anything that occurs in the soul will cause some corresponding phenomenon in the body.

"I trust you will agree with me that the concept of oneness within the microcosm of the human being—which serves as an analogy and model of the true oneness of the macrocosmos—is not aligned with the pantheistic view that all that exists is nature and matter. Quite the contrary, all that exists is spiritual. Yet further, everything is divine. As the Alter Rebbe notes briefly (*Tanya, Igeret Hakodesh*, Epistle 9) in his interpretation of the verse 'one nation on earth' [Samuel II 7:23] that even 'earthly' matters are not separated from the 'One.'

"It is worth mentioning that those who championed a materialistic worldview, whenever it was discovered how a soulful emotion was associated with changes in the body, such as electrical charges, etc., they would rejoice in this discovery as though they found a treasure [in support of their worldview]. However, in truth, not only is there no contradiction, but quite the contrary: this is the logical outcome of the absolute truth of the oneness of the Creator.

"By oneness, I mean that G-d is one and there is none else besides Him—not simply that there is no other divinity besides Him, but that there is literally nothing else, no existence aside from His.

"Indeed, this is one of the most fundamental ideas of the teachings of Chasidut, as explained in Shaar Hayichud Veha'emunah by the Alter Rebbe."

(Much of the letter's translation is taken from Rabbi Tzvi Freeman's eloquent article on this subject, "Why I'm Not Excited That Science Hasn't (Yet) Found Consciousness in Your Brain," accessible at chabad.org/6007982.)

Similarly reads another letter (*Igrot Kodesh,* Vol. 14, p. 147):

"The news has reached me that you find yourself in a house of healing [i.e., a hospital], and my hope is that by the time this letter reaches you your situation will have already improved, and you will soon be able to report this good news yourself....

"One of the foundational lessons of Chasidut is to take an approach of 'raise it *with* him' [Exodus 23:5]—i.e. *with* the body [and not to be in conflict with it]. Since divine service must be healthy and wholesome, it is clear that the body must also be healthy and wholesome. Especially considering that the Jewish people are referred to as 'one nation on earth' [Samuel II 7:23], in the sense [*Igeret Hakodesh,* Epistle 9] that they bring oneness also in 'earthly' matters. They do not only prioritize 'form' over 'matter,' but in fact transform matter itself into form, creating true unity."

On this note, Dr. Mel Alexenberg, an experimental artist and distinguished professor of art and Jewish thought who created the first computer-generated digital art in 1965, related the following:

"I first met the Rebbe in 1962. I had a fascinating discussion with him on the relationship between art, science, technology, and Judaism, which has been my life's work. He was very interested in these kinds of things...

"That first meeting led to many others, and to a voluminous correspondence between us. I cannot remember exactly at which meeting it came up, but the Rebbe told me one thing that became a central part of my thinking. He pointed out that, in Hebrew, the words for 'matter' and 'spirit' are interchangeable; that is the letters that spell *chomer*, meaning 'matter,' also spell *ruach*, meaning 'spirit' —all you have to do is drop one letter.

"'What is the difference between the spiritual and material world?' he asked rhetorically. 'It's a matter of perspective. If you look at the world one way, you see a material world. But if you make a switch in your head, if you change the quality of your perception, if you look at things in a new, fresh way, then the same world becomes spiritual. The spiritual world and the material world are not two worlds. The quality of your relationship to the material world makes it spiritual.'

"Because of this insight, a lot of my artwork—as a matter of fact almost all of my artwork—begins with Hebrew words and Torah concepts."

59. *Igrot Kodesh*, Vol. 11, p. 202. See also *Igrot Kodesh*, Vol. 5, p. 280.

The unity of body and soul was a central theme in the Rebbe's advice to medical professionals—that alongside meticulous physical care, it is vital to focus and tend to the emotional state of the patient, not only for its own sake, but also because it has a real impact on their physical capacity to heal.

For example, the following 1957 letter (to Dr. William Mendelsohn from New Haven):

"I was gratified to learn from [name omitted] that you gave him your special attention, particularly in connection with the surgery that you performed on him.

"A physician is, of course, the authorized agent through whom G-d sends a cure to a sick person, and needless to say, it is not only the physician's skill that is important, but also his cordial attitude towards his patients, in conformity with the accepted view that a physician's profession is not just a calling, but is a sacred mission of bringing a relief and a cure to the suffering. Hence a personal attitude, and even a personal bond with the patient, often goes a long way towards bringing him the necessary relief and cure. Although in the case of a surgeon a subjective attitude may, in a sense, present a problem, since the surgeon must operate with perfect calmness, without being distracted by personal emotion, in practice, the surgeon who combines intellect and feeling in perfect harmony enjoys G-d's blessings, so that he is not only not distracted by his feelings, but rather on the contrary, is greatly helped thereby.

"Parenthetically, one of the significant lessons and influences of *tefillin* which, as you know, is placed both on the arm facing the heart and on the head facing the brain, is to teach us and help us to harmonize the two and to subjugate both to the services of G-d and mankind, making the complete and perfect man.

"All this is in keeping with the idea of monotheism, of which our Jewish people has been privileged to be the bearer throughout the ages. This is the idea that a perfect unity pervades everything, the macrocosm as well as the microcosm. Accordingly, in human life we do not consider the body and soul as two separate universes, but two aspects of the same microcosm. Even science, in modern times, has become aware of this truth, realizing that physical and spiritual health are intimately connected.

"I trust, therefore, that in treating your patients physically, you also help them spiritually, which in general terms, means to strengthen their bond with the Source of life, the Creator of the universe, and the Giver of the Torah, the way we are taught in our Torah, the Law of Life, [which teaches us] how to realize and strengthen the said bonds in the most effective and in the fullest measure.

"I do not want to say thank you for your personal attention to [name omitted], but instead I would rather extend to you my prayerful wishes that for many, many years to come the Almighty grant you the strength and the skill to help those who turn to you, both physically and spiritually. And as G-d's reward is in kind, but in a very generous measure, may the

Almighty reward you and all of yours with good health, both physically and spiritually..."

In this spirit, the Rebbe would often emphasize how important it is for physical healing that the patient maintain their hope and will to recover and not succumb to pessimism. See, for example, the following English letter (dated 1 Kislev, 5733):

"I received your letter. While I am pleased to read in your letter a quotation about G-d being the Creator of the world who also guides all its destinies, etc., this very good impression is weakened by the tone of your letter later on, where you state that you want to be 'realistic,' based on the prognosis of physicians regarding your condition.

"I want to tell you, first, that even from the realistic point of view, we must recognize the fact that very many times the greatest physicians have made mistakes in diagnosis. Moreover, in recent times we see that new discoveries are made daily in the medical field, with new 'wonder' drugs and methods, which have revolutionized medical treatment.

"Secondly, observing life in general, we see so many things that are strange and unbelievable—that to be truly realistic, one cannot consider anything as impossible.

"In a condition which is, to a large extent, bound up with the nervous system and the resistance of the organism, even medical opinion agrees that the stronger the patient's faith in the cure, and the stronger his will to get better, the stronger becomes his ability to recover.

"Needless to say, this is not said in the way of an admonition. But, inasmuch as by individual Divine Providence, you have learned of me, and I of you, I think I am entitled to convey to you the above thoughts which I was privileged to hear from my father-in-law of saintly memory in similar cases.... With blessing and hoping to hear good news from you..."

Being as a patient's mindset is an integral part of their healing, the Rebbe was concerned that technology might distract doctors from paying attention to their patients' inner world. In a 1973 private audience with Dr. Mordechai Shani, the director of Sheba Medical Center, the Rebbe expressed this concern.

Here is Shani's recollection:

"Another issue that we discussed was the place of technology in medicine. Back in the 1970s, before the age of the personal computer, technology was not yet a central nor dominant tool of the medical world. The problems related to technology in medicine would not become apparent for years to come. But here, too, the Rebbe was ahead of his time.

"He said something tremendously forward-thinking: 'It is up to you, the doctor, to determine whether technology will be used for the benefit of humanity.' He worried that technology might create distance between the doctor and the patient. 'At the end of the day,' [the Rebbe] said, 'the attention of the doctor, the human being, is most important, and while technology can be a helpful tool, it cannot become a replacement for listening and caring.'

"He was so very right. If a doctor works strictly according to protocol, he will often administer many unnecessary tests or, worse, misdiagnose. The most important starting point is to listen to the patient and try to understand what his or her needs are. But, unfortunately, for many doctors today, technology has become the central means of practicing medicine, instead of a helping tool, sometimes to the detriment of the patient. So the Rebbe had every reason to be concerned..."

60. *Igrot Kodesh,* Vol. 7, p. 194, and Vol. 4, pp. 157, 341.
61. *Kovetz Hayechidut–Vaad Talmidei Hatmimim,* p. 55-56.
62. The Rebbe would point to the ruling in *Shulchan Aruch Harav* (*Hilchot Nizkei Guf Venefesh, se'if 4*), that "a person does not have the right to hurt their body..."

See, for example, *Igrot Kodesh,* Vol. 5, p. 60, and Vol. 14, p. 203—"It is certainly superfluous to elaborate on the necessity to listen to the directives of the doctor.... The central idea here is, in the words of our Sages, that 'a person does not have the right to hurt their body, because the body belongs to G-d—an amazing expression which, with even brief reflection, is absolutely mind-boggling. And may it be that this profound teaching of our Sages should have its desired effect on you to be more careful with your health...'"

A 1975 English letter, dated 1 Shevat, 5735, explains similarly:

"I was sorry to hear that you have not been in the best of health. I trust that you are carrying out the instructions of your doctor, especially as this is also a basic teaching of our Torah, as it is written, '*Verapo yerapei*—the doctor should heal' [Exodus 21:19, as interpreted in *Berachot* 60a].

"No doubt you have also heard the saying of our Sages that a person's physical body is 'G-d's property,' which was given to the person in trust to take care of. Thus, it is obvious with what care a person has to guard one's health and body, which is G-d's property.

"Needless to say, this must not be overdone at the expense of the soul, which is more than G-d's 'property,' but actually a part of G-dliness above (as explained at length in *Tanya*, ch. 2)..."

Many letters also point to the teaching of Maimonides (*Mishneh Torah, Hilchot Dei'ot* 4:1) that "the body being healthy and wholesome is of the ways of G-d," and the verse "Watch yourselves very well" (Deuteronomy 4:15), which the Talmud (*Berachot* 32b) also interprets as an instruction to guard one's health.

See, for example, the following English letter (dated 20 Teves, 5744):

"I believe I have already had occasion to write the following point to you, but because of its importance, I will repeat it. I am referring to the *mitzvah* of taking care of one's health, which is one of the most important commandments of Hashem, as explained at length in the Rambam (*Mishneh Torah, Hilchot Dei'ot*, end of ch. 3 and beg. of ch. 4; see there)...

"Inasmuch as in all situations one is required to rely on authority, I trust that you are following the instructions of a doctor, bearing in mind that the Torah has given a physician the power to heal. One must not rely upon one's own judgment when it comes to matters of health. Besides, it is one of the good customs in this country to have a physical checkup from time to time."

63. *Igrot Kodesh,* Vol. 7, p. 75. This letter points to words from Maimonides (*Mishneh Torah, Hilchot Rotzei'ach* 1:4) that connote this perspective.

64. Job 5:7.
65. See *Sefer Hamaspik L'Ovdei Hashem,* in his treatise on *hitbodedut.*
66. *Bava Metzia* 77a.
67. *Sichot Kodesh 5739,* Vol. 2, pp. 316-17.
68. See *Igrot Kodesh,* Vol. 14, p. 491. For a broader overview of the Rebbe's views on retirement, see Joseph Telushkin, *Rebbe* pp. 128-9 and its endnotes.
69. See English letter dated 12 Nissan, 5734 (chabad.org/826460). See also *Igrot Kodesh,* Vol. 27, p. 231, and Vol. 28, p. 348; *Petakim,* Vol. 2, p. 180, and Vol. 3, p. 128. ("For many reasons, and especially to improve your state of mind, you should find a job, at least part-time. And even better if it is a job that will give you satisfaction.")

The following is a response to a rabbi who consulted with the Rebbe about an individual he was helping, who was unemployed and struggling with depression. The handwritten response (*Teshurah Begun-Mockin,* 5774) begins as follows: "He should do *whatever it takes* to get a job, or work, for a few hours every weekday (except Shabbat and festivals). In the first stages the *type* of work makes no difference *at all.* [Additionally,] for a certain amount of time every day he should help others for no reward. *Certainly* the *yetzer hara* will want to persuade him that no such work exists, it's not in his power, and so on—however, this is a complete *falsehood* of the *yetzer hara.* If he will invest effort, he will find such opportunities *and he will succeed...* If he has been taking anti-anxiety pills, etc., until now—he can continue doing so."

In addition to productive occupation serving an innate psychological need, staying occupied (or getting a job) can be a helpful distraction from negative thoughts, as suggested in various letters. See, for example, *Igrot Kodesh,* Vol. 28, p. 347. To help alleviate the mind from fears, the letter recommends: "Be as occupied as possible—be it a job, *mivtza'im,* and so on." See also *Petakim,* Vol. 2, pp. 80, 246; and *Likkutei Sichot,* Vol. 36, p. 324.

Occasionally, when addressing people in need of emotional rehabilitation, letters recommend specifically *physical* work.

See, for example, *Likkutei Sichot,* Vol. 36, p. 325: "It is critically important that his time not be empty. He should be occupied with tasks that do not require deep thought. The best would be for him to do some physical labor, at least part-time." Several letters advise young people in need of rehabilitation to join a Torah-observant kibbutz where they will be physically productive and have proper structure. See *Igrot Kodesh,* Vol. 17, p. 19, and Vol. 18, p. 426. See also *Igrot Kodesh,* Vol. 28, p. 348.

In special instances, it seems the Rebbe counseled getting occupied with tangible tasks to help people lost in their own minds get back in touch with reality. See, for example, *Igrot Kodesh,* Vol. 16, p. 241; and *Petakim,* Vol. 2, p. 131.

Interestingly, in one letter (*Igrot Kodesh,* Vol. 31, p. 338), the Rebbe counseled parents whose son was struggling psychologically that he learn a trade from which to make an income independent of his parents, and this might help him change his self-image and outlook on life.

Taking outdoor walks to relieve stress is also advised. See, for example, *Igrot Kodesh,* Vol. 7, p. 322; and *Igrot Kodesh,* Vol. 18, p. 275.

70. Photocopy of handwritten response.
71. *Petakim,* Vol. 1, p. 123.

See also *Otzar Hamelech 3,* p. 198: "The ability to be—and actually being—organized, self-disciplined, and self-controlled, are essential in everyone's life, especially when you're young and preparing yourself to set up your life." *Igrot Kodesh,* Vol. 32, p. 94: "What's most important is that you lead an orderly life as much as possible and, by extension, with a minimum of stress." *Igrot Kodesh,* Vol. 20, p. 315: "In general the life of a person needs to be specifically in an orderly fashion. And specifically such is the way of holiness, in contrast to the 'opposite force' [*sitra achara*], which functions in a manner of chaos. And I mean order in all areas—waking up, studying Torah, eating and drinking, etc. and, certainly and importantly, with regards to things concerning your relationship at home, for [as our Sages taught] great is the peace between husband and wife [see *Vayikra Rabbah* 9:9] for then the divine presence rests amongst them [see *Sotah* 17a].")

See *Igrot Kodesh*, Vol. 17, p. 169, on how having an orderly schedule during the day can help sleep at night. See *Igrot Kodesh*, Vol. 20, p. 119, on how not having daily structure can lead to various extreme thoughts (in this case, that people hate him and are out to get him). See, for example, *Igrot Kodesh*, Vol. 14, p. 18, on the obvious physical health benefits of maintaining a proper schedule of eating and sleeping.

72. Photocopy of handwritten response.
73. In a similar spirit, a few letters advise that to keep a fixed study schedule it is helpful to get a study partner, as the obligation to the other person will keep you on track. See *Igrot Kodesh*, Vol. 10, p. 119; Vol. 14, p. 243; Vol. 20, p. 311.
74. *Igrot Kodesh*, Vol. 24, p. 179.
75. English letter.
76. *A Chassidisher Derher*, no. 48, p. 52.
77. *Moreh Nevuchim* II, ch. 40.
78. *Megillah* 23b.
79. *Igrot Kodesh*, Vol. 18, p. 534.

See also *Igrot Kodesh*, Vol. 23, p. 264. "Human beings are not isolationist by nature, and 'it is not good for man to be alone' [Genesis 2:18]. People naturally search for a social life in which, and through which, and with the help of which, they can actualize their own completion." See there for a lengthy analysis of the *kibbutz* model of communal living.

Citing the verse "It is not good for man to be alone" (Genesis 2:18), which refers to the importance of Adam finding a mate in Eve, the Rebbe would sometimes encourage both men and women to work towards getting married, not only for its own sake, but also because it would significantly enhance their own emotional wellness. See, for example, *Igrot Kodesh*, Vol. 12, p. 46; Vol. 23, p. 360; Vol. 24, p. 180.

Although the Rebbe posited that everyone should maintain at least *some* level of social interaction, a few letters seem to counsel spending *significant time* in the company of others for therapeutic reasons, to help get through a difficult period. See, for example, an English letter dated 11 Nissan, 5720: "Another good method [in coping with personal problems] is to try to be in the company of other people as much as possible." See also *Igrot Kodesh,* Vol. 27, p. 101, for a letter to a young widow who tragically lost her husband and asked advice about her children. Among other things, the Rebbe wrote: "Try to make it that your children should be in the company of other children their age as much as possible." See also *Petakim,* Vol. 1, p. 130: "To expedite your healing and make it easier for you to distract your thoughts, it is advisable to work outside your house, at least a few hours a week; and it should be a job that necessitates interacting with others."

For a letter advising a father how to help his son out of his reclusiveness, see *Igrot Kodesh,* Vol. 26, p. 2.

80. *Igrot Kodesh,* Vol. 19, p. 371.

This letter emphasizes two points: First, take a step-by-step approach (because leaping ahead is often counterproductive); and second, don't get dispirited by the arduous path. If you keep taking one step after another, your goals will surely be attained. These two points were a recurring theme in the Rebbe's counseling. Many letters would point to the verse "Little by little will they be driven out from before you" (Exodus 23:30) as an eternal principle that overcoming negativity is usually a gradual process, but ultimately is crowned with success. Following are a few specific examples:

For spiritual growth, self-improvement, and overcoming negative traits and behaviors—see *Igrot Kodesh,* Vol. 7, pp. 75, 79; Vol. 11, p. 82; Vol. 14, pp. 451, 459; Vol. 17, p. 27; Vol. 18, p. 544. See also *Igrot Kodesh,* Vol. 11, p. 97.

To improve a negative mood—see *Igrot Kodesh,* Vol. 13, p. 487; and Vol. 22, p. 323.

To train oneself to live according to a schedule—see *Igrot Kodesh,* Vol. 11, p. 244; Vol. 20, p. 119.

For returning to study after an extended break—see *Igrot Kodesh,* Vol. 14, p. 243. Similarly, to a young man who wrote of his struggle with concentrating on his studies, see *Igrot Kodesh,* Vol. 11, p. 161: "Add every day only a few minutes more than the day before [not more].") See there for some other interesting advice.

See *Igrot Kodesh,* Vol. 20, p. 311, for a letter about the importance of going step by step to a young man who wrote that he can't seem to hold onto the good resolutions and goals that he sets.

See also: English letter, dated 17 Iyar, 5719 (The Time for Teshuvah, accessible at chabad.org/1907086)—"It would be well to find an opportunity, of course without him knowing that I suggested it to you, to emphasize to him again that the normal way for a person to make progress is to advance step by step, rather than expect of himself radical changes all at once. Even if progress seems slow, this is the way of progress in his circumstance."

See also: English letter dated 20 Teves, 5717, (Are Setbacks Cause for Frustration? accessible at chabad.org/1950496)— "As for the setbacks you mention, and especially your feeling of deficiency in your studies, it should be remembered that the Torah teaches us that the conquest of setbacks and the general settling down in life usually can be accomplished in stages. You will recall that the Holy Land was also conquered by degrees, and as it was in the case of the physical conquest, so it is in the case of spiritual conquest. For just as it is said of the Holy Land that 'the eyes of G-d are upon it from the beginning of the year to the end of the year' [Deuteronomy 11:12], so are the eyes of G-d upon everyone of us individually, watching over us constantly and helping us in our determination to accomplish our conquests. Therefore, one should not be discouraged by the slowness of the progress, or even by an occasional setback."

81. Psalms 1:3.
82. Psalms 128:3.
83. *Igrot Kodesh,* Vol. 26, p. 454.

Mishkovsky's letter to the Rebbe and some of the details here are translated from the book *Harabi Sheli: Nashim Mesaprot*, p. 163 and on.

84. See *Avodah Zarah* 17a.
85. *Igrot Kodesh,* Vol. 9, p. 306. Following are additional excerpts from the letter:

"It is 'easy for the intelligent to know' [Proverbs 14:6], and we can also observe this in reality, that the purpose of life doesn't lie in gleaning enjoyment from fleeting material pleasures. Rather, 'Man is born to toil' [Job 5:7], and it is through one's work in the eternal Torah and *mitzvot* that one attains spiritual satisfaction, especially when one is active in helping others. This is the literal meaning of the Torah being called a 'Torah of Life' [*Sim Shalom* in the Amidah prayer]—for it gives a good life in this physical world as well...

"If this was always true, all the more so in our times when it was exposed for all to see the emptiness and lack of substance and taste in various fallacious ideologies, when not money nor power stood by a person in their time of need. Thus, in our generation, it is easier to see the truth in its simplicity now that many distracting doctrines, which muddled clear thinking, have been depleted.

"All of us who survived the horrific slaughters [of our people] as 'brands plucked from a fire' [Zechariah 3:2] must view ourselves as emissaries not only to fulfill our own role, but also that of all those who perished before their time.

"And just as regarding the Jewish people as a whole, the parts which kept the ways of the Torah have survived until this day, while all the groups that left its path have either been lost entirely, or are dwindling—the same is true in the life of an individual Jew...

"The foundational point that emanates from all the above is that the Torah and *mitzvot* have kept the Jewish people from perishing, despite [the Jewish people] being 'a minority among the nations' [Deuteronomy 7:7] and in every generation there being those who 'rose up to wipe us out' [*Passover Haggadah*]. And the Torah and *mitzvot* are the golden thread that unites all the generations of the Jewish people from the giving of the Torah until this day..."

86. English letter from 5725, published in *Healthy in Body, Mind, and Spirit* (SIE), Vol. 3, chapter 3, accessible at chabad.org/2308532.
87. *Mishneh Torah, Hilchot Gerushin* 2:20.

The following is how the letter explains this source in the Rambam:

"You ask me about my reference to the Rambam and where it contains in substance, though in different terms, the concepts of the conscious and subconscious of modern psychology. I had in mind a passage in *Hilchot Gerushin*, end of chapter. 2, in the Rambam's Opus Magnum ('Yad Hachazakah').

"The gist of that passage is as follows: There are certain matters in Jewish Law, the performance of which requires free volition, no coercion. However, where the Jewish law requires specific performance, it is permitted to use coercive measures until the reluctant party declares 'I am willing,' and his performance is valid and considered voluntary. There seems here an obvious contradiction: If it is permitted [to] compel performance, why is it necessary that the person should declare himself 'willing'? And if compulsory performance is not valid, what good is it if the person declares himself 'willing' under compulsion?

"And here comes the essential point of the Rambam's explanation:

"Every Jew, regardless of his status and station, is essentially willing to do all that he is commanded to do by our Torah. However, sometimes the Yetzer (Hara) prevails over his better judgment and prevents him from doing what he has to do in accordance with the Torah. When, therefore, Beth Din compels a Jew to do something, it is not with a view to creating in him a new desire, but rather to release him from the compulsion which had paralyzed his desire, thus enabling him to express his true self. Under these circumstances, when he declares 'I am willing,' it is an authentic declaration.

"To put the above in contemporary terminology: The conscious state of a Jew can be affected by external factors to the extent of including states of mind and even behavior which are contrary to his subconscious, which is the Jew's essential nature. When the external pressures are removed, it does not constitute a change or transformation of his essential nature, but, on the contrary, merely the reassertion of his innate and true character."

88. English letter dated 21 Sivan, 5725, (accessible at chabad.org/1899570).
89. English letter from 5720.
90. Carl Jung. *Modern Man in Search of a Soul* (1933), p. 229.
91. *Viktor Frankl on Religion & Ultimate Meaning 1990* (YouTube).

92. On Frankl's own telling, the Rebbe's encouragement came to him at a critical moment. For a full and sourced account of this episode, see *Mrs. Mozart, Viktor Frankl, & The Lubavitcher Rebbe* on TheYeshiva.net, and *The Message the Rebbe Sent to Famed Psychiatrist Dr. Victor Frankl* (JEM).

93. In a 1960 audience (recorded in HMS, titled "Do What Your Zeide Says To Do"), the Rebbe encouraged Dr. Abraham J. Twerski, a then unknown religious psychiatrist, to move to New York City. He explained that observant psychiatrists were woefully missing in New York, adding that "there are many people here whom I would like to send to a psychiatrist because they need psychiatric help, but I can't send them to a psychiatrist who is going to say that religion is a neurosis and will tell them that they have to drop their religion." The Rebbe then asked him if he had read Frankl's works. When Twerski answered in the negative, the Rebbe encouraged him to do so. See also *Mrs. Mozart, Viktor Frankl & The Lubavitcher Rebbe* on TheYeshiva.net for two other accounts of the Rebbe encouraging individuals studying psychology to take interest in Frankl.

94. *Igrot Kodesh*, Vol. 26, p. 158.

In the summer of 1962, a man wrote a letter to the Rebbe describing the mental health struggle of a friend. He asked for prayers on his friend's behalf and guidance as to his own role in helping him.

The Rebbe began his reply (*Igrot Kodesh*, Vol. 22, p. 227) by writing that he had recently prayed for the friend's healing at the gravesite of his father-in-law, the previous Lubavitcher Rebbe. He then continued to encourage the man to hold onto his hope that his friend would indeed overcome his present condition. "Our Sages taught us that a person should never despair [see *Berachot* 10a], and this is especially emphasized in Chasidic teachings. Knowing this should encourage you to not slacken in your efforts to influence your friend in the right direction, in a tactful manner. As I've written in the past, we find in similar situations that indirect influence has a better chance of bringing positive results than direct intervention."

The Rebbe then added a point he should keep in mind when seeking out professional care for his friend:

"There is a specific class of psychologists who commence their treatment by deriding G-d, spirituality, honor of one's parents, and the like. If that is the type of psychologist your friend is seeing, much research and scrutiny is required to determine the benefit he may receive from them, and even if it is substantial, whether that benefit won't be outweighed by the long-term harm.

"There are of course many psychologists who heal effectively using unconvoluted methods. This is especially the case since one professor [Frankl] found the inner courage to declare that (contrary to the well-known individual who founded this form of therapy [Freud]) faith in G-d and an overall religious inclination give meaning to life and are of the most constructive paths to healing. Nevertheless, for a number of reasons, this approach has not permeated many professional circles, and it is thus worthwhile to find out more about the psychologist…

"With blessings that you should be able to share good news regarding all the above."

In this regard, it is noteworthy that multiple letters advising people to see psychologists emphasize that the psychologist should be a person of faith. See, for example, *Igrot Kodesh,* Vol. 31, p. 338; English letter dated 24 Tammuz, 5726; *Here's My Story* (JEM) from 14 March, 2018, "Health Psychiatry," accessible at chabad.org/3974318. See there also for an account of the Rebbe discouraging a psychiatrist from submitting himself to a years-long intensive psychoanalysis, although that was considered a requisite to becoming a good psychiatrist at the time. ("I don't see what you'll get out of it.")

*

On this note, the following are three letters about the important role of psychologists.

The first letter:

Responding to a licensed psychologist from Canada who asked "if a therapist carries the status of a physician according to the *Shulchan Aruch* (*Code of Jewish Law*)" this 1987 letter answers:

"Anyone who is trained (and formally attested) to bring

therapeutic relief to a human being has the status of a physician in that area of his training and expertise.

"Furthermore, since medical science has become so specialized, the area of therapy, and also dietetics, have in recent years been researched and systematized, etc., much in the same way as an eye doctor and an ear doctor have become specialists in their particular field. This is especially true in regard to dietetics, in view of the importance attached to diet by the Rambam (*Mishnah Torah, Hilchot Dei'ot*) almost 800 years ago, which only recently has become increasingly recognized.

"With regard to the problem of the complex nature of human behavior and the difficulties inherent in empirical investigation—surely, as you know, all empirical sciences, and certainly medical science, face this problem. But the *Shulchan Aruch*, well aware of this problem, rules [see, for example, *Orach Chaim* 328:10-16] that one has to deal with the existential reality of the available criteria as to what is medically useful and has been verified as such, etc.

"Regarding the question of repression of anger and sadness, and the like—you surely know the approach of Chasidut, especially Chabad, and how much emphasis is placed on the *tikkun hamidot* (development of character, self-control, etc.) and how to overcome sadness and the like.

"As in many other areas, there are two aspects to consider: a) the aspect relating to physical health, and b) that relating to spiritual health. Since both are, of course, interrelated, they can be harmonized. For example, the matter of sadness is a mental state that affects physical well-being, and at the same time, there is the directive to 'serve Hashem with joy' [Psalms 100:2]. The latter in itself testifies to the general ability of a human being to overcome sadness, for otherwise the Torah would not have given such a directive.

"In conclusion, I would like to add the important point that precisely in our days it has become increasingly revealed and recognized in many areas of human life that the *mitzvot* of the Torah that are obligatory in the everyday life in our time (as distinct from those *mitzvot* that are related to the

Beit Hamikdash) are of direct benefit to physical and mental health."

*

The second letter, is an excerpt of a 1980 English letter (dated 17 Shevat, 5740) to a certified social worker from New York:

"May G-d grant you success in your professional services to bring relief and healing to those who turn to you for help.

"Your qualifications as a clinical social worker, holding certificates also in psychotherapy and in mental health consultation, etc., as outlined in your curriculum vitae, surely present a wide range of professional services which, I am sure, you render with warm personal interest and consideration for your patients. And there is no need to emphasize to you how important such an attitude is therapeutically in the medical profession in general and in your field in particular.

"Nor is there any need to point out to you that those of your patients for whom belief in G-d is a meaningful factor in their lives—and not merely in an abstract way, but in terms of actual commitment to religious observances and practices in the everyday life, in accordance with the *Shulchan Aruch*, the code of Jewish living and conduct—would derive much benefit from your encouraging and strengthening them in this belief. Clearly, strong trust in G-d goes a long way to relieve and even dispel anxiety and helps one attain inner peace and confidence; moreover, it helps to overcome a split-personality syndrome which is so often at the root of mental disorders.

"Above all, the Torah teaches us that the performance of *mitzvot*, though a 'must' for its own sake, is also the channel to receive G-d's blessings materially, physically, and spiritually."

*

The third letter:

This is a 1984 English letter (12 Adar, 5744) to a mother who seems to have wanted the Rebbe to advise her newlywed daughter—who seems to have had her own relationship with the Rebbe and to have already consulted with him—to get divorced from her husband, due to the (mental?) health challenge now plaguing him. Although her daughter's psychiatrist advised her against divorce, the mother was concerned for her daughter and wanted the Rebbe to override this counsel. Here is the response:

"Your letter reached me this morning. Though it is Erev Shabbos [the eve of Shabbat], Erev Purim [the eve of the holiday of Purim], I hasten my reply, because of the subject matter, especially as it involves a mother's concern for her daughter.

"To begin with the essential point: namely, my answer to the daughter's question was to the effect that she should follow the psychiatrist's advice. It certainly was not, G-d forbid, an attempt at evasion. It was based on common sense, since the psychiatrist would, in my opinion, be the only qualified person to give advice on the basis of his knowledge and experience. My answer was based on the directives of the Torah [see *Mishneh Torah, Hilchot Rotzei'ach Ushmirat HaNefesh,* 12:14] that one should be cognizant of one's responsibility to give the proper advice after due deliberation of all the factors involved.

"In light of the above:

"1. Insofar as I know your daughter from her correspondence, as well as her husband, it is my opinion that the solution you suggest now (a) will certainly cause a shock and trauma, probably accompanied by a feeling of guilt on the part of your daughter; (b) as to how long the traumatic state would last—this would be difficult to assess, even for a psychiatrist.

"2. I am surprised to note from your letter that your daughter knew nothing about the health of her husband. I beg to differ, for I have strong reason to believe that although she may not have been aware of all the specific details, she was aware that he had a health problem, etc.

"3. No doubt you know, and certainly doctors know, that the health condition in question affects people in different ways. With a great many people it is transient; in the case of many others it takes the form of 'ups and downs,' with a wide range in the form and duration of the 'downs.'

"4. From your daughter's writing to me—though I am not at liberty to divulge anything of a confidential nature—I can say this much, that she still has a good feeling towards her husband and more, is in love with him. Therefore, even assuming that the traumatic state and guilt feeling would eventually be overcome, it is very likely that when she hears that he has recovered, or at any rate, that the 'down' state has improved substantially, it would reawaken her guilt, with all its consequences.

"5. All the above considerations assume even greater weight in view of the fact that she is carrying her husband's child, which of course, adds a new dimension to the whole situation.

"Much more can be said in regard to the situation, but I trust that the above will suffice to explain to you why I cannot take upon myself the responsibility of advising her the solution which you suggest in your letter and why I think a psychiatrist would be the only suitable person to assess the situation and to recommend a course of action that would be most advisable, considering all the factors."

95. *Igrot Kodesh,* Vol. 17, p. 33.
96. Here is the excerpt of this point in the letter:
    "Parenthetically, I prefer some such term as 'special' people, not simply as a euphemism, but because it would more accurately reflect their situation, especially in view of the fact that in many cases the retardation is limited to the capacity to absorb and assimilate knowledge, while in other areas they may be quite normal or even above average."
97. Accessible at chabad.org/1924131. See also "The Rebbe on Autism" (YouTube) and "The Rebbe on Autism—Part 2" (YouTube) for an encounter where the Rebbe advises the importance of an autistic child doing the mitzvah of *tzedakah* (charity) and having a charity box in his room. (The Rebbe adds that while autistic children "are not busy with people, they are busy with G-d.") For a general overview of the Rebbe's approach to special-needs individuals, see Rabbi Ari Solish, *Inclusion and the Power of the Individual.*
98. English letter from 5725, published in *Healthy in Body, Mind, and Spirit* (SIE), Vol. 3, chapter 3, accessible at chabad.org/2308532. See there also for another undated letter expressing a similar theme. See also *Igrot Kodesh,* Vol. 24, p. 178; English letter dated 26 Teves, 5725.

    See also *Igrot Kodesh,* Vol. 10, p. 38:

"Medical students in particular, considering that nowadays even science recognizes the important role of heredity in human life, should be explained that the soul's health, in regards to a Jew, is intrinsically connected to the inheritance of the Torah from the time of Mt. Sinai. A Jew cannot be mentally and spiritually whole if they are, Heaven forbid, sundered from the source to which their parents and grandparents were so closely connected for countless generations."

A 1959 English letter (dated 9 Adar II, 5719) elucidates this inner, subconscious calling with the metaphor of radio signals:

"I received your letter of March 8th in which you write about the highlights of your life and about your family status and material circumstances. You write that you have read and learned that a man has to seek G-d, and you ask if it is not the case also that G-d should seek man.

"You are quite right, and indeed G-d seeks out not only certain individuals but calls unto everyone through the agency of the divine soul which animates every Jew. But, inasmuch as the soul is encased in a physical body, it sometimes happens that the divine signals which are sent to the divine soul are either not received at all or are received in distortion by the physical 'static.' Nevertheless, the signals are there, but often remain buried in the subconscious, and from there, impulses, thoughts, and stimuli beg to be admitted into the conscious state. Modern science is increasingly recognizing the importance of the subconscious state of mind. Yet, this has been recognized in our Torah and its commentaries for thousands of years.

"And, as in the case of a receiver which can receive signals only if it is in good order and properly attuned, and will not receive anything at all if the switch is off, so in the case of the body. However, as far as the soul is concerned, which is part of G-d above [*Tanya*, ch. 2], and always remains loyal to her Heavenly Father [ibid. ch. 24], it is always receptive to the subconscious. That is why under certain propitious circumstances, the body and soul may suddenly become illuminated with the light of the Torah and *mitzvot*. That is why, also, an individual may suddenly experience an inner desire to return to G-d, and so on. All this is discussed at great length in the teachings of Chasidut [see, for example, *Likkutei Torah,* p. 2b], which explains in this way [*Maamarei Admor Ha'emtza'i, Vayikra,* Vol. 1, p. 9] the statement of our Sages [*Zohar,* Vol. III, p. 126b] that "every day a heavenly voice comes forth calling: 'Return to Me, My errant children' [Jeremiah 3:14,22].

"Needless to say, although G-d constantly seeks man and calls to him, this does not minimize the necessity of man seeking G-d, as it is written, 'And you shall seek G-d' [Deuteronomy 55:6]. For unless man reciprocates and makes an effort on his part, the signals are likely to remain ineffective. And the way man can apprehend and respond to the divine signals is by observing the Torah and *mitzvot* in everyday life..."

*

Another component in the Rebbe's counseling on the topic of mitzvot is the joy a person can draw from appreciating that *mitzvot* connect them with the infinite G-d. See, for example, *Here's My Story* (JEM), "If It's Good, Do It," for the account of Rabbi Chaim Nisenbaum: "Once, I recall asking the Rebbe how to lead my life in a more joyful way. I told him that it was not in my character to be happy-go-lucky and it was especially hard since I was never satisfied with my accomplishments. The Rebbe answered simply: 'When you find yourself being unhappy, remind yourself that you are just a little creature to whom the Creator gave the ability and the privilege to connect to Him via the *mitzvot* of the Torah.' Until today, whenever I am not happy, I think about the Rebbe's words and that changes my attitude."

Another aspect the Rebbe would often mention is that *mitzvot* have the power to draw divine blessings into all areas of life, including emotional health. See, for example, *Igrot Kodesh, Vol. 22,* p. 323: "And if a person always blessings from G-d—the Creator of man and his Guide—one certainly needs additional blessings [to improve one's emotional state]. The channel and vessel for these blessings is to live one's daily life in the light of our Torah, the Torah of Life, and to fulfill its *mitzvot,* about which it is said, 'You will live through them' [Leviticus 18:5]. It has no bearing whether one understands the connection between living this way and the blessings [one needs]. This is similar to physical healing where it doesn't matter so much if a sick person understands how the medicine will heal them, especially if it only heals after a while—it is only important that they actually take the medicine."

For how doing *mitzvot* is psychologically beneficial for the morale of Jewish military personnel, see *Igrot Kodesh*, Vol. 26, p. 457.

*

In addition to the observance of *mitzvot* more generally, many letters mention specifically the healing power of Torah study.

Drawing on the verse "G-d's commands are just; they cause the heart to rejoice" (Psalms 19:9), the Rebbe would emphasize how the study of Torah can greatly rejuvenate a person's spirit. See, for example, *Igrot Kodesh*, Vol. 10, p. 33: "Even a small amount of light banishes much darkness, and how much more so when there is a great amount of light. When you will study our sacred Torah assiduously and diligently, establishing fixed times for Torah study, fixed in your soul as well, then your feelings of hopelessness and even melancholy will cease. For our holy Torah gladdens the heart and soul, as the verse states, 'G-d's commands are just; they cause the heart to rejoice' [Psalms 19:9]." See also *Petakim*, Vol. 2, p. 118.

Some letters emphasize the uplifting power of the study of Chasidut. See, for example, *Igrot Kodesh*, Vol. 8, p. 2: "You should study Chassidic discourses which eventually rejuvenate the heart and elevate the soul, and by default uplift and extract them from the dirt and mire. A good place to begin is *Kuntres Umaayan* [a Chasidic work by the Rebbe Rashab, written in 1903]." See also *Igrot Kodesh*, Vol. 12, p. 321.

A handwritten response (*Teshurah Raichik*, 5773, p. 10) to a yeshiva student who was dejected about his spiritual state, counsels similarly: "Let yourself immerse (*tovel*)—which has the same Hebrew letters as losing yourself (*bittul*)—in the study of Nigleh and Chasidut in overflowing abundance, and 'you will forget your poverty.'" (This response employs language from the following verses in Proverbs (31:6-7): "Give strong drink to the hapless, and wine to the embittered. Let him drink, and forget his poverty, and remember his misery no more." It also invokes imagery from Maimonides [*Mishneh Torah, Hilchot Mikva'ot* 11:12], who speaks of the metaphorical meaning of the *mitzvah* of *mikvah* [immersion in a ritual bath] as also alluding to immersion in the "waters of pure knowledge." It also references a teaching from the Alter Rebbe [*Siddur Im Dach* 159:d], which explains that in Hebrew, the letters of the word for immersion, *tovel, are* the same letters as the word for losing one's ego, *bittul.)*

99. English letter dated 24 Adar, 5734, included in *the Letter and the Spirit,* Vol. 5, p. 80.
100. *Here's My Story* (JEM), "From Rolling Stones to Wrapping Tefillin."
101. English letter from *In the Days of Repentance, 5719.*
102. Ibid.

Reuven Yelen was born to a Polish Jewish family in 1915. He studied in *cheder,* and in his early teens assumed leadership roles in the burgeoning Zionist youth movement of the time. In 1934, he made his way to British-ruled Palestine and participated in underground activities to pressure the British to open the country's closed borders to Jews escaping Europe. He was imprisoned by the British for a while, and, after fighting in the war of 1948, settled down as the director of a government healthcare program, while remaining involved in the educational arm of the Zionist movement.

Responding to a letter of his in 1962, the Rebbe wrote the following pointed lines (excerpted from a longer letter):

"If in all times and places there was an essential need to give meaning to everyday life, a meaning based on Torah and tradition, all the more so in this generation, where many movements and ideologies, from the far left to the far right, have brought about bitter disappointment. This is especially pronounced regarding the [Israeli] youth who [in contrast to their parents] have not seen a life enlightened by the values of the Jewish people, the eternal nation, and they feel they were left hanging in a void empty of all content. This leads to the most undesirable symptoms, [particularly] when life enters a normal trajectory, dubbed by the world as 'gray' life, in which there are no special [revolutionary] operations that give opportunity to uncover one's internal strengths, powers of heroism, devotion, and so on.

"And, begging your pardon—a double responsibility rests upon the parents of these youths to fill what they have omitted in the education of their children until today. And 'If not now, then when?' (*Avot* 1:14). And what will they answer on the day of accounting when their children demand to know why they weren't given foundational, eternal values that give meaning to life and provide encouragement through the hard and unglamorous fight for survival?

"As you certainly know, it is not the path of Chasidut to lecture. On the whole it attempts to focus on themes that encourage and elevate the soul.... Every man and woman has endless internal strengths—if one only wants to utilize them to create a life worthy of its name. And then nature, or, as the world calls it, 'the laws of nature,' not only don't inhibit one from creating such a life, but, moreover, a person is able, obliged, and fortunate to elevate nature itself beyond nature" (*Igrot Kodesh,* Vol. 19, p. 307).

*

See also *Igrot Kodesh,* Vol. 27, p. 189, for a letter encouraging Rabbi Simchah Raz to publish a biography on the "*tzadik* of Jerusalem" (Rabbi Aryeh Levin, 1885-1969): "I haven't met him in person, and my acquaintance with him was only through correspondence by mail and hearing reports of his most exalted activities. Thus, it is hard for me to give an opinion on the specifics of what to emphasize in his biography.

"However, it is of vital importance to publicize his way of life and accomplishments. Especially in our times, when the youth are wandering in tangled paths, and have only succeeded in 'shattering the [false] idols' [see *Bereishit Rabbah* 38:13] of the previous generation, but not as of yet in finding their own way in life; and because of their great yearning for true meaning, and because of their great fear of emptiness, they 'grope around in the dark' [see Deuteronomy 28:29] and hang on to all types of ideologies. Thus, it is of tremendous value to have a book from which they can learn about a man who has just lived among them, and, though educated in the past generation, had deep bonds with the most progressive of our times.... Though I cannot give an opinion on the details, when I read the draft you sent I have become even more convinced of the book's vital necessity. May you be blessed for taking it on yourself."

*

It was 1960, and a young Canadian woman wrote a letter to the Rebbe asking for his counsel on her conundrums surrounding dating and marriage.

She laid out her practical dilemmas. Should she remain in Montreal, where she was already settled? Or should she move to New York, where there are more suitable young men? She divulged her reflections about what values she sought in a potential life partner, expressing her preference for a man who was "religious and modern." And she added that while she wanted to know the Rebbe's thoughts, she might not accept them, and she feared it would then be unbecoming of her to continue corresponding with him.

The Rebbe began his response (English letter dated 25 Adar, 5720) by assuring her that while "I try my best to give the best possible advice as it seems to me," it is by no means binding or intended to deprive anyone of their own free decision; thus, "you may continue to write to me in the future too, without obligation or apprehension." He then addressed her practical dilemmas, telling her that since it's hard to make consequential decisions while acclimating to a new location, it might be best to continue living in Montreal and traveling to New York on occasion to date. He then proceeded to offer perspective on what to prioritize in her search for a religious and modern partner.

After noting that "in our confused times, 'modern' may mean different things, and it is indeed used to describe viewpoints and attitudes which are often quite contrary and extreme"—for example, one modern trend is to lead a more spiritually committed life of immersion in Torah study, and another modern trend is to reject the conventions of society, as personified by the beatniks—he then continued with the following:

"The real point I want to make is this. We live in very transient and changeable times; some may speak proudly of our Atomic Age, but the present age has not increased the sense of security and stability, especially for the younger generation; rather, on the contrary.

"Young people are now more than ever groping for real meaning in life, instead of constant frustration. When one is about to enter married life and build a home, one surely wants it to be a *binyan adei ad* (an everlasting edifice), as the text reads [*Sheva Brachot—Ketubot* 8a]. [Marriage] involves a total commitment of two young people to each other for the rest of their lives, their lives being still ahead of them.

"It is therefore necessary to find a partner for life who is secure, stable, and steadfast in his outlooks, whose integrity and reliability as far as the most essential things in life are concerned will not waver or be affected by the changes in outlook outside the home. In other words, a most "un-modern" type of person.

"But in the final analysis what is important is not to be modern but to be happy and to enjoy a happy and harmonious life together with one's chosen partner in life. Experience has shown that the more religious a young man is, the more stable he is and the greater therefore the chance of lasting happiness with him. It is necessary to weigh really essential things and values against non-essential, external aspects, and if one has to make concessions, common sense should clearly indicate where the concessions should be made..."

*

On April 11, 1956, two terrorists entered a school and killed five students and their teacher in the Israeli village of Kfar Chabad, founded only six years earlier. The attack was devastating and deeply disheartening to the village, the entire Chabad community, and Israel as a whole. In response, the Rebbe sent twelve yeshivah students to Israel as his personal *shluchim* (emissaries) to bring comfort, encouragement, and revival. Splitting up into pairs, they crisscrossed Israel for a month, talking to residents, especially the youth, and bringing a message of hope. Following their visit, the Rebbe wrote the following (*Igrot Kodesh,* Vol. 13, p. 476) to Mr. Zalman Shazar, a prolific writer and poet, who served at the time as a member of Israel's parliament (and later as its president):

"I hesitated if I should write the following lines, but I will nevertheless do so, at least briefly.

"Based on the reports I received from the *shluchim* on their return from the Holy Land, the fear I expressed in our conversation on your last visit—that Israel's younger generation feels bitterly disappointed in many areas, and, to a considerable measure, they feel without proper footing in life—has been confirmed, to my greatest anguish, and to an even worse extent than I thought. For it seems that this disappointment caused a substantial element of the youth to turn all their aspirations towards physical and mundane pleasures, such as a nice home with elegant furniture, a comfortable and quiet job, and so on. (Though, to my delight, at the present, it is mostly not prohibited pleasures, but rather what the *Tanya* [ch. 7] refers to as *klipat nogah*.) And their whole passion is invested in this to the point of withdrawal from all spiritual achievements. And if a considerable amount of the youth are in this state, it is understood that there is a minority that has fallen lower—below *klipat nogah*.

"As we discussed in the past, in a person's life the exact state of the present is not so important. What's most important is the direction they are going towards. Thus, what is most painful—and frightening—in the above is that for the last few years the path of Israel's youth has all been moving in one direction: from the spiritual to the less spiritual, and from there to the physical, and from the physical to the materialistic.

"Of course my intention is not at all to pain you, which is why I wrote these lines as briefly as possible. I have come to you with these lines only in the hope that you will use your influence on those with the means to finally mend this situation, and certainly to refrain from anything that pushes the youth in this [negative] direction..."

103. See, for example, *Tanya,* chs. 12-13, and *Zohar,* Vol. III, p. 224a.

In a 1969 letter (*Igrot Kodesh*, Vol. 26, p. 72), written as campuses across America were ablaze with revolt, the Rebbe identified the widening chasm between intellect and emotion as the underlying cause for the internal turmoil and discontent of the era's youth. See there for how the unity between intellect and emotion is the "key to unity in the world, and is also deeply connected to the unity of G-d...."

104. *Igrot Kodesh*, Vol. 18, p. 480.

105. The Arizal's *Likkutei Torah, Parshat Bereishit*, paragraph beginning "*Uneva'er maalat Adam Harishon.*" See also *Tanya, Igeret Hakodesh*, Epistle 12; *Torah Ohr*, p. 5d.

For other letters explaining that complete satisfaction and perfection is not possible in this world, see *Igrot Kodesh*, Vol. 15, pp. 14, 72.

Some letters reference the *Tanya*'s words, "All affairs of this world are severe and evil, and the wicked prevail in it" (ch. 6; originating in *Eitz Chaim, sha'ar* 42, ch. 4). See, for example, *Igrot Kodesh*, Vol. 17, p. 339: "It is clear that the reason why the Torah, which is called the 'Torah of Life' [*Sim Shalom* prayer in the Amidah], taught us that our world is a world of *kelipot* and its affairs are 'severe and evil, and the wicked prevail in it' is not to cause despair or weakened vigor, nor even to justify diminished activity.... Rather, one of the intentions in this statement is to forewarn that a person should not become downhearted and dispirited when they encounter difficulties [*he'eleimot v'hesteirim*]....") See also *Teshurah Nagel*, 5756, p. 72.

To see this approach applied to interpersonal relationships, see *Igrot Kodesh*, Vol. 19, p. 63: "One should recognize reality as it is—there is no perfection in our world. Therefore, one shouldn't search and dig for the defects of those individuals that one meets, especially considering that the examiner is also not perfect. However, when one looks with 'a good eye'..." See also *Igrot Kodesh*, Vol. 4, p. 272; and Vol. 5, p. 103: "In our world there is nothing that is perfect. The same is true for man. There is no human being who possesses all the good qualities. Thus, one shouldn't wait to meet the [perfect] person they picture in their mind...." Ibid., Vol. 9, p. 297; Vol. 15, p. 95; Vol. 16, p. 101;

Vol. 16, p. 168; Vol. 21, p. 334. Also see *Here's My Story* (JEM), "The Very, Very Good Idea," accessible at chabad.org/4771652.

A letter from 1954 (*Igrot Kodesh,* Vol. 9, p. 121) elaborates:

"Chasidut explains that since the sin of the Tree of Knowledge all things are composed of a mixture of good and bad. However, the way to deal with this according to the path of Chasidut is to busy yourself with accentuating the side of good and light. This allows your service to be done with great joy. (In contrast to the path of *Mussar* [a Jewish spiritual movement founded in the 19th century that advocates self-refinement through meditating on the repugnancy of materialism and bad character traits], which emphasizes distancing oneself from the negative—which can easily lead to gloominess, etc.).

"The same is true when it comes to relating with others [in this case, coworkers or employees]: utilize their strengths and talents to the utmost degree, and then—either organically or with a small effort—the non-positive components will diminish."

This lesson can be applied to any relationship, such as the parent-child bond. See *Igrot Kodesh*, Vol. 9, p. 320, for a letter to a daughter about tension in her relationship with her mother, due to (what she perceived as) her mother's inherent character flaws:

"Even if one finds that their mother doesn't relate to them properly, however, when they reflect on 'the pain of raising children' [*Eruvin* 100b] that their parents endured—especially their mother—beginning with pregnancy, birth, caretaking, education, etc.—it becomes easier to contain [negative] feelings towards her shortcomings, even if they are entirely justified, and all the more so that they might be imagined or exaggerated.

"However, considering that not always is the mind in control of the heart [and thus the above reflection won't always be effective in real time], it is advisable that most of the time you spend with your parents should be in the company of others. In the company of others quarreling is usually refrained from; and in this way peaceful and loving interactions will become habitual…."

On the topic of helping children empathize with their parents, see the English letter dated 25 Adar, 5720: "One final remark. You write that your parents are worried about your desire for independence. This should be understandable enough, in the light of what has been said earlier, inasmuch as your parents realize what is happening outside. When the Almighty blesses you with your own home and your own children, you will appreciate the parental feeling and desire to spare one's children the trials and tribulations and problems which they had experienced and overcome."

Interestingly, in a handwritten response (*Mibeit Hamalchut*, Vol. 4, p. 73) to a teenage girl who was bothered by her own disrespectful behavior towards her father, the Rebbe suggested that she write on a piece of paper the words of the commandment "Honor your father and mother," through the end of the verse (Exodus 20:12), and for a period of time ("until the holiday of Shavuot") she should keep it in her pocket ("except on Shabbat") and read it to herself every so often.

106. English letter, dated 22 Elul 5716 (accessible at chabad.org/1910419). The letter continues:

"One of the basic things, however, is to have a clear vision on the fundamental issues, and to cultivate attitudes. You surely know the explanation of the [Biblical] words *bashamayim mimaal ve'al haaretz mitachat* ['in the Heavens above and on the earth below'—Deuteronomy 4:39], that in 'Heavenly' (spiritual) matters one should look 'above,' comparing themselves to one who is on a higher spiritual plane and strive to attain it, while in 'earthly' matters one should see the less fortunate, and thus better appreciate the blessings of the Creator and Master of the world."

For another letter that gives similar advice, see *Igrot Kodesh*, Vol. 5, p. 237.

107. *Igrot Kodesh,* Vol. 20, p. 41. The letter continues to illustrate that focus is always a choice, no matter how good or bad the circumstances are, through contrasting Adam's ungrateful complaining while in Paradise [*Avodah Zarah* 5b] with the heroic attitude of some Jewish men and women in the Nazi concentration camps.

In a 1957 talk (*Likkutei Sichot,* Vol. 1, p. 175), the Rebbe pointed to a Talmudic source (*Bava Batra* 145b) to illustrate the power of our perspective over our circumstances: On the verse "All the days of a poor man are wretched, but he who has a cheerful heart always has a feast" (Proverbs 15:15), the sage Rabbi Yehoshua ben Levi (3rd century CE) commented: "'All the days of a poor man are wretched'—this refers to a person with a narrow perspective. 'He who has a cheerful heart always has a feast'— this refers to a person with a broad perspective." See there for elaboration.

Another source the Rebbe would sometimes invoke to counter the depressing sentiment of "if only things were a little bit different" were the verses "I have placed before you today life and good, and death and evil... and you shall choose life..." (Deuteronomy 30:15,19). Characteristically, the Rebbe saw these verses as an eternal divine lesson. G-d tells us, "I have placed before you *today*"—in precisely your current situation—that choice between "life and good" and the opposite. "And you shall choose life"—the divine urging empowers you that even right now, with all of today's messy complexities, you can choose the goodness within your life (instead of wishing things were different). See, for example, *Igrot Kodesh,* Vol. 12, p. 51:

"We were each given our task in times that are suited to us, in places that are suited to us, and in areas that are suited to us, as the verse states explicitly (Ecclesiastes 3:11) [—'He brings everything to pass precisely at its time; He also puts eternity in their mind, but without man ever guessing, from first to last, all the things that G-d brings to pass'].... The thought of how [good] it would be 'if only things were different' is an abstract intellectual exercise which has no relevance, and, moreover, is likely to weaken one's resolve to improve the present situation. It is clear that even in the present situation [with all of its complexities] it is in the hand of each individual to fulfill the verse, 'Look, I have placed before you [life and death]... and you should choose life.'" See also *Igrot Kodesh,* Vol. 18, p. 215; Vol. 22, p. 122.

A 1955 letter (*Igrot Kodesh*, Vol. 11, p. 383) points to an irony in history that proves this concept:

"I must, however, differ from the expression in your letter that viewing the world joyfully provides a defensive cover under which you can hide from the truth. Rather, it is a means by which a person can make their life significantly easier; as it is already well known, and medical science acknowledges this to an ever-greater extent, the entire condition of the individual, [not only psychologically, but] physiologically as well, is impacted by the manner in which they perceive events surrounding them.

"Indeed, it is most significant that among the founders of optimistic approaches to life, there were quite a number whose lives were filled with experiences that we would term travails. Conversely, among the pessimists, we find many whose lives were abundantly good and were lacking nothing... except for satisfaction and joy in their lives. As I am aware of the experiences and events that transpired with your parents in their childhood, [and who nevertheless maintained a sense of optimism and joy,] they may possibly also serve—to a certain extent—as an example for you regarding the above.

"It is thus no wonder that Chasidut, which popularized the best and most exalted [ideals], has as one of its foundational principles that one can find in every situation a way to serve G-d. And that, in general, serving G-d should be done with true joy, for only then will it reach its fullest potential."

See *Igrot Kodesh*, Vol. 22, p. 296, for a letter on the power of perspective in transforming one's attitude to their job. For a wide-ranging overview of the Rebbe's teachings on this subject, see Rabbi Mendel Kalmanson, *Positivity Bias*.

108. *Igrot Kodesh*, Vol. 20, p. 41.

A Hebrew letter (*Teshurah Butler-Lowenthal*, 5783, p. 9) dated 8 Tishrei, 5718, explains this succinctly:

"...For all the factors causing lack of inner peace, etc., are temporal things. And the vast majority of them are profoundly miniscule even when compared to a person's lifespan on earth. All the more so are they entirely insignificant relative to the eternal, as well as a person's actions that are connected with the eternal. And all the more so [are they insignificant] relative to [a person's actions] that are connected to He who is beyond the categories of time entirely, as the known teaching of the Maggid has it [see *Siddur Im Dach* 75:d], that time itself is a creation...."

109. Accessible at chabad.org/4855474. The letter continues:

"In light of the above, moreover, this helpful feeling is further enhanced given its universal nature. All good actions unite to make the world as a whole progressively better. Even when a religious and moral relapse seems very much in evidence, with many yet to become wiser and more religious, the world as a whole is essentially becoming more purified with every passing year, every day and every minute, for no instant passes without many good deeds."

As a source for the eternal nature of our good deeds, many letters point to the Alter Rebbe's words: "In the upper spheres, this union is eternal, for G-d, blessed be He, and His will transcend time" (*Tanya*, ch. 25).

110. *Igrot Kodesh*, Vol. 13, p. 249. See also *Igrot Kodesh*, Vol. 9, p. 242.

111. See *Maamarei Admor Hazakein* 5562, Vol. 1, p. 51; *Maamarei Admor Ha'emtza'i, Nach*, p. 27. Chasidut sources this idea in the words of the prophet Isaiah (29:19), "Then the humble shall have increasing joy through G-d."

In a Chasidic discourse delivered in 1951 (*Torat Menachem 5712*, Vol. 1, p. 121 (chabad.org/4280185)), the Rebbe explained Isaiah's words with the following: "A person who feels self-important will not experience complete happiness, as he feels entitled to to everything he has. Moreover, he easily becomes dejected when lacking something, because he thinks it is owed to him.

"However, a humble person will find true happiness in what he has, knowing that it's not owed to him. And even if he lacks something, he's not depressed about it because he feels he's not entitled to more, and he views what he already has as a gift from Above. This is how humility leads to happiness." See also *Likkutei Sichot*, Vol. 1, p. 176.

112. The morning blessings were introduced by the Sages of the

Talmud (see *Berachot* 60b) and can be found in all traditional Jewish prayer books.

For other letters that mention the morning blessings as an exemplar of the importance of gratitude, see *Igrot Kodesh,* Vol. 18, p. 215, and an English letter dated 28 Cheshvan, 5739.

Other letters (see, for example, *Igrot Kodesh,* Vol. 11, p. 321) point to the Sages' interpretation (*Bereishit Rabbah* 14:9) of the closing verse in Psalms, "Let every soul praise G-d" (150:6). The sage Rabbi Chaninah (2nd century CE) taught that the verse can also be read, "For every breath—praise G-d." (The word for soul, *neshamah,* shares the same etymological root as the word *neshimah,* breath.)

113. *Petakim,* Vol. 1, p. 147.

    See also *Igrot Kodesh,* Vol. 12, p. 270: "Hundreds and thousands of people pray every day to be blessed with children, and would give everything they own to have a single child, but have not as of yet merited this...

    "But you, the recipient of this blessing, don't recognize the wealth and happiness in the blessings you have, and write twice in your letter that you haven't experienced any good in life!" See also *Petakim,* Vol. 1, pp. 111, 114, and Vol. 2, pp. 122, 130—"I was greatly surprised to read in your letter that you don't see anything to be happy about, after you also wrote, 'Thank G-d, we have two very sweet and religious daughters'!"

114. Psalms 100:2.

    See, for example, *Igrot Kodesh,* Vol. 4, p. 293; Vol. 6, pp. 82, 210; Vol. 9, p. 103; Vol. 10, p. 376; Vol. 14, pp. 278, 481; Vol. 15, p. 232; Vol. 27, p. 231. (See also *Igrot Kodesh,* Vol. 13 p. 228: "The [gloomy] spirit of your letter is a great wonder. For it is entirely out of line from the constant mandate that has been commanded to every Jew, and, if you will, to every being in creation, to 'serve G-d—the Creator of the universe—with joy...'")

    Some letters point to the verse in Deuteronomy (28:47): "...for you did not serve G-d, your Lord, with joy and a glad heart..." Many letters also highlight a ruling from Maimonides: "The joy in the fulfillment of *mitzvot* and the love of G-d who commanded them is [in itself] a great virtue (*avodah gedolah hee*).... There is no greatness or honor other than celebrating before G-d, as the verse [Samuel II 6:16] states: 'King David was dancing wildly and whistling before G-d' (*Mishneh Torah, Hilchot Lulav* 8:15)."

While the verses and Maimonides speak of joy when serving G-d, the letters consistently emphasize that this is actually a mandate for all times (not only times of prayer and study), because a person can serve G-d in all areas of their life. As Maimonides writes elsewhere (*Mishneh Torah, Hilchot Dei'ot* 3:3, quoted in *Tur* and *Shulchan Aruch, Orach Chaim* 231), "Whoever walks in such a path all his days will be serving G-d constantly, even in the midst of his business dealings... even when he sleeps.... On this matter, our Sages instructed and said: 'And all your deeds should be for the sake of Heaven' (*Avot* 2:12). This is what Solomon declared in his wisdom: 'Know Him in all your ways' (Proverbs 3:6)."

Combining this passage from Maimonides, the Rebbe would explain, with his aforementioned words about the importance of ecstatic joy when serving G-d—we are left with an emphatic halachic ruling from Maimonides that we are to strive to live our daily lives with unabated joy.

A 1978 letter (dated 15 Av, 5738), addressing "all participants in the Chasidic Song Festival [of] Sydney, Australia," reads as follows:

"To 'serve G-d with joy' is a basic tenet of the Jewish way, greatly emphasized in the Torah and Talmud. Our Great Teacher, the Rambam, declares: 'The joy that a Jew should rejoice in doing a *mitzvah*, and in loving G-d who commanded the fulfillment of the *mitzvah*, is a great service (end of Hilchot Lulav). Elsewhere, he reminds us that divine service is not limited to Torah study, prayer, and doing *mitzvot*, but embraces all of a Jew's daily activities, as it is written, 'Know Him in all of your ways.'

"Chasidut, in particular, extols the importance of serving G-d with joy. While both the mind and the heart—the intellect and the emotions—must fully participate in serving G-d, the intellect has its natural limitations, but the emotions go deeper and farther. It is a matter of experience that joy and enthusiasm

break through barriers and inspire one to accomplish things that would otherwise be unattainable."
115. *Tanya*, ch. 31.
116. *Igrot Kodesh*, Vol. 14, p. 396.
117. *Igrot Kodesh*, Vol. 8, p. 299.

   A 1954 English letter (dated 25 Tammuz, 5714) to a young man reads similarly:

   "Referring to your letter, I am surprised that it contains a cry of anguish from a repentant and breaking heart, etc., despite my writing to you several times that this is not the way to approach G-d. For it has been revealed to us that the true way of worship is to worship G-d with joy. All thoughts that interfere with this way of worship, thoughts that bring sadness and bitter remorse, especially when magnified by imagination and constant self-appraisal—all such thoughts must be dismissed, for far from helping, they hinder in true worship.

   "I therefore underline again, that this is not the time for *cheshbon hanefesh*, soul-searching, and the like, but to get on with one's business, be contented and full of joy to the extent of even overflowing and bringing joy all around" (chabad.org/1897842).
118. *Igrot Kodesh*, Vol. 27, p. 425.

   See Elkanah Shmotkin and Boruch Oberlander, *Early Years* (JEM) pp. 71-73, for an overview of this relationship, including memories from both Avraham and his sister Vardina (a respected composer and pianist). See also *Igrot Kodesh*, Vol. 32, p. 254, for a letter to Vardina that also discusses Avraham's writings.
119. *Dvar Hapo'elet*, 31.3.1940. Reprinted in *Karov Eilecha*, no. 269, p. 10.
120. Deuteronomy 20:19.
121. *Igrot Kodesh*, Vol. 32, p. 115. See *Karov Eilecha* ibid. for a photograph of the response.

   Another response (*Igrot Kodesh*, Vol. 26, p. 86) to a poet, Rochela Bavli, reads as follows:

   "With blessings for success in your song—both the song of writing and the song of living. For, according to our Torah, as elucidated in the teachings of Chasidut, a person's life is a song (in potential), and it is upon us to bring this song from potential to actuality, and that it should be a sanctified song. As the 'sweet psalmist of Israel [King David]' alludes in his words (Psalms 104:33): 'I will sing to G-d all my life *[ashirah laHashem bechayay]*'. The [Hebrew] letter *bet* being a multi-functional prefix, it can also be read, 'I will sing to G-d *through* my life.'" (Emphasis added.)

*

An anecdote in connection to poetry and this chapter:

Zvi Yair Steinmetz was a Romanian Jewish poet from a Chasidic background. His first volume of poetry, titled *Bridges*, was printed in Hungary in 1942, two years before the country's Jews were annihilated by the Nazis. Premonitions of catastrophe are present in his poems, as well as his internal struggle to make sense of it.

He survived the Holocaust by hiding, and ultimately made it to the United States in 1952. Soon after, he met the Rebbe. Steinmetz, who throughout his existential journey longed for a spiritual home, developed a soulful bond with the Rebbe. Throughout the years, the Rebbe encouraged him to publish his poetry.

One poem titled "The Foundation," was Steinmetz's attempt at describing the inner world of the Rebbe. One paragraph reads as follows:

All rivers of sorrow flow
Along the channels of his heart
On to the valley of understanding;
Therefore
His fountain of joy
Does not falter.

When he showed this poem to the Rebbe, on the first stanza the Rebbe commented that it is true that *"binah memateket gevurot"* (understanding sweetens strictness, which can also mean that understanding helps heal sorrow; from the Arizal's *Taamei Hamitzvot, Shaar Parah Adumah; Tanya*, ch. 31). However, about the second stanza—"Therefore his fountain of joy does not falter"—the Rebbe remarked in Yiddish, *"Halvai volt azoi geven*—I wish that were the case...."

(The original Hebrew is available in Yair's book *Meirosh Tzurim*. The translation here is by Rabbi Yanki Tauber (chabad.org/1897842). This anecdote is recorded in *Kovetz Tishrei 5782*, no. 3.)

While on this note, the following is an account of another interaction between the Rebbe and Steinmetz about a poem on joy.

In a poem titled "Eternal Joy," Steinmetz ended by writing (in reference to G-d): "Therefore, for all eternity, strength and joy are His vicinity."

When he sent the poem to the Rebbe, he remarked that its conclusion—"strength and joy are His vicinity"—seems to run into a tension between two medieval Jewish sages about how to read a passage in the Talmud.

An enigmatic Talmudic dialogue (*Chagigah* 5a) reads as follows:

"The verse states, 'My soul shall weep in secret for your pride, [says G-d].' (Jeremiah 13:17)... But is there crying before the Holy One, Blessed be He? Didn't Rav Pappa say: There is no sadness before G-d, as it is stated: 'Honor and majesty are before Him; strength and joy are in His vicinity' (I Chronicles 16:27)? This contradiction is not difficult to answer. This verse refers to the innermost chambers. That verse refers to the outer chambers."

The leading medieval Jewish sages interpreted the Talmud's cryptic answer in opposite ways.

Rashi (1040-1105) explained that in "the outer" divine chamber no sadness is possible, and only "strength and joy" resides. It is in "the inner" divine chamber that sadness is possible. Rabainu Chananel (c. 980–1055) interprets the Talmud's answer in the exact opposite way: The inner divine chamber is where there is only joy. It is in the outer chamber where there can be an element of "weeping and sadness."

Steinmetz referenced this discussion about the joy and sadness of Heaven in his note accompanying his poem, and asked if Chassidic teachings offered any insight into this Talmudic debate.

The Rebbe wrote in response: "See *Or Hatorah, Eicha*, p. 22

[in current printings *Or Hatorah, Nach,* Vol. 2, p. 1052], where both opinions are brought and explained. Additionally, see *Or Hatorah, Divrei Hayamim* [in current printings *Or Hatorah, Nach,* Vol. 1, p. 709]. It is explained there."

These writings of the Tzemach Tzedek (the third Lubavitcher Rebbe, 1789–1866) elucidate the Talmud with a Chasidic lens:

The inner and outer chambers represent different forms of G-d's relationship with the world. When the divine presence is in the outer chamber—when it is "extroverted" and revealed and felt in the world—then there is a state of divine joy. However, when for whatever sublime reasons the divine presence must recede into itself and remain only in the "inner chambers," leaving the world in a state of exile and spiritual darkness—then G-d weeps for us... "There is sadness." This explains Rashi's interpretation.

The Tzemach Tzedek offers another explanation: Negative elements take their life force from the "outside chambers" of G-d. From an external layer of divinity, negative elements can feed off energy and channel it to wrong places. Thus, the "outer chamber" can lead to negativity in the world, inevitably leading to divine "sadness." However, from the truly transcendent levels of the Divine *(atika kadisha),* only goodness emanates, and it can never translate into negative manifestations. Thus, in the "inner chamber" there is only "strength and joy in His vicinity." This sheds light on Rabainu Chananel's interpretation and on Steinmetz's poem.

A photocopy of this handwritten note can be found in *Teshurah Greenberg-Zalmanov,* 5772.

122. *Igrot Harambam,* Vol. 1, 1.311 (Jerusalem: Maaliyot, 1987).
123. *Avot* 4:22. For other letters that reference this Mishnaic saying in the context of the inevitable hardships of life, see *Igrot Kodesh,* Vol. 4, p. 248; Vol. 22, p. 344.
124. See *Guide for the Perplexed* 3:13.
125. *Igrot Kodesh,* Vol. 4, p. 261.
126. *Tanya,* ch. 12.
127. *Igrot Kodesh,* Vol. 22, p. 288.
128. *Sanhedrin* 100b. Rav Yosef quotes it from *Ben Sira* (an ancient

Jewish text, approx. 3rd-2nd century BCE) and adds that it is something worth teaching the public. The beginning of the statement, "Grieve not about tomorrow's trouble," is a verse from Proverbs (27:1). The Talmud in *Yevamot* (63b) also quotes this teaching from *Ben Sira*.

129. This theme appears in countless letters.

In Good Hands, a book by Rabbi Uri Kaploun, compiles 100 letters and talks from the Rebbe on *bitachon* (chabad.org/2313435).

A 1982 English letter (12 Tevet, 5742) clarifies a central point: "As I have often emphasized, all the teachings in our Torah, *Torat Emet* [the Torah of Truth], are true and they are not just tranquilizers. In other words, we have complete trust in G-d not merely because it gives us a good feeling of security but because such trust is justified. Thus we are assured that 'G-d is your keeper; G-d is your shade (protection) at your right hand' [Psalms 121:6], and much more in this vein...."

130. *Chovot Halvavot, Shaar Habitachon*, beginning of chapter 1.

Many letters advise studying this treatise to help cultivate *bitachon*. See, for example, *Igrot Kodesh*, Vol. 4, p. 319; Vol. 11, p. 162; Vol. 15, p. 295 ("Study it again and again...."); and Vol. 28, p. 347 ("It is available in English as well").

131. *Igrot Kodesh*, Vol. 11, p. 70.

See also Vol. 8, p. 262: "When a person not only knows, conceptually, but thoroughly feels that G-d is the Master of the universe, including our world, including every individual man or woman, and that He is the essence of goodness, and thus surely desires to shower only goodness and kindness on each and every individual—feeling this, the psyche becomes infused with an inner calm, which also immediately improves physical health...."

132. Deuteronomy 15:18.

133. See, for example, *Derech Mitzvotecha, Mitzvat Tiglachat Metzora*.

134. *Petakim*, Vol. 2, p. 129.

135. English letter, 22 Tammuz, 5738.

136. *Mishlei Yaakov*, 114.

137. *Igrot Kodesh*, Vol. 4, p. 248.

138. This recommendation recurs frequently in the Rebbe's letters. Usually, he advised checking one's *tefillin* or *mezuzot* to ensure that they are in proper shape and kosher. This requires sending them to a qualified scribe with halachic training to check on the condition of the writing in the scroll, the boxes, and the straps. Occasionally, as in this response, he would recommend checking *tzitzit* too.

Forever seeing a correlation between the spiritual and physical (see footnote 58), the Rebbe explained (*Sichot Kodesh 5737* Vol. 1, p. 73) that physical and emotional health can be increased by the fulfillment of the *mitzvah* of *tefillin*, which represents the bond of the mind and heart with the Divine (see *Shulchan Aruch, Orach Chaim,* 25:5), and the *mitzvah* of *mezuzah*, which represents the bond of the home with the Divine (see *Zohar,* Vol. III, p. 263b).

The Rebbe pointed to the words of the *Shulchan Aruch* (*Yoreh De'ah* 285:1), which does not usually explain the reasoning of *mitzvot,* but in the case of *mezuzah* uncharacteristically states: "One who is careful with the *mitzvah* of *mezuzah* lengthens his own days and those of his children." Additionally, the Rebbe referred to the teaching of the sage Rabbi Elazar Hagadol (*Sanhedrin* 71a) that one single kosher *mezuzah* can salvage an entire condemned city. These sources highlight the material benefit of acquiring kosher *mezuzot* (and similarly *tefillin*) for those who don't have them yet. Or, for those who already have *mezuzot* and *tefillin,* the benefit of getting them checked by a qualified scribe on occasion.

A little background: The *Shulchan Aruch* (*Yoreh Deah* 291:1) writes that one must check their *mezuzot* twice in every seven-year period to confirm that they are still kosher. Regarding *tefillin,* it stipulates (*Orach Chaim* 39:10) that a pair of *tefillin* that is used only periodically must also be checked twice every seven years, but, if they are used consistently, they are not required to be checked (because they deteriorate less when in constant use). However, multiple halachic authorities (see, for example, *Mishneh Berurah,* ibid. 26) clarify that it is nevertheless highly recommended to check them frequently.

In a 1974 talk (*Sichot Kodesh 5734 Vol. 2,* pp. 377-379) the

Rebbe explained that this recommendation is all the more pertinent today because in the past the question was only if the *tefillin* or *mezuzot remained* in good shape. But today, there is rampant fraud, and unsuspecting customers are sold *mezuzot* and *tefillin* written on paper (instead of parchment), or with a digitized inscription (instead of handwritten), or even with entirely empty cases. Thus, sending them to a scribe to check is often about uncovering something that was never kosher in the first place.

The Rebbe added that in modern times, the method of producing parchment has changed, and inscriptions on some parchments actually rub out quicker than they used to, heightening the importance of checking one's *tefillin* and *mezuzot*.

Additionally, the Rebbe pointed to the *Mateh Efraim* (581:10; quoted also in *Kitzur Shulchan Aruch* 128:3), which lauds those who check their *mezuzot* and *tefillin* annually, particularly in the month of Elul (the month preceding the High Holidays). This broadly indicates that when a person needs increased blessings—whether before the High Holidays or for personal reasons—it is recommended to check one's *tefillin* and *mezuzot*.

Another recommendation that recurs in the letters is for Jewish women to light Shabbat candles on Friday before sunset, and to give a coin to the t*zedakah* (charity fund) of Rabbi Meir Baal Haness preceding the lighting.

139. *Here's My Story* (JEM), "Unlocking the Gate of Trust," accessible at chabad.org/4515703.
140. See *Sefer HaSichot 5687*, p. 113; *Likkutei Dibburim*, Vol. 1, p. 159.

One letter (*Igrot Kodesh*, Vol. 3, p. 364) points to Talmudic roots for the idea of "think good and it will be good": the Talmud (*Horayot* 12a) discusses whether one should check for omens before embarking on a long journey to determine if they will return safely. The Talmud rejects doing so because, irrespective of the questionable validity of the omens, "perhaps he will be disheartened by what he sees and this [pessimistic perspective of his] will in itself cause a negative outcome."

Another letter (*Igrot Kodesh*, Vol. 10, p. 358) connects "think good and it will be good" with the following teaching of the *Zohar* (Vol. II, p. 184b): "Come and see, the lower world is a receptacle of the higher world. And the higher world gives to him only in accordance with his state. If he has a shining face down here, then he is shined upon similarly from above. And if he is gloomy, he is in turn dealt strictly from above. The verse says, 'Serve G-d with joy' (Psalms 100:2). A person's joy draws to joy to him from above...."

See also *Igrot Kodesh*, Vol. 4, p. 119: "It is in vain that you are pining yourself, for the worry only ruins.... In general, it would be prudent to publicize to our fellow Chasidim the *Zohar*'s words about the destructiveness of gloomy pessimism, which can be found in *Zohar*, Vol. III, p. 184b: 'Come and see, the lower world...' See there. In addition to gloomy pessimism's negative effect on divine service, studying Torah, and physical health, it has a destructive effect, G-d forbid, on the very thing one is pessimistic about...."

141. For more letters about the power of cultivating positive expectations for the future, see *Igrot Kodesh*, Vol. 3, p. 333; Vol. 4, pp. 130, 198; Vol. 8, p. 358; Vol. 9, p. 280; Vol. 14, p. 346; Vol. 16, pp. 213, 252; Vol. 17, p. 341; Vol. 18, pp. 174, 182, 188; Vol. 19, p. 72; Vol. 20, pp. 7, 195; *Petakim*, Vol. 3, p. 123. See also *Living Torah* (JEM), program 588, accessible at chabad.org/3144781.

For a broader overview of this idea, see *Positivity Bias*, ch. 12, accessible at chabad.org/4405212.

142. *Here's My Story* (JEM), "From Despondent to Confident."
143. English letter.

See also: chabad.org/1942759.

"As in all areas of fruitful endeavor, it is more effective and successful, and at the same time less strenuous, when it is carried out with confidence and a happy disposition." See also "Business Worries: The 'Wheel' of Fortune" (chabad.org/289094): "But a lack of faith does not help it. Besides, there is also the psychological effect, and a lack of courage and assurance brings with it a lessening of initiative, etc."

144. *Igrot Kodesh*, Vol. 16, p. 49. For another letter that explains the tangible effects of looking positively at one's children, see *Igrot Kodesh*, Vol. 12, p. 286, addressing a grandfather who felt

that his children and grandchildren were not living up to the values he taught them: "When you look at them with a good and positive eye, not only will *you* start noticing their positive attributes, but your [positive] perspective will itself empower *them*, and thus the negative elements will become smaller and fewer." (Emphasis added.)

This was also a point the Rebbe made about relationships more broadly.

See, for example, *Igrot Kodesh*, Vol. 18, p. 323, written to a teenager:

"A general piece of advice for making friendship easier: Contemplate that there is no person who is absolutely perfect—yourself included. You should therefore not require and insist that your friends be perfect in all areas....

"Additionally, our Sages have testified that 'the daughters of Israel are beautiful' [*Mishnah Nedarim* 9:10: 'A man refused to marry an impoverished woman. Rabbi Ishmael took her into his home, took good care of her, and then called the man back. He immediately consented. Rabbi Ishmael cried, saying, "The daughters of Israel are beautiful, but poverty disfigures them."'] And every one of your schoolmates is the daughter of Sarah, Rivkah, Rachel, and Leah; thus, they surely possess many good qualities, and with time you will come to recognize them as well. Moreover, becoming friendly with others will help you grow, too. The more you explain this idea to yourself, the easier it will be for you to make friends, and the more quickly your isolation will dissipate."

Similarly, see *Igrot Kodesh*, Vol. 18, p. 151: just as a salesperson looks for the point of contact with their customer, not the point of dissonance, we should apply the same in relating to others.

For how this idea explains why we have only one nose and mouth but two eyes, see *Igrot Kodesh*, Vol. 4, p. 193. See *Igrot Kodesh*, Vol. 13, p. 173, for a letter explaining how to view the defects of fellow community members. See also *Igrot Kodesh*, Vol. 19, p. 193; and Vol. 28, p. 85.

145. *Igrot Kodesh*, Vol. 13, p. 228.

See also *Igrot Kodesh*, Vol. 22, p. 322, for another letter that sees the world's natural order as a reason to be optimistic that one's own situation will also fall into place with the right effort. It is in response to a man who wrote that he feels internally unsettled (the details are unclear). After advising him to speak to a professional, the Rebbe continues:

"You should reflect on the presence of a Creator and Conductor of the world, for we see clearly that the world is not *hefker* [abandoned] and 'this palace has an owner' [see *Bereishit Rabbah* 39:1]. The order we find within the inanimate realm and so on, which constitutes most of the world around us, implies there must likewise be order in smaller parts of the universe, including in [an individual] human being; for it is unreasonable to say he has no order, or that disarray prevails in him.

"Why, this is also the approach of science—that the laws which regulate ninety-nine percent of a given phenomenon are assumed to certainly apply to the one percent that hasn't yet been tested or cannot be seen.

"All this leads to the conclusion that ultimately, in the end, order and good prevails. And this provides assurance and encouragement that, although temporarily the good in you is veiled by a particular challenge or internal issue, a person was certainly given the strength to overcome it if they only want to. However, as is the nature of the world, change happens step-by-step and not from one extreme to another all at once.

"Reflecting on the above—especially as you write of your background and investment in the sciences—should bring you encouragement of spirit, an increase in self-confidence, and general optimism. All this will in turn boost your vitality and improve your condition. But, as stated above, this will be a step-by-step process...."

A long 1952 English letter to a young woman (dated 8 Cheshvan, 5713) has a similar theme. Following is an excerpt:

"I want to dwell on item 6 of your letter which contains the key to all your other problems. In this paragraph you mentioned that you feel depressed and cannot see any reasons for a brighter future. You ask how you can really get rid of your fears.

"When a person will reflect, in a rational way, on creation, and the order and precision and laws that are to be found in nature, the conclusion is inescapable. There is a tremendous system of order in the universe, governed by strict laws. There can therefore be no doubt that the world is regulated by plan, order, and purpose.... The very fact that there is order, purpose, and law in the universe must lead one to the conviction that all this is good, since evil is the opposite of order and structure, and is associated with chaos.

"No matter how much importance a person attaches to one's own self and one's own problems, they must recognize that if there is order in such a complicated universe, how much easier it is to bring about law and order in one's own small universe—a thought which should lead to satisfaction and peace of mind....

"In the light of the above, you may be quite certain that there is a good answer to all your problems and that eventually all the complications will be resolved satisfactorily. Needless to say, one must seek to solve one's problems—but there can be no room for a feeling of depression, and certainly no room for a feeling of despondency, which can be nothing but destructive.....

"If you will develop a more optimistic view on life it will give you a more cheerful disposition, your job will not appear so difficult and tedious, and you will not feel so unhappy about it...."

Similarly in a 1956 letter (*Igrot Kodesh,* Vol. 13, p. 172) to an immigrant from the Soviet Union, who wrote of the various phases of his life's journey and the experiences he endured, as well as his thoughts and emotions. The Rebbe responded to him with a similar theme. Following is an excerpt:

"Everyone knows from physics, chemistry, astronomy, etc. (recognized not only by Jews or believers but even by non-believers), that every tiny atom has its exact laws, and everything operates in accordance with these intrinsic laws. The earth, rocks, plants, animals, and everything that surrounds us also have definitive laws and established systems, despite being far more complex and vast than one person and their family.

"Now, imagine entering a magnificent building with thousands of rooms. Each room is in precise order, to the point where even a newcomer appreciates its perfect arrangement. However, about one small room the visitor is unsure if its contents—furniture and so on—are arranged properly in their places. A person with common sense will certainly reason that since all thousands of chambers of this vast building are in the best order, undoubtedly the room they do not yet appreciate, being part of this splendid building, certainly also has a meaningful design, despite the fact that they do not presently understand it.

"I assume it would be superfluous to explain the analogy any further. I only wish to add one point: If each one of us, including yourself, were to ponder objectively how their years have passed—in what places they were, what happened to them—they will find dozens and thousands of instances where they were led in a particular direction. [In your case,] beginning ten years ago, and from then on, this has been consistently in the direction from left to right.

"However, being that G-d desires a person to do things of their own free will, He therefore allows each person the ability to choose their own path. It is therefore unsurprising that being only human, we sometimes make mistakes and veer off the path, and instead of the path being a straight one, we make some zigzags.

"But if we give it thought, and don't want to fool ourselves, we see to it that the number of zigzags should become fewer and less frequent. Then we arrive at the goal which G-d has designed for every human being, and for every Jew, that they and their family should be truly happy, and happy also in this world. And this can be attained by living in light of how the Torah, which is called the Torah of Life, teaches us...."

146. A 1953 English letter (*Teshurah Simpson,* 5771, p. 11), responding to a young man who inquired about various foundational Chasidic teachings, elucidates this theme:

"...(3) Regarding the Four Worlds, which you regard not as actual worlds but as different levels attainable by a person, this is not so. They are actual worlds—but not in the sense of being in different localities, because they penetrate each other....

"By way of illustration: When we observe another person with any of our senses (sight, hearing, etc.), we notice and see him as a complex unit made up of different physical phenomena. This immediate sense perception is then analyzed by us intellectually, and we realize that each physical movement we see has a corresponding spiritual and psychological origin in the heart or brain. E.g., when we see a person putting on *tefillin*, we are immediately aware of the movement of one his hand's in regard to the other, but on closer reflection we understand that behind that movement there is a will and knowledge of the *mitzvah*, and that these inner aspects motivate the outer physical movements. Thus we conclude that there exists a second 'man'—a complex unit of spiritual phenomena, which is the cause of and which permeates the physical complex. And as in the case of in a human being—the microcosm ('small world'), so we can get an idea of the macrocosm ('big world').

"For further reference, see *Likkutei Torah*, [Shir HaShirim,] p. 49a. There is also a letter from my father-in-law, of sainted memory, on the subject of the Four Worlds, which is to be found in copy among the yeshivah students.

"(4) With regard to what you call the 'hierarchy' of the worlds, we may refer to the illustration mentioned earlier concerning the influence of the 'inner' human world on his outer phenomena, showing the action of cause and effect. It should be added that, as often happens, the effect subsequently reacts upon the cause, as we see, for example, in the case of prayer, where the very reciting of the words fans the inner inspiration and warmth to a greater degree. In a similar way, the action and counteraction of the worlds are reciprocal; the lower worlds receive influence from the upper worlds, but in return also contribute light to the higher worlds.

"In the Index of *Derech Mitzvotecha*, as well as in the index of *Sefer Hamaamarim 5710*, you will surely find further elaboration on the above subjects from different angles."

147. *Igrot Kodesh*, Vol. 6, p. 286.

148. *Here's My Story* (JEM), "Rabbi Yehoshua Gordon," accessible at chabad.org/4448935.
149. *Bereishit Rabbah* 3:7.
150. See *Torah Shleimah, Bereishit, siman katan* 423, for an extensive treatise on this *midrash* replete with numerous sources. See also *Igrot Kodesh*, Vol. 13, p. 145, where the Rebbe discusses this *midrash* in correspondence with Rabbi Yitzchak Halevi Herzog (Israel's first Chief Rabbi). The reference to the above *Torah Shleimah* is from this letter.
151. See *Shaar Maamarei Rashbi, Idra Rabbah* 44b; *Eitz Chaim, Shaar 9—Shaar Shevirat Hakeilim* (*The Gate on the Breaking of the Vessels*).

    Eitz Chaim explains that the Torah's description (Genesis 36:31-39) of "the kings who reigned [and died] in the land of Edom before any king reigned over the children of Israel" allude to the *sefirot* of *Tohu*—the spiritual world of Chaos. This is because Esau and Edom mystically correspond with the sublime (but ultimately unsustainable) spiritual dimension of Chaos; and Jacob and Israel correspond with the spiritual dimension of *Tikkun*—Order. (See *Torah Or, Parshat Vayishlach*, for an extensive exploration of this Kabbalistic interpretation.)
152. See *Sefer Hamaamarim 5649*, pp. 233-261, for a detailed explanation of the worlds of Chaos and Order, both conceptually and as they reflect themselves in a person's inner world. The analogy of a child can be found ibid., p. 237.

    A foundational approach of Chabad Chasidut is to see a person's internal world as a reflection of—and therefore a gateway to understanding—transcendent levels of Divinity. A 1964 English letter (2 Cheshvan, 5725), responding to a psychology professor from Chicago, reads as follows:

    "I would also welcome an opportunity to meet with you when you are in New York, as I feel we would have some topics of mutual interest to discuss, especially in view of the fact that your field is that of psychology. For, as you may be aware, there is a close affinity between the teachings of Chassidus and the study of the psyche, more specifically the study of the soul.

    "As a matter of fact, one of the basic doctrines of Chabad Chasidut is derived from the concept that the understanding of G-d as revealed in nature and even beyond can best be attained by the study of the essence and functions of the human soul. This is based on the Biblical verse "From my flesh I see G-d" (Job 19:26). And while our mind is limited, and no created being could possibly understand the Creator, through our soul, which is 'truly as part of G-dliness Above' (*Tanya*, ch. 2), we can grasp those relatively infinitesimal aspects of G-dliness that come within our limitations..."

153. Proverbs 24:16.
154. *Igrot Kodesh*, Vol. 19, p. 106. See also *Igrot Kodesh*, Vol. 27, p. 553; *Petakim*, Vol. 3, p. 128. See also *Igrot Kodesh*, Vol. 10, pp. 118, 396; Vol. 11, p. 82; Vol. 13, p. 487.
155. *Igrot Kodesh*, Vol. 15, p. 353.

The letter continues: "However, to help it pass sooner, it would be beneficial to meditate on the above [the great merit you have to work in education] and especially to keep in mind Torah's foundational idea of divine providence, elucidated so beautifully in Chasidic teachings, which means quite literally that the Creator of the universe looks with an individual interest over every person and over the minute details of their life.

"My hope, considering the education you received, is that even these lines, though brief in quantity, will suffice to help you appreciate the truth—that we find ourselves in a world about which its Creator has said, 'And He saw that it was good' [Genesis 1:31], and as our great teacher the Rambam [Maimonides] has elucidated in his works [see *Moreh Nevuchim* 3:13]. But a person mustn't 'search out too many schemes' [see Ecclesiastes, 7:29] which conceal and distort this reality...."

156. *Living Torah* (JEM), program 742, "A Time for Everything" (chabad.org/4199232). See also *Igrot Kodesh*, Vol. 4, p. 65.
157. *Yevamot* 25b; *Ketubot* 18b; *Sanhedrin* 9b, 25a.

It is important to note that this Talmudic principle applies only to questions of punishment and penalty. Regarding all monetary disputes, a plaintiff's admissions are considered solid evidence (see, for example, *Gittin* 40b). Additionally, in some exceptional cases, a Jewish court can rely only on the admission of the suspect (see *Teshuvot Harivash*, responsum 234).

158. The classic explanation (see, for example, *Rashi, Sanhedrin* 9b) is that Rava is referring to the general Torah ruling that unequivocally disqualifies all relatives of a suspect from being witnesses, even to testify to his guilt (*Sanhedrin* 27b, derives this principle from Deuteronomy 24:16). Rava is simply expanding this general rule to apply to every individual about themselves, as well. After all, a person is—quite literally—their own relative.

Others (see *Tosefot, Bava Metzia* 3b) explain that a person, being only a single individual, cannot on their own take down the assumption of innocence that is their natural status *("chezkat kashrut")*; for that, a proper pair of witnesses is necessary. Thus, even in cases where a relative's testimony would theoretically be admissible, Rava's rule still applies.

Maimonides (*Mishneh Torah, Hilchot Sanhedrin* 18:6) provides an explanation based on human psychology—that there are individuals who want to harm themselves and thus speak of crimes they never committed.

The particular psychological explanation of Rava's ruling found in this chapter is based on how the Rebbe explained it in multiple letters. (Whether this understanding is meant as an actual explanation of Rava's teaching or is only drawing on it as an allegorical interpretation remains unclear.) In addition to the letters quoted in the chapter, see also, for example:

Igrot Kodesh, Vol. 10, p. 202: "...self-love [is] blinding, so that sometimes one exaggerates the not-good parts of themselves and sometimes the good parts, as in the ruling in our Torah that a person is trusted neither to consider themselves righteous nor to consider themselves wicked."

Igrot Kodesh, Vol. 15, p. 62, to a teacher who wrote that he is not having an effect on his students: "On this and about this our Sages have said that a person is their own relative and is biased and thus is not trusted to testify about themselves, neither their own merit nor [to their guilt]."

Igrot Kodesh, Vol. 18, p. 142: "One needs the opinion of someone on site, because, a person is their own closest relative,' as our Sages say, and thus cannot judge their own situation accurately; as our Sages explain, because of a person's proximity to themselves they aren't trusted to testify about themselves—whether to their own virtues or their weaknesses...."

See also *Igrot Kodesh,* Vol. 16, p. 336.

The following letter (*Igrot Kodesh,* Vol. 20, p. 284) explains that Rava's principle can sometimes apply to parents' judgment of their children (i.e., because of their emotional closeness, parents cannot always see their children objectively, sometimes also seeing their defects worse than they are):

"In response to your letter detailing various thoughts about your son's education...

"Since this decision depends on multiple factors, and especially your son's individual personality, it would be advisable to consult with others who know him well. Very often, parents themselves are not so reliable when it comes to assessing their children. The concern is not only that they might tilt the assessment too much to the right [i.e., exaggerate their children's virtues] but also, because of their closeness, they might tilt it in the opposite direction [i.e., overblow their defects]. This is similar to the teaching of our Sages [*Sanhedrin* 9b] that a person is not trusted to declare themselves righteous, and also not to [declare themselves wicked]. And may G-d, who looks after every individual with divine providence, help you to choose what is truly best for your son, both physically and spiritually."

*

As a way to mitigate the distorted perspective that comes from being "our own closest relative," the Rebbe would often recommend seeking the advice of others in order to gain objective insight. Pointing to King Solomon's teaching (Proverbs 11:14) that "with a multitude of counselors salvation is found," he would encourage people to consult with understanding friends to hear their perspective.

See, for example, *Igrot Kodesh,* Vol. 20, p. 127: "Since a 'person is their own relative,' and thus isn't always able to assess their own strengths accurately, or the external pressures that are affecting them, it is worthwhile to consult with your friends who are knowledgeable in all the above."

See also *Igrot Kodesh,* Vol. 22, p. 141, to a man who felt people were maliciously targeting his business: "Oftentimes it can seem that someone is going after you even though it isn't necessarily so in reality—or at least not to the extent that it appears. Since 'a person is their own relative,' you should consult with your friends who live there about the matter."

See also *Igrot Kodesh,* Vol. 7, p. 291.

159. *Igrot Kodesh,* Vol. 16, p. 283.
160. Exodus 23:7.
161. *Igrot Kodesh,* Vol. 12, p. 149.
162. *Berachot* 61a.
163. See, for example, *Likkutei Dibburim,* Vol. 3, p. 516, and *Sefer Hasichot 5708,* p. 177. The Rebbe would often connect this Chasidic term with the words of the Talmud (*Shabbat* 105b), "This is the craft of the *yetzer hara*—today it tells him do this, tomorrow it tells him to do that, until eventually it tells him to worship idols," indicating the shrewd and strategic process the *yetzer hara* uses to get someone going down the wrong path. See, for example, *Torat Menachem,* Vol. 1, p. 106 (chabad.org/2988063); ibid., Vol. 7, p. 92 (chabad.org/2987856); ibid., Vol. 33, p. 475 (chabad.org/2987979).

A 1954 letter (*Igrot Kodesh,* Vol. 9, p. 297) reconciles the above Talmudic statement, which implies that the *yetzer hara* is strategic and shrewd, with an apparently contradictory teaching from the Sages. On King Solomon's words, "Better a poor but wise youth than an old but foolish king" (Ecclesiastes 4:13), the Midrash (*Kohelet Rabbah* 4:13) comments that "an old but foolish king" refers to the *yetzer hara.* Because it is first to enter a person's heart and because people tend to listen to its advice, it is "old" and a "king," but it is also a fool. The letter reconciles these descriptions: the *yetzer hara*'s foolishness lies in what it advocates for, and its wisdom lies in its tactics.

The above letter also finds other biblical sources for the *yetzer hara*'s craftiness. In Kabbalistic teachings, the serpent who seduced Eve is seen as a spiritual predecessor to the *yetzer hara.* The Torah describes the serpent with these words: "Now the serpent was the shrewdest of all the wild beasts" (Genesis 3:1).

See also *Igrot Kodesh,* Vol. 19, p. 226: "The dictum of our Chasidic masters is known: just as it is important to know your own flaws, it is equally important to know your own virtues [see *Sefer Hasichot 5687,* p. 114]. This is especially so given that one of the tactics of the *yetzer hara* is to instill dejection into a person's heart by saying, 'Since you're not succeeding anyway, who cares?'

"Although the *yetzer hara* is 'a craftsman' [*Shabbat* 105b], 'G-d has created an antidote to the *yetzer hara* in the form of the Torah' [see *Kiddushin* 30b], especially the teachings of Chabad Chasidut, which bring his tactics to light, including the aforementioned tactic [of amplifying a person's weaknesses], whose purpose is only to bring a person down."

164. *Pesachim* 50b.
165. *A Chasidisher Derher,* Cheshvan 5778, p. 39.
166. *Igrot Kodesh,* Vol. 19, p. 106, and Vol. 18, p. 147.
167. See *Igrot Kodesh Admor Mehorayatz,* Vol. 4, p. 67; and *Hayom Yom,* entry for 23 Sivan.
168. *Igrot Kodesh,* Vol. 15, p. 305.

See also *Igrot Kodesh,* Vol. 13, p. 270, written in response to a Chasidic activist who lamented his inability to produce anything perfectly: "You should examine where such thoughts come from.... The barometer is explained in the teachings of my saintly father-in-law: Any thought that holds you back from actual work, as exalted as it seems to be, is only a scheme of the animalistic soul. And since, as it seems from your letter, these reflections inhibit you from your activities in 'disseminating the wellsprings'—it is clear that their source is impure and detrimental...."

See also *Igrot Kodesh,* Vol. 12, p. 287:

"I was told of your dejected spirit over your [perceived dismal] spiritual state....

"My saintly father-in-law taught that the prohibition against speaking *lashon hara* applies also to oneself; and we know the difference between slander and *lashon hara* from the Rambam—that the latter is prohibited even when the things being said are entirely true [*Mishneh Torah, Hilchot Dei'ot* 7:2].

All the more so [in our case] when it is an exaggeration. And exaggeration is an understatement.

"Chasidic teachings explain that for a planted seed to sprout into a tree and bear fruit of its own, it needs to first decompose in the earth; i.e., there needs to be the effacement of its first existence in order for it to grow exponentially.

"However, when is this decomposition a blessing? When it happens inside fertilized earth that is suited for planting and growing. But if one places a seed on the table and then decomposes it, not only is this not constructive to growth, it actually ruins the seed. And this is the difference between *merirut* [bitterness, which is constructive]] and *atzvut* [sadness, which is destructive], as explained in *Tanya* [chapter 31].

"The barometer by which you can know, without deceiving yourself, what kind of 'decomposition' and dejection you are experiencing is to check the actual results: If this dissatisfaction leads to increased Jewish activities, that means it is the type of 'decomposition' that will lead to growing something worth many times the original 'seed,' but if it leads to weakening or even stopping such activities altogether, then it's clear that it is the other type..."

See also *Igrot Kodesh,* Vol. 15, p. 330; Vol. 17, p. 181; Vol. 27, p. 142 (about continuous thoughts of remorse for past actions).

*

In this spirit, it is important to take note of a related theme in the Rebbe's counseling: the consistent prioritization of action over reflection and rumination. The Rebbe posited this both as a principle (that action is objectively the most important bottom line) and as a strategy (that action, more than thought, has the power to change a person's spiritual and emotional state).

There are a few Torah sources for this approach that the Rebbe frequently pointed at. One was the teaching of the Mishnah: "The essential thing is not study, but deed" (*Avot* 1:17). Another was the axiom from the *Zohar* that "*asiyah le'eila*—deed is above all."

The *Zohar* (Vol. I, p. 115a) derives this principle from the verse "And G-d took note of Sarah as He had promised, and

G-d did for Sarah as He had spoken" [Genesis 21:1]. The *Zohar* observes that in the first half of the verse, where G-d only "takes note," His name is written *"vaHashem,"* with a prefix, whereas in the second half of the verse, where G-d "takes action," His name is simply *Hashem*, with no prefix. Mystically, when G-d's name is spelled simply, with no add-ons, it indicates a higher level of G-dliness than when His name is written with a prefix. That is how the *Zohar* derives that deed is above all.

The *Zohar* (Vol. III, p. 108b) also extracts this principle from the Jewish people's response to G-d when he gave them the Torah. First they said "We will do," and only later did they add "We will hear [understand]." Although hearing and understanding would seem to be the necessary precursor to doing, the *Zohar* observes that the verse records first "we will do." This indicates that deed is, in fact, what matters most.

See, for example, the following 1957 letter (*Igrot Kodesh*, Vol. 15, p. 248) to a man who wrote that he sometimes questions if there is value in his positive actions, considering his ulterior motives:

"The directive of our Sages is already known—'A person should always engage in Torah study, even not for its own sake, for through this, one will come to engage it for its own sake' [*Pesachim* 50b]. If this is true of everyone, all the more so is it true of one who is already bothered by the purity of their intentions and is thinking about it—such a person will certainly ultimately 'do it for its own sake.' And this is true even if an external motive actually played a role; all the more so [in your case] when this itself might be in doubt.

"What is most important going forward is to remember the Mishnah's teaching that 'it is the deed that is essential.' In the words of the holy *Zohar*—'*Asiyah le'eila*,' i.e., deed is above all. Although self-reflection and soul-searching are necessary, we know my saintly father-in-law's analogy—that a businessperson who keeps leaving their business to get busy checking their account balance, calculating whether the incoming cash flow covers expenses, and so on, not only will not benefit their business, but very much the opposite. As the verse states, 'There's a time for everything' [Ecclesiastes 3:1]."

For other letters that touch upon this analogy from the Previous Rebbe, see *Igrot Kodesh,* Vol. 8, p. 267; Vol. 11, p. 98; Vol. 14, p. 486. See also *Igrot Kodesh,* Vol. 4, p. 404.

169. English letter dated 5 Tishrei, 5720.
170. *Living Torah* (JEM), disc 168.
171. The prohibition is rooted in the verse "You shall not go around as a gossipmonger amidst your people" (Leviticus 19:16). The Sages have also taught (see *Rashi* ad loc.) that the verse "Cursed be he who strikes his fellow in secret" (Deuteronomy 27:24) also alludes to talking bad about another, which on some level is "striking them in secret."
172. *Igrot Kodesh,* Vol. 7, p. 194. The letter continues: "This can be more profoundly understood based on the distinction between the prohibition against slander *[motzi shem ra]* and the prohibition against speaking bad about someone. The former, commentaries explain, pertains only to spreading a false narrative about someone. The prohibition against *lashon hara,* on the other hand, applies even if it is true...." As sources for this distinction, the letter references Rambam's *Peirush Hamishnayot, Pirkei Avot* 1:17, as well as *Mishneh Torah, Hilchot Dei'ot* 7:2. The Rebbe later added to the letter an additional reference to *Sdei Chemed, Klalim* 30:63, which delineates various proofs for this distinction.

See also, for example, *Igrot Kodesh,* Vol. 6, p. 76: "Regarding your lamentation over your spiritual state—that your inspiration and growth lasts only for a bit and then recedes [and thus seems to you to be disingenuous]—we know the dictum of my saintly father-in-law, that the prohibition against speaking *lashon hara* is not only about another but about oneself too.

"It is also known how Chasidut interprets [*Torah Or, Parshat Vayeishev,* p. 28c] the verse [Psalms 126:1] 'We will be like dreamers'—that even if soon after a positive inspiration one finds themselves in an opposite state [seeming to prove that it wasn't truly heartfelt], G-d forbid, the inspiration may nevertheless have been entirely authentic. Just like in a dream where opposites truly coexist.

"Either way, even if the situation is in fact as you described it, lamentation is no solution, and taking action is most effective...."

Igrot Kodesh, Vol. 15, p. 152:

"Regarding what you wrote, that you have a 'clogged' heart, and so on.

"We know the dictum of my saintly father-in-law that the negation of *lashon hara* doesn't apply only to talking badly about someone else, but applies to oneself too. And just like it is important for a*vodat Hashem* [divine service] not to overlook one's flaws, it is also important to know one's strengths [*Sefer Hasichot 5687*, p. 114]. We see clearly that one of the tactics of the *yetzer hara* is to instill dejection and despair in a person who is serving their Creator, by saying, 'Who are you anyway, and what difference will your efforts make?' and so on..."

Igrot Kodesh, Vol. 18, p. 347:

"Certainly this [dismal description] is not aligned with reality. We already know the dictum of my saintly father-in-law that the negation of *lashon hara* doesn't only apply to talking badly about someone else, but applies to oneself too. And we know the dictum of his father [the Rebbe Rashab] that just as it is important to know one's flaws, it is equally important to know one's virtues [*Sefer Hasichot 5687*, p. 114]. And it is worth noting—when it comes to being a positive influence on others, sometimes knowing your virtues is more important than knowing your flaws..."

See also *Igrot Kodesh*, Vol. 6, p. 100; *Heichal Menachem* Vol. 2, p. 95.

173. *Igrot Kodesh*, Vol. 20, p. 13.
174. *Here's My Story* (JEM), "A Memorable Deal," accessible at chabad.org/4449210.
175. *Igrot Kodesh*, Vol. 16, p. 13. See also *Igrot Kodesh*, Vol. 12, p. 65; Vol. 23, p. 158; Vol. 27, p. 231. See also English letter dated 21 Sivan, 5724.

It is important to make note of another, more existential type of *hesach hadaat*: to take a pause from analyzing the self more broadly and instead turn the mind toward thinking about G-d, His greatness, and His role for you. See, for example, *Igrot Kodesh*, Vol. 4, p. 404; Vol. 8, pp. 3, 341; Vol. 14, p. 23.

176. English letter. See also the English letter dated 24 Shevat, 5732, which uses the same analogy.

One letter (*Igrot Kodesh*, Vol. 14, p. 395) draws a comparison to the Talmudic concept of *isurei achshevei*—something that in normal circumstances is considered too negligible to have legal value, if an explicit prohibition is leveled *against it*, the prohibition itself gives what was otherwise insignificant new importance, and it may then take on new legal value. For example, leftover dough in the cracks of a mixing bowl is halachically considered null and does not have the status of food. However, on Passover, when even tiny amounts of leaven are prohibited, the prohibition itself bestows new value on the dough, and for the duration of Passover, such leftover dough assumes the status of food also for other legal matters entirely unrelated to Passover (see *Pesachim* 46a). Similarly in the human mind—even when a thought on its own has little power or substance, when one wages a fierce battle *against the thought*, the battle itself can give it newfound prominence and power over the person.

Another letter (*Igrot Kodesh*, Vol. 15, p. 200; see also Vol. 14, p. 276) ties the meaning of *hesach hadaat* as it is used here—specifically not to battle but instead to change focus entirely—to the particular meaning of the term *hesach hadaat* in its Talmudic origins: "And *hesach hadaat* means, as explained in various places in the Talmud, to not battle it either, for that too would be the opposite of *hesach hadaat*. Rather, it means to divert the mind to something else unrelated."

The letter does not explicate what Talmudic sources it is referring to. However, in a 1953 talk (*Torat Menachem 5713*, Vol. 3, p. 90 (chabad.org/2987900)) the Rebbe pointed to two Talmudic sources that indicate that so long as the mind remains in the "vicinity" of a given thought (even if it is not explicitly engaged in thinking the thought), it would not be considered *hesach hadaat*. *Hesach hadaat* is only if the mind moves to unrelated places.

The first source the Rebbe points to is a Talmudic and halachic ruling regarding *tefillin*. The Torah (Exodus 28:38) implies that the High Priest should never take his mind off his sacred headplate because the divine name is inscribed on it. The Sages (*Menachot* 36b) derive from this verse that when one wears *tefillin*, which has the divine name inscribed on it multiple times, certainly one may not have *hesach hadaat* from the *tefillin*.

However, strangely enough, the Talmud rules (*Sukkah* 26a) that one is allowed to take a nap with their *tefillin* on. This would seem to contradict the above Talmudic ruling—after all, how can you sleep without having *hesach hadaat* and taking your mind off your *tefillin*?

The great medieval Jewish sage Rabbi Asher ben Yechiel, also known as the *Rosh* (c. 1250 – 1327), answers this contradiction as follows (*Berachot* 3:28): To be considered *hesach hadaat*, it is not enough to just not think about the *tefillin*. So long as a person is in a more serious mode because he is wearing his *tefillin*—he is in the "vicinity" of the *tefillin*—he cannot be considered to have had *hesach hadaat* and to have taken his mind off it. Thus, when one takes a snooze in a serious posture, with their *tefillin* on, though of course they are not actively thinking about their *tefillin* every second, they haven't really moved away from it either. True *hesach hadaat* would only be if a person mentally disengages from his *tefillin* entirely, i.e., by frolicking irreverently, going into a deep sleep, or similar actions that imply total disconnection from the *tefillin*.

The second source the Rebbe pointed to is in the Jerusalem Talmud. When speaking of the scenario of *hesach hadaat* (see, for example, Jerusalem Talmud, *Berachot* 7:4), it continually uses the phrase *hisi'a da'ato*—he *transported* his mind. This language emphasizes, even more clearly than does the Babylonian Talmud, that *hesach hadaat* is defined by moving the mind away from its original focus, to such an extent that it is considered to have changed its location entirely ("transported").

Another source to which various letters refer (see, for example, *Igrot Kodesh,* Vol. 12, p. 176, and Vol. 23, p. 334) is a letter written by the Tzemach Tzedek (*Igrot Kodesh Tzemach Tzedek,* p. 169), where he records a conversation he had with the Alter Rebbe about a Talmudic teaching (*Yoma* 88a), and explains that sometimes the thought and angst and tension about *negating* something in fact draws the person closer to it than had they not thought about it at all.

177. *Likkutei Sichot,* Vol. 36, p. 323.

This idea—that we have a natural inner health, and diverting ourselves from the negativity that "covers it" often enables it to resurface—is echoed in multiple letters.

See, for example, *Igrot Kodesh,* Vol. 10, p. 118:

"Since it is unfounded, it will not be long-lasting—'appeared overnight and perished overnight' [Jonah 4:10]—that is, provided you do not incite onto yourself morose thoughts that are contrary to the nature of man... You surely know, also from your own experience, what we verily observe: that if at times it is difficult to overcome a certain mood, it is advisable to distract your attention from the mood, not by battling it, but by focusing your thoughts elsewhere. The general motto for this is: 'G-d made man upright, but they [humans] have sought out many schemes' (Ecclesiastes 7:29). Since it comes from 'they,' therefore 'they' have the ability to nullify it more easily."

See also *Igrot Kodesh,* Vol. 14, p. 395, for the same idea in a slightly different context:

"The explanation [for why diversion can be effective] is that such doubts and questions come from outside the person. It is said regarding every one of the children of Israel that they are 'believers the sons of believers' [*Shabbat* 97a], and something that was passed on as an inheritance for dozens of generations is certainly strong and stable. However, for various side reasons, it doesn't always have a conscious effect, and it is possible that opposing forces will cover and conceal it. Through battling [these opposing forces], the battle itself reinforces their existence and lends them importance... However, distraction and not paying them any attention—not getting into a dialogue with them at all, and instead occupying oneself with entirely unrelated concepts—weakens the grip of these foreign and opposing forces on the person's psyche and train of thought."

On this note, see also *Igrot Kodesh,* Vol. 14, p. 400—the beginning of a long letter to a man who wrote about his lack of inner peace:

"It is explained in various sources that such feelings come from 'the other side,' meaning they are not rooted inside a person's soul but are rather from outside. From this it is understood that a person is able to ultimately rid themselves of such feelings.... Although not every person and situation are the same, which is why it doesn't take everyone the same amount of time to accomplish this."

See also *Torat Menachem 5718,* Vol. 2, p. 148 (chabad.org/3008973): "The innovation of Chasidut is to explain not only the reason for an emotional ailment but also that, in essence, you are beyond it, and it's not 'yours'—and this knowledge itself brings healing."

178. English letter dated 20 Tammuz, 5725.
179. *Igrot Kodesh,* Vol. 16, p. 13. See also *Igrot Kodesh,* Vol. 12, p. 65; Vol. 23, p. 158; and Vol. 27, p. 231. See also, English letter dated 21 Sivan, 5724.
180. *Igrot Kodesh,* Vol. 14, p. 22.

The letter adds: "And although when the thought occupies your mind there seems to be no difference whether or not it reflects a factual reality, in truth this is not so: there always exists within a person a 'reality checker' that examines his feelings and the degree of their authenticity and certitude. The results of this assessment affect the person even when their [conscious] capacity to make a 'reality check' is concealed, or to use the common vernacular, lies within the subconscious."

181. Vol. 14, p. 22.
182. *Petakim,* Vol. 1, p. 130. See also *Igrot Kodesh,* Vol. 16, p. 14.
183. *Igrot Kodesh,* Vol. 32, p. 1.
184. *Pesachim* 54b.
185. *Igrot Kodesh,* Vol. 10, p. 320.
186. *Igrot Kodesh,* Vol. 18, p. 93.

See *Igrot Kodesh,* Vol. 9, p. 158, for similar advice to a teenage yeshiva student who suffered from random lapses of concentration and memory while studying: "If you experience this in the middle of studying a given Torah text, you shouldn't pressure your mind, but should instead release the tension by studying something else that you enjoy in Torah, and only then

come back to the original study topic." See also *Igrot Kodesh,* Vol. 8, p. 302.
187. Photocopy of response.
188. *Otzar Hamelech 3,* p. 226.
189. *Likkutei Sichot,* Vol. 36, p. 285. See also *Igrot Kodesh,* Vol. 14, p. 451, and Vol. 15, p. 353; *Heichal Menachem* Vol. 2, p. 94.

In a similar vein, the Rebbe would often counsel "straight-forwardness" as the optimal approach, invoking the following teaching from the Sages:

The Torah commands us to blow a *shofar* (animal's horn) on Rosh Hashanah (the Jewish New Year). The Talmud (*Rosh Hashanah* 26b) records an argument between the Sages as to whether it's better to use a *shofar* made from a curved horn or a straight one.

One sage, Rabbi Yehuda, opined that a curved horn should be used, while the other (anonymous) sage maintained that a straight one is best. The Talmud proceeds to explain their reasoning. Rabbi Yehuda believed the *shofar* should embody how a person should humbly "bend" themselves before G-d in prayer on Rosh Hashanah. The other sage thought that the shape of the *shofar* should impart a different important message: *"Kol deposhit tfei maalei tfei"*—the straighter (i.e., praying with simplicity) the better.

Multiple letters invoke this expression to teach a broader life lesson: *"Kol deposhit tfei maalei tfei"*—oftentimes, the more straightforwardly we approach life, the better.

See, for example, *Igrot Kodesh,* Vol. 20, p. 143, for a letter to a young man who seems to have been ruminating about whether he would be happy in marriage (it seems he wanted to get married, but felt unsettled by the possible future scenarios in his particular situation):

"There is a known lesson from the Sages: *maaseh rav* [the strongest proof is practical precedent—Shabbat 21a]. And we see in reality, in many situations similar to yours, that when the individual got engaged and, after not too long, also married, they were able to establish themselves in an organized and stable life, to the point where [in retrospect] they were themselves surprised at the hesitation and ambivalence they experienced before getting engaged.

"It has already been said multiple times that life doesn't operate like exact mathematics where you can put down all the variables black and white on a paper and form a precise plan. On the contrary, in the vast majority of cases, *'Kol deposhit tfei maalei tfei.'* And may it be the will of G-d, Who looks after every person with individual providence, that, at least from now on, you will 'walk confidently on your path' [Proverbs 3:23], with firm trust in divine providence..."

See also *Igrot Kodesh*, Vol. 12, p. 218:

"In response to your letter—which you began writing last Monday.

"I have told you a few times—if I recall correctly—that you shouldn't meditate and ruminate about the things you write about, i.e., analyzing the state of your psyche, how so-and-so relates to you, etc. Rather, you should remember the 'great principle' [Jerusalem Talmud, *Nedarim* 9:3] of 'Love your fellow as yourself' [Leviticus 19:18], and therefore you should look at another person with a 'good eye' [see *Avot* 5:19]. You should remember the teaching of the Mishnah, 'I was created to serve my Creator' [*Kiddushin* 82a], and to do that properly the body must be healthy (as Maimonides elaborates in chapters 3 and 4 of *Hilchot Dei'ot*). Thus, you need to have an organized schedule for eating, drinking, and sleeping.

"Similarly at work, you should go about it straightforwardly, without getting into complex internal dialogues and logical argumentation for and against every big or even small thing. And where there seems to be doubt, for the most part it is a symptom of entering into complex ruminations about it, instead of just 'taking it smoothly.' And in the minority of cases where doubt nevertheless persists, through consulting good friends and acquaintances the doubt can usually be solved. And the teaching of our Sages has already been applied to this, *'Kol deposhit tfei maalei tfei.'*

"The same applies also in regards to [your desire to] set aside times for Torah study—you don't need to make complex timetable plans, and worry about where you will find the time and spirit; rather, simply begin. And then you will see that it is not hard; in the Torah's words, 'It is very close to you, for your mouth and heart to do it' [Deuteronomy 30:14]."

See also *Igrot Kodesh,* Vol. 19, p. 394:

"Regarding what you wrote about wedding arrangements: In general I am very uncomfortable with the waste of money on halls and so on—expenses which do not bring benefit even from a physical standpoint. And although our Sages have greatly lauded bringing joy to a bride and groom and said that everyone is obligated to participate in this [see *Berachot* 6b]— we see clearly that the joy is even greater when the wedding is not in a hall that costs a fortune, but rather, when it is arranged with the approach of *'Kol deposhit tfei maalei tfei.'* However, whatever the case may be, the wedding arrangements must be done in a pleasant manner and with the full agreement of both sides..."

See also *Igrot Kodesh,* Vol. 12, p. 113; Vol. 13, p. 200; Vol. 15, p. 5.

190. *Petakim,* Vol. 1, p. 131; ibid., p. 124.

Another area where the Rebbe counseled individuals to disengage and take a break was in situations of doubt regarding the suitability of a date for marriage. Often the Rebbe would recommend taking a break from seeing each other (and sometimes even a break from all contact) to help the man or woman better assess their true thoughts and feelings. See for example *Igrot Kodesh,* Vol. 14, p. 316; and *Petakim,* Vol. 2, p. 155.

191. Proverbs 27:19.
192. *Igrot Kodesh,* Vol. 17, p. 330. See also ibid., Vol. 11, p. 162; Vol. 12, p. 66; Vol. 18, p. 169; Vol. 27, p. 227.

See also ibid., Vol. 22, p. 351, in response to a teenager who (it seems) wrote about friendships that were holding him back from personal growth, but from which he couldn't find the strength to extricate himself: "We observe that when a person begins to spend time with good friends, non-constructive friends naturally distance themselves on their own, even without much effort."

On a related note, the following is an English letter (dated 11 Shevat, 5744) to a woman who felt jealous of her husband's love for his daughter from a first marriage. The letter advises her to deflect the jealousy by focusing on love:

"With regard to the matter of your husband's daughter from a previous marriage, and that you feel a little jealous because of your husband's love for his daughter, I would call your attention to the following, though it is also self-evident.

"In view of your good relationship with your husband, which, as mentioned before, will surely get only stronger, an important factor in this will be when your husband will note your good relationship and sincere affection towards his daughter. Thus, because he naturally loves his daughter, and would also like you to love her, his affection for his daughter— far from detracting from his affection for you—will make him all the more appreciate your attitude towards his daughter and strengthen your mutual relationship even more.

"There is surely no need to remind you that 'Ve'ahavta lerei'acha kamocha' [love your fellow as yourself] is the 'great principle' of our Torah, which makes it the duty and privilege of a Jew to love a fellow Jew, even a stranger, 'kamocha'—like yourself. How much more so should one love a Jewish child, since all children are particularly sensitive and want to be loved, and they instinctively feel whether such love is genuine. How much more so has one to love a child whose parents have been separated, and whose father has married another wife. All this, as mentioned, is really self-evident. I am confident that you will not find it difficult to love that child, once you make up your mind that she is in no way in competition with you, but, on the contrary, could further strengthen the mutual relationship all around..."

193. See, for example, *Sanhedrin* 22a.
194. *Mibeit Hamalchut,* Vol. 2, p. 49.
195. *Igrot Kodesh,* Vol. 6, p. 357. See also, for example, ibid., Vol. 19, p. 429.

Sourced in a Chasidic teaching of the Alter Rebbe (*Likkutei Torah, Kedoshim* 30:d), many letters add that committing Torah words to memory has an overall uplifting effect on one's thoughts, even when one is not consciously reviewing them.

See *Igrot Kodesh,* Vol. 5, pp. 235, 259; Vol. 8, p. 197; Vol. 18, p. 98.

Some letters invoke another teaching of the Alter Rebbe: Responding to a student who lamented the negative thoughts populating his mind, he said, *"in a pustke kricht"*—things "crawl" in a barren space. Emptiness invites negativity, while filling the mind with light naturally diminishes it. See *Igrot Kodesh,* Vol. 5, p. 170; Vol. 6, p. 208. In a talk delivered on Purim 1963, the Rebbe repeated this teaching and choked up with tears. For the transcript, see Torat Menachem 5723, p. 221 (chabad.org/4296324).

196. *Petakim,* Vol. 3, p. 187. See also ibid., Vol. 1, p. 129, and Vol. 2, p. 246.
197. Proverbs 6:23.
198. The sentence "A little light dispels a lot of darkness" is from *Tanya* ch. 12. ("A little physical light banishes a great deal of darkness, which is displaced automatically and inevitably without any effort on the part of the light.") The Rebbe would often add, "all the more so a lot of light."
199. *Igrot Kodesh,* Vol. 13, p. 92. See also ibid., Vol. 15, p. 348; and Vol. 16, p. 13.
200. This adage is referenced by the Maharsha (*Gittin* 58a) and by Rabbi Yosef Caro *(Maggid Meisharim, Parshat Mikeitz).* Some find roots for it in the Midrash (*Devarim Rabbah, Va'etchanan 2*), which says: "A trouble which is only of the individual is indeed a trouble; a trouble which is not only of the individual is not a trouble."

However, some later Jewish scholars take issue with it.

"If a devastating plague ravages the entire world," argues the Talmudist Rabbi Zev Shafran (1866–1929), "and others suffer as I do, does that make me any better off? Why, that is only jealousy and mean-spiritedness toward my fellow!" He interprets the proverb to mean that when others, who do not have your problem, nevertheless share your pain and pray for you, that provides consolation. In this sense a trouble shared is half consoled (*Shu"t Ravaz, Yalkut Hachanochi, siman* 31)."

Similarly, the Kabbalist Rabbi Eliezer Papo (1786-1827) quips (in *Pele Yo'etz, Erech Ahavat Re'im*) that "a trouble shared is the consolation of fools." If you learn that others *do not* have your issue—now *that* is half a consolation, he writes; but certainly not learning that other people are suffering.

The Rebbe, in contrast, quotes the proverb approvingly on multiple occasions, though sometimes adding that "woe is to such consolation." See, for example, *Igrot Kodesh,* Vol. 17, p. 340. See also *Igrot Kodesh,* Vol. 12, p. 224, and Vol. 19, p. 37.

201. *Petakim,* Vol. 2, p. 155. (The response adds (amongst other points): "Talk it over openheartedly with your friends, and ask them also to find out the feelings of the other party [the woman he was meeting]. If you are in an emotionally charged state, *delay* debating the merits of your doubts until you are more collected. It is also understood that if you have such doubts—you should not make an irreversible move without having clarified them.)

Similarly reads a comforting 1957 letter (*Igrot Kodesh*, Vol. 14, p. 316) to a young woman who was plagued by doubt, to the extent of non-stop crying, as to whether the man she was dating was for her:

"It is a normal occurrence to have doubts in these areas. Not only is it quite usual, it is understandable as well—this a major step in life, and, since there is no perfection in this world [including in people], there is always room for doubt. Of course these concerns must be considered with the necessary seriousness, but this needn't affect your spirit in such a [negative] way." The letter then suggests taking a three- or four-week break from meeting him, or even corresponding with him, and she should then assess her feelings.

Similarly, here is an excerpt of a 1962 English letter (accessible at chabad.org/1956914) addressing a woman who expressed her general anxiety as she was approaching marriage, considering that she was "treated like a baby her whole life" : "A feeling of anxiety in such a case is not unusual, even where the person has not been treated like a baby. For marriage is an important and serious step which affects the rest of one's life, and, as it is stated in the text of the blessing [recited under the marriage canopy], it is a *binyan adei ad*, an everlasting edifice.

It is, therefore, natural that young people should approach this with a feeling of some anxiety and awe...."

202. Some specific examples:

Disturbing thoughts—see *Igrot Kodesh,* Vol. 14, p. 22.

Difficulty finding the right person to marry—see *Petakim,* Vol. 2 p. 142.

Marital strain—see *Mibeit Hamalchut,* Vol. 2, p. 50. "The situation you describe is present by many other couples as well—on a similar level, on a lesser level, or even on a more severe level. (Although, understandably, people try to conceal or downplay it, which allows one to think they are experiencing an entirely abnormal situation.)" This response also advises going to marriage counseling, among other things. See also *Petakim,* Vol. 1, p. 180.

Depression—see *Petakim,* Vol. 3, p. 130.

Trouble following along in class—see *Igrot Kodesh,* Vol. 11, p. 349.

Downturn in business—see *Igrot Kodesh,* Vol. 26, p. 499.

Difficulty concentrating—see the handwritten response quoted in *Healthy in Body, Mind, and Spirit* (SIE), Vol 3, ch. 4 (accessible at chabad.org/2308537). Similarly, on having a hard time concentrating in prayers—see *Here's My Story* (JEM), "The Power of One Blessing." The Rebbe said: "Many people have the same problem; you're not the only one!" He also offered practical advice: "Focus on one blessing every day."

Coping with loss and tragedy—see Rabbi Mendel Kalmanson, *A Time to Heal,* ch. 1.

Agoraphobia—see *Igrot Kodesh,* Vol. 32, p. 1.

To a doctoral student who worked for a long time on a thesis and then needed to redo it—see *Here's My Story* (JEM), "No Reason to Be Discouraged." "As you have surely heard from others, it is not at all unusual to start working on a thesis and spend considerable time and effort on it only to find that a revision is necessary."

See also *Igrot Kodesh,* Vol. 22, p. 122, and Vol. 25, p. 17.

It is interesting to note that some letters highlight to the recipient that many other people are currently going through the same problem, while other letters emphasize that many have had this issue *and have overcome it.*

*

The following are a few letters which, in slightly different contexts and with different emphases, reassure the recipients of the normalcy of their experiences:

Igrot Kodesh, Vol. 15, p. 166 (to a young woman who appears to have been concerned over her sensitive disposition): "Regarding what you write that you are sensitive—there is nothing to overthink about this; it is normal; and this is the way it should be. As the verse states: 'G-d made man upright, but they have sought out many schemes' [Ecclesiastes 7:29]."

Igrot Kodesh, Vol 18, p. 251: "It is certainly superfluous to remind you that you should not be dejected if in the past there were mistakes in how you handled various issues—because this is normal in all areas of human endeavor. Our Sages have taught, 'One does not arrive at the true meaning of Torah without stumbling first' [*Gittin* 43a]. And usually a person learns from past mistakes many times over about how to properly act in the future…"

Igrot Kodesh, Vol. 16, p. 362: "This [mistake] should be no reason for feelings of inferiority and dejection…. [Concerning] the greatest of our people, it has been said that 'one does not arrive at the true meaning of Torah without stumbling first.' On the contrary, mistakes of the past, when overcome, shed light and teach lessons for the future.

"Moreover, even if this mistake was made not as a beginner but after a significant amount of work [and experience], nonetheless we are told that the Sages would sometimes tell their students, 'What I told you earlier was mistaken' (*Bava Batra* 127a). This was after they were sitting at the helms of educational institutions for dozens of years and after teaching a great number of disciples.

"The reason this anecdote was handed down to us is not only for the sake of tales and history, G-d forbid, but is intended to teach a twofold lesson: 1) We shouldn't conceal our mistakes, even though '[self-]love covers all faults' [Proverbs 10:12]. 2) We shouldn't get disheartened [when we realize that we erred] and slacken in our work. On the contrary, we should draw even greater inner strengths to not only fix the past but to do even more than before. As the analogy is given [see *Igeret Hateshuvah*, ch. 9] of a rope that is severed and then knotted together again—in the place of the rip, the rope becomes twice as thick...."

203. *Petakim*, Vol. 1, p. 129.
204. *Igrot Kodesh*, Vol. 18, p. 426.
205. *Igrot Kodesh*, Vol. 27, p. 528, and Vol. 25, p. 17.

See also *Igrot Kodesh*, Vol. 14, p. 384, for a letter to a teenager who felt that her relationships with her siblings were very strained due to the age gap between them.

For other letters on the period of adolescence and its emotional challenges, see *Healthy in Body, Mind, and Spirit* (SIE), Vol. 3, ch. 7 (chabad.org/2308546).

206. English letter dated 12 Tishrei, 5727.
207. *Yoma* 75a.
208. Quoted in *Here's My Story* (JEM), "Special Delivery" (chabad.org/2981604). See also *Igrot Kodesh*, Vol. 12, p. 202, and Vol. 19, p. 107. See also *Mibeit Hamalchut*, Vol. 2, p. 50.

A 1950 letter (*Igrot Kodesh*, Vol. 3, p. 402) begins as follows: "There's no reason for you to apologize for writing to me [and bothering me with your problems]. I am always happy to learn what is happening in the lives of fellow Chasidim. If there is good news, it causes [me] delight and joy. And if, Heaven forbid, the opposite is true, at the very least this itself—that we are in contact through letters—can encourage the spirit and lessen the feelings of dejection and loneliness...."

209. See *Sefer Hasichos 5748*, Vol. 1, p. 240 and footnote 128.
210. *Teshurah Hoch-Garelik*, 5783, p. 21.
211. See, for example, *Tanya, Igeret Hakodesh*, p. 117b.
212. See, for example, *Zohar*, Vol. I, p. 158a; *Tanya*, chs. 6, 32.

In a 1986 talk (*Sefer Hasichot 5747*, Vol. 1, p. 48, footnote 84) the Rebbe connected this Chasidic idea (that the negative forces within two people will never unite) with the Talmudic axiom that "a person does not sin for the benefit of another individual" (Bava Metzia 5b).

213. Brought in *Hayom Yom*, entry for 20 Teves. It can also be found

in *Igrot Kodesh Admor Mehorayatz,* Vol. 2, p. 383. See also *Reshimat Hayoman,* p. 457.

In a 1987 talk (*Torat Menachem 5747,* Vol. 3, p. 87) the Rebbe explained that while the Mitteler Rebbe was primarily referring to two friends discussing their personal *spiritual* matters with each other, something of this unique power applies also when two friends discuss their *material* dilemmas.

214. *Igrot Kodesh,* Vol. 11, p. 147; see also ibid., p. 17, for further references. Both letters point to the teaching of the Mishnah (*Avot* 1:6): "Acquire for yourself a friend." See also *Igrot Kodesh,* Vol. 17, p. 181.
215. *Ta'anit* 7a.
216. Leviticus 19:18.
217. *Ar'enu Niflaot,* p. 185.
218. Jerusalem Talmud, *Nedarim* 9:3.
219. Isaiah 41:6.
220. *Chayal B'tzava Ha'Rabi,* p. 214.
221. *Here's My Story* (JEM), "There is No Point of No Return."

See also the following English letter, dated Chanukah 5721:

"I received your letter, in which you ask my advice with regard to certain educational problems, especially how to influence the children to get rid of undesirable habits, etc.

"Needless to say, these problems cannot be adequately discussed in a letter. However, experienced teachers and educators are usually their own best guides, for, as the saying goes, 'None is wiser than the man of experience' [*Akeidah, Parshat Noach, shaar* 14, s.v. *Hashlishit; Ma'avar Yabok, shaar* 2]. Besides, it is difficult to give advice from a distance, especially as the psychology of children may vary in certain aspects from one country to another. Nevertheless I would like to make one general point which can be universally applied in educational problems, a point which is emphasized in the teachings of Chasidut. I refer to the effort to make the children aware that they possess a soul which is a part of G-d, and that they are always in the presence of G-d (as explained in chapters 2 and 41 of the *Tanya*).

"When this is done persistently, and on a level which is suitable to the age group and background of the children, the children come to realize that they possess a great and holy quality which is directly linked with G-d, the Creator and Master of the world, and that it would therefore be quite unbecoming and unworthy of them to do anything which is not good. At the same time they come to realize that they have the potential to overcome temptation or difficulty, and if they would only make a little effort on their part they would receive considerable assistance from on high to live up to the Torah and *mitzvot*, which constitute the will and wisdom of G-d.

"As for the problem of some children having a habit to take things not belonging to them, this may fall into one of two categories: a. The attitude mentioned in the Mishnah in *Pirkei Avot* [5:10]: 'Mine is thine and thine is mine.' In this case, the effort should be made to educate the child that just as it is necessary to be careful not to offend or shame another person, so it is necessary to be careful not to touch anything belonging to somebody else. b. An unhealthy condition which should be treated medically by specialists who know how to handle such an aberration.

"I would like to add one more point, which is also emphasized in the teachings of Chasidut, namely, to be careful that in admonishing children the teacher or parent should not evoke a sense of helplessness and despondency on the part of the child; in other words, the child should not get the impression that he is good-for-nothing and that all is lost, etc., and therefore he can continue to do as he wishes. On the contrary, the child should always be encouraged in the feeling that he is capable of overcoming his difficulties and that it is only a matter of will and determination...."

222. *Zechariah* 3:7.
223. See, for example, the commentary of *Metzudat David* ad loc.
224. See *Torah Ohr,* p. 30a, for a discourse on this verse; *Likkutei Torah, Parshat Re'eh* 38d; *Derech Mitzvotecha*, p. 140b.

The Rebbe would quote this idea frequently, often emphatically, as a defining feature of a human being and as one of the reasons our soul descends to earth instead of remaining in its original pristine state in the spiritual worlds above.

See, for example, *Igrot Kodesh,* Vol. 12, p. 36: "The Chasidic interpretation of the verse that refers to man as a 'walker' [Zechariah 3:7] is already known—that this is a person's task, and this is a sign of their inner vitality, that they grow and develop from day to day. We see clearly that this depends only on a person's will, for the ability to grow is always accessible, to reach a higher level today than yesterday, and so on from day to day. If this is true of all people, all the more so with regards to the younger generation, whose energy is not yet spent and still percolates inside them, and whose initiative is strong..." See also *Igrot Kodesh*, Vol. 13, p. 367, and Vol. 14, p. 257; *Torat Menachem*, Vol. 5, p. 56 (chabad.org/4280217), and Vol. 10, p. 110 (chabad.org/2987598)—this source brings into sharp focus the direct correlation between the capacity for failure and the capacity for exponential growth, in contrast to angels who have neither. Ibid. Vol. 34, p. 6 (chabad.org/2988015).

The Rebbe would also often refer to the Talmudic statement (*Berachot* 64a): "Torah scholars do not stagnate, not in this world and not in the next, as the verse states [Psalms 84:7], 'They walk from strength to strength.'"

Additionally, the Talmud (*Eruvin* 54a) says, "Grab and eat, grab and drink, as the world from which we walk is like a wedding feast." The Rebbe explained that "the world from which we walk" alludes to the unique feature of this world—that here, unlike in the higher realms, we can truly move forward instead of standing still. And this unique opportunity creates the urgency to metaphorically "grab and eat, grab and drink" while one still can.

On a related note, multiple letters reference the analogy of the Rebbe's father-in-law, the Previous Rebbe, that when you're walking on level terrain, you can stop and just stand in place, but when you're climbing up a steep mountain, you can't just hunker in place. Moving upwards is what keeps you from falling down. And our volatile times are like a steep mountain. See *Igrot Kodesh*, Vol. 7, p. 353, and Vol. 18, p. 274.

225. *Igrot Kodesh*, Vol. 18, p. 479.
226. *Igrot Kodesh*, Vol. 8, p. 128.
227. *Tanya, Shaar Hayichud Veha'emunah*, ch. 1, elucidates this teaching of the Baal Shem Tov.

Rabbi Nachman (1772–1810) was an early Chasidic master, and a great-grandson of the Baal Shem Tov, who lived in the Ukrainian town of Breslov. He was known to spend his time immersed in Torah study, ecstatic prayer, and earnest meditation. Over time, a group of dedicated students gathered around him to learn from his teachings, until his early passing at the age of thirty-eight. One of them, Rabbi Nosson, transcribed the following moment:

"[Our teacher said:] 'Even if someone finds himself in the lowest pits of Hell and darkness, may G-d spare us, he should nevertheless keep himself from despair.... The main thing is to encourage oneself in every way possible, for there is no such thing as despair!'

"He drew out these words, 'for there is no such thing as despair,' saying them emphatically, with profound and awesome depth, in order to instruct each and every person throughout the generations to not despair under any circumstances, no matter what they go through" (*Likkutei Moharan*, Vol. II, 78:7:3).

This moment, and its poignant message, became a central theme in the Breslov Chasidic tradition for centuries to come.

Moshe Maisels (1901–1984) was a thinker and writer who grew up in the vibrant Breslov community of Warsaw (before it was decimated in the Holocaust, along with the 400,000+ other Jews in the Warsaw ghetto). Although recognized for his acute mind and pointed pen—serving as the editor-in-chief of several distinguished Jewish newspapers—he was a humble spirit who notoriously evaded the limelight. However, his increasing retreat from the public (he moved from journalism to publishing to academic pursuits) was also motivated by a deep despair. He felt the losses his generation had suffered caused an inevitable void of spiritual leadership for the younger generation and there was nothing that could be done about it.

In a letter written to Maisels in 1962 (*Igrot Kodesh*, Vol. 22, p. 179), the Rebbe encouraged him that "despite being a hidden person who holds on tightly to the words of the Sages that 'there is nothing better for a person than silence,'" [*Avot* 1:17] he should more fully utilize his talents for the benefit of the public. And "the fact that in our generation the creative powers of our people has been greatly diminished only increases the responsibility of each and every individual who has been gifted with talent..." The letter continues:

"I was told that your family, as well as your personal perspective, is associated with the Breslov [Chasidic tradition] and its worldview. I mention this here because a common justification for not being active is that there is no hope for success and the effort is thus a waste. But this spirit is diametrically opposed to the slogan of Breslov: "No despair!"

"Finding ourselves in the [Hebrew] month of Adar, this too is related to the above. The whole idea of the Purim miracle was that in the natural means there seemed to be absolutely no hope for salvation. And the miracle happened specifically in a way of *v'nahapoch hu* [Esther 9:1]—radical transformation from one extreme to the total opposite extreme...."

"Even if," continues a follow up letter (*Igrot Kodesh*, Vol. 22, p. 281),

"to our eyes it seems, as you put it in your letter, that a great emptiness prevails in the world, an inner emptiness—nevertheless, who is it who can judge and decide that their personal perception is in fact the objective reality, to the point that they can lock themselves [metaphorically] into their own little room....

"If I have elaborated too much, please accept my apologies; [but] I will not conceal my hope that perhaps as a result of this [elaboration], despite the disappointment you express in your letter, you will go out of your normal framework and begin being active wherever your influence reaches."

See *Kovetz Hayechidut, Vaad Talmidei Hatmimim*, Tishrei 5782, no. 3, p. 85, for a letter where the poet Zvi Yair Steinmetz records a conversation he had with Maisels, in which Maisels told him that he identifies with the words of the writer Leib Rochman (a prominent Yiddishist who came from a Polish Chasidic background and survived the Holocaust in hiding) that "the miracle and wonder of the Jewish people after the Holocaust is the Lubavitcher Rebbe."

(In this regard, it is interesting to note a 1975 conversation between former Israeli Prime Minister Menachem Begin and one of his early financial supporters and friends, Sam Moss [a Holocaust survivor who later lived in Australia]. Moss asked Begin, "Who do you think is the greatest leader of the Jewish people alive now?" Begin responded that, in his opinion, it was the Lubavitcher Rebbe. When Moss asked him why he thought so, Begin answered, "He lifted up the generation after the Holocaust. He helped the Jewish people believe in themselves again." See *Here's My Story* (JEM), "The Survivor Who Wouldn't Sit Down," accessible at chabad.org/4047408).

*

On a similar note to this correspondence with Maisels, another type of despair the Rebbe tried to drive out of people was the despair of activists and educators who felt all their work and efforts were for naught.

For example, the following 1955 letter (*Igrot Kodesh*, Vol. 12, p. 4) to a despondent educator:

"Although from time to time I hear of your activities [from others], it was a pleasure to receive a letter from you directly; though, of course, I am unhappy about the spirit expressed therein, namely your dejection that, to your eyes, you do not see any positive effects from your work with the youth.

"It is understood that if an activist is fully satisfied it doesn't bring the best results; for it is prone to weaken his resolve, as his evil inclination says to him, 'You did enough, you succeeded, now let others come and take over.' However, the opposite extreme—feeling entirely hopeless or even dejected—also leads to bad results. In fact, it is worse, because the withdrawal from work caused by despair is much greater [than that of satisfaction].

"Now, to the heart of the matter—that [you feel] the youth in whom you invested so much energy are nevertheless swept up in the wave of assimilation—we are assured that 'no serious [educational] effort returns empty-handed' [*Hayom Yom*, entry of 12 Tishrei], though it doesn't always succeed on the level one aspired and hoped for. Furthermore, very often, for various reasons, these results are only evident much later. It is often delayed until the student settles down to family life, when he is in less of a state of flux, and he then takes account of everything that he's gone through in life as well as his present situation, and then the period when he received guidance from so-and-so in a given place makes its way into his self-accounting and can be the factor that tips the scale toward the good.

"Moreover, the Talmud [*Yevamot* 62b] relates the story of Rabbi Akiva, one of the greatest of the Sages, and one of the pillars of our Oral Torah, that for forty years he was a teacher, an influencer, an educator, and the leading sage, and he had 24,000 students, and these were students relative to Rabbi Akiva's stature, meaning that they were on such a level of intellect and character that their educator had to be someone like Rabbi Akiva. And then, for a specific reason, they all perished, and the Torah was at risk of being forgotten from Israel. Rabbi Akiva nevertheless went ahead and taught another five students, and it was they who restored the Oral Torah and disseminated it to the Jewish people in their times, and this has been continually passed on from generation to generation until it reached us and our children and grandchildren for all eternity.

"It is clear that our Torah is not simply a story book; rather, the word Torah means a lesson [*horaah*—see *Zohar*, Vol. III, p. 53b], meaning that everything in it teaches us and shows the way for every man and woman. This story provides a living example that a person is to utilize and maximize his talents, and whatever obstacles are hurdled against his work, he cannot lose spirit. Even if, Heaven forbid, it is a setback on the level of the above story, where many years of labor seem to fleshly eyes to be entirely lost and in vain, nevertheless, it is upon him to continue his holy work with vitality and joy, and in the end he will certainly succeed. It might be as in the above story, that with a great number he sees no success at all, or no lasting results, but then with a small number he will have such tremendous success that it fills the void and deeply gratifies him for all the toil he invested. In the words of the verse referenced by our Sages in the above story, 'Sow your seed in the morning, and don't hold back your hand in the evening, since you do not know which is going to succeed' [Ecclesiastes 11:6]."

In a 1972 talk (*Torat Menachem 5732*, Vol. 2, p. 129 (chabad.org/5989361)) the Rebbe relayed this lesson through a quote from King Solomon: "Cast your bread upon the water, for after many days you will find it" [Ecclesiastes 11:1]. It might indeed take many days, the Rebbe explained, but cast your bread and the result is assured—you will find it.

Some letters also point to the verse "Water wears away stone" [Job 14:19], as the Sages interpret it [*Avot D'Rabi Natan*, 6:2]: If one drop of water after another ultimately penetrates even a stone, all the more so the human heart. See, for example *Igrot Kodesh*, Vol. 8, p. 342; Vol. 11, p. 241; Vol. 21, p. 302. Other letters add the assurance—and condition—of the medieval Jewish leader, Rabbeinu Tam (1100–1171), that "words that come from the heart enter the heart" [*Sefer Hayashar, Shaar* 13; *Shelah* 69a]. See also *Igrot Kodesh*, Vol. 7, p. 144; Vol. 10, p. 126; Vol. 12, p. 370; Vol. 14, p. 356.

228. *Sefer Hamaamarim 5643*, p. 97.
229. *Torat Menachem 5743*, Vol. 3, p. 1223 (chabad.org/6011409).
230. *Sefer Hasichot 5750*, p. 598.
231. English letter dated 1 Iyar, 5711. See similarly *Igrot Kodesh*, Vol. 4, p. 267.

Another English letter from 1951 (dated 6 Nissan, 5711) highlights a different lesson of hope gleaned from Passover:

"For a long time the children of Israel were enslaved in Egypt, in physical and intellectual bondage, and the danger of complete assimilation was grave, as the Torah tells us [see *Zohar Chadash, Yitro*]. So low had they sunk that when Moses brought them the message of deliverance from Egyptian bondage, 'they did not listen to him because of lack of spirit and hard labor' [Exodus 6:9].

"However, after their liberation from enslavement, they reached, in comparatively very short time, the highest spiritual level which is humanly possible to attain, making them all, men, women and children, fit for divine revelation at Mount Sinai, and worthy of the highest knowledge and inexhaustible source of wisdom and faith for all generations to come. This shows that potentially every person has it in him to rise from the lowest depths to the loftiest spiritual heights in a comparatively short time, provided he has the sincere and wholehearted desire and will to do so."

*

This leads us to an important point: We always have the capacity to start anew—not only after a period of stagnation but even if we messed up bitterly. Many letters counsel the teaching of the Sages that "nothing stands in the way of *teshuvah* [repentance]" (Jerusalem Talmud, *Pe'ah* 1:1). No matter how far one has fallen, they should not despair, because with sincere regret and firm resolution to behave differently, they can begin anew. And we are assured by covenant that G-d is forgiving and accepts those who repent with open arms.

See, for example, *Igrot Kodesh*, Vol. 26, p. 68, for a letter addressing a woman who wrote remorsefully about a "bad incident" involving a married spouse and another person (it's not entirely clear if she was the spouse or the other person, or what level "incident" this was):

"In answer to your letter of Jan. 5th,

"Since you describe the incident as a 'bad' one, certainly there is no need to further expound on the incident itself, how it hurts not only the three people involved, as you write, but also the couple's children, as it is the nature of sons and daughters to sense an upheaval in their parents' relationship. Additionally, the effects of the incident endure—one cannot know if it will be for weeks, months, or even longer—while the 'pleasure' was only momentary and only of two people.

"On the other hand, every one of the sons and daughters of Israel has been commanded to repel a sense of despair [see *Berachot* 10a], because nothing stands in the way of *teshuvah*. And *teshuvah* means [*Mishneh Torah, Hilchot Teshuvah* 2:2] complete regret of the past from the depths of your soul and thus a firm resolution for the future. This includes being careful of anything that can place the relevant individuals in a tempting setting again, and every additional caution in this regard is praiseworthy.

"And G-d, 'who sees the heart' [Samuel I 16:7] and knows

that your repentance as detailed above is real and authentic, 'pardons in abundance' [Isaiah 55:7], and grants a complete pardon as only G-d can, including to diminish the pain and shame caused to all those involved in this incident. As the verse puts it, 'Is the arm of G-d too short [to fulfill a request]?' [Numbers 11:23]. And your heart's wish is indeed to diminish the pain, etc.

"Based on what is explained in the teachings of Maimonides, who was a healer of both body and soul [in addition to being a spiritual leader, he was a prominent physician], it is understood that any incident requiring repentance must be utilized for increasing goodness and uprightness between man and G-d and between man and his fellow, as the Creator of man has outlined in His Torah, which is called the 'Torah of Life,' meaning, it is a guide for life. My intention is simply daily behavior in light of the Torah and being more careful with this than you were before. And, as mentioned above, nothing stands in the way of the will.

"With blessings for success in all the above, and to have good news to share about this."

Other letters point to a teaching of the *Zohar* (Vol. I, p. 129a): "Fortunate are those who repent, for in one hour, in one day, in one moment, they become close to G-d. This is not the case even for the completely righteous, who become close to G-d [only] in a [matter of] years. Abraham didn't reach [the status of] 'elevated days' until he aged [Genesis 24:1]. King David as well, as the verse states, 'And King David was old [and only then did he achieve 'elevated] days' [Kings I 1:1]. But those who repent immediately enter and bond with Him—with the Holy One blessed be He."

See, for example, *Igrot Kodesh,* Vol. 12, p. 290: "Even one who finds themselves in the lowest of the lowest places can transform themselves from one extreme to another, sometimes even, as the *Zohar* expresses it, 'in one hour, in one moment.'" See also *Igrot Kodesh,* Vol. 14, p. 284; Vol. 19, p. 226; Vol. 23, p. 170.

Some letters point to the concluding statement of a Talmudic story [*Avodah Zarah* 17a] about the wayward sage

Elazar ben Durdaya [approx. 2nd century CE] who fell from greatness to lowly places of lust and passion:

"They said about Rabbi Elazar ben Durdaya that he was so promiscuous that there was not one prostitute in the world with whom he did not engage in sexual intercourse. Once, he heard that there was one prostitute in one of the cities overseas who would take a purse full of dinars as her payment. He took a purse full of dinars and went and crossed seven rivers to reach her. When they were engaged in the matters to which they were accustomed, she passed wind and said, 'Just as this passed wind will not return to its place, so too Elazar ben Durdaya will not be accepted in repentance.'

"[This statement deeply moved Elazar ben Durdaya, and] he went and sat between two mountains and hills and said, 'Mountains and hills, pray for mercy on my behalf, so that my repentance will be accepted.' They said to him: 'Before we pray for mercy on your behalf, we must pray for mercy on our own behalf...' He said: 'Heaven and earth, pray for mercy on my behalf.' They said to him: 'Before we pray for mercy on your behalf, we must pray for mercy on our own behalf...' He said: 'Sun and moon, pray for mercy on my behalf...'

"[Finally,] Elazar ben Durdaya said, 'Clearly, the matter depends on nothing other than myself.' He placed his head between his knees and cried loudly until his soul left his body. A divine voice emerged and said: 'Rabbi Elazar ben Durdaya is destined for life in the World to Come.'

"When Rabbi Yehuda Hanasi heard this story, he wept and said: There are those who acquire their world [their portion in the World to Come] only after many years of toil, and there are those who acquire their world in one moment... And he further said: Not only are those who repent fully accepted, but they are even called 'Rabbi' [—as the divine voice referred to Elazar ben Durdaya as *Rabbi* Elazar ben Durdaya]."

See, for example, *Igrot Kodesh*, Vol. 9, p. 285: "Explain to him that nothing is ever lost, and 'no banished one will remain banished' [Samuel II 14:14], and though one shouldn't wail about the past [*Mishnah, Berachot* 9:3] and about the time that has gone to waste—from now on, every moment should be precious.... And, as can also be logically understood, 'One can acquire their world in one moment' [*Avodah Zarah* 17a]... And the question as to why his bygone years happened as they did—'Why dig in to the secrets of the All-merciful?' [*Berachot* 10a]..."

See also *Igrot Kodesh*, Vol. 4, p. 56; Vol. 23, p. 176 (in the footnote).

Other letters take this theme a step further. Drawing on the Talmud's teaching (*Yoma* 86b) that through "repentance from love" one not only earns forgiveness but can, in fact, transform their mistakes into positive accomplishments, the Rebbe would counsel people that not only is their future not lost, but *even their past is redeemable!* Sincere *teshuvah* has the capacity to transcend the limits of time. This 1967 English letter (*Michtav Klali*, period of Selichot, 5727, accessible at chabad.org/744109) elaborates:

"There is an accepted rule that no thing can become totally extinct. It applies also to human thought, word, and deed. This is to say that the thoughts, words, and deeds of yesterday, and of the day before, and prior to that, do not vanish without a trace; their influence lingers on, affecting the shape of things today and tomorrow, as evidenced in actual results, both in regard to the self and to the environment.

"Another point in this connection is this: Although at first glance it may appear that an action in the past is no longer under human control—i.e. the past is gone, and no person can retrieve it and alter it—this is really not so. For G-d has given man a divine power by means of *teshuvah* to alter not only the course of the future, but also the power to directly affect the past as well: to change it, even to the extent of reversing it altogether, so much so that 'willful transgressions are deemed as inadvertent errors,' and can, moreover, be converted into positive accomplishments [*Yoma* 86b]."

See similarly *Igrot Kodesh*, Vol. 19, p. 448.

On a related note, see *Here's My Story* (JEM), "Service-Oriented Teshuvah." When a rabbinical student who had recently become religiously observant asked the Rebbe for advice on how to mend his past mistakes, the Rebbe responded:

"Help other people not to falter and transgress in the ways that you did."

Reflecting on this answer from the Rebbe years later, he said, "I heard it, I absorbed it, and I remembered it. But, honestly speaking, it took me years to figure it out. I've thought about it a lot, and the reason I am sharing it here is because I think it is important advice. This was the Rebbe's instruction to a *baal teshuvah*, but it could apply to many people in a variety of situations. The Rebbe wasn't telling me to work on myself—which of course is important, but it was not what I needed to focus on at that time. He was telling me to help others improve and, by doing so, I would end up improving myself as well."

*

In 1954, Gad Frumkin, an Israeli jurist and scholar who served as one of the few Jewish Supreme Court judges in Mandatory Palestine, wrote a letter to the Rebbe, and sent along a gift—his translation of the Mecelle (the civil code of the Ottoman Empire) into Hebrew. The following is an excerpt of the Rebbe's response to him:

"It is fascinating that our sacred Torah's legal code contains a fundamental difference from the legal codes of other nations—namely, the blanket absence of incarceration as a *punishment*. (The case where one is placed in a vaulted room [Sanhedrin 9:5] isn't intended to be incarceration as a legal punishment, as the Mishnah explains there.)

"This, too, illustrates the Torah's perspective on the great value of action and the preciousness of life. In the words of the verse, 'Days are formed, and not one of them [is superfluous],' indicating that all moments in a person's life are significant. Because punishment in the Torah's view is not for the purpose of revenge, but rather to correct or repair, therefore, there is no room to deprive a person of the capacity to act, even if it is done for the benefit of the public, as is the logic of prison. (With the sole exception of someone who is entirely unfit to fulfill their individual task, whose punishment is death.)

"We can learn from this three fundamental principles:

1. The tremendous value of every moment in a person's life.

2. The tremendous value of the individual.

3. Even though a person has sinned—they are a human being, and they continue to have a unique mission from the Creator of the universe."

232. See Exodus 7:7.
233. Recorded in the book *Short Stories From The Rebbe*, pp. 187-189.
234. *Likkutei Sichot*, Vol. 39, p. 297.
235. The response does not specify where in *Tanya* it is referring to. In conversation with a few Chasidic scholars, a few possibilities were suggested:

In chapter 1 of *Tanya* the Alter Rebbe explains the danger of considering oneself a wicked person because it can lead to carelessness about one's actions.

In chapter 27, the Alter Rebbe explains that if one finds themselves thinking inappropriate thoughts, they mustn't feel sadness and despair; instead they should see it as a joyful opportunity to do the *mitzvah* of diverting their mind from these thoughts. This can be understood as a tool for helping a person avoid falling into victimhood and self-pity over the proliferation of negative thoughts, and instead feel responsible and empowered.

In chapter 31, the Alter Rebbe addresses a person who is depressed over their lowly spiritual state, and sees themselves as a mere piece of flesh and blood full of crass cravings and misdeeds. He emphatically counsels a meditation to counter this, to uplift their spirit and change this gloomy and pitiful self-perception.

236. *Megillah* 6b.

This teaching of the Sages is brought in countless letters. Many letters cite it as an assuring promise: "If you toil, you will [certainly] succeed." As one English letter puts it: "The road from hope to reality lies in effort and determination, as our Torah, the Torah of life, declares: 'Try, and you will succeed.'"

Some letters point out that the Hebrew words of the Sages, "If you toil, you will *find—umatzata*," indicate that the success you discover will be on an entirely different level than the amount of effort put in—just like when you find a precious object (in contrast to when you buy it with hard-earned money), there is an element of surprise, of beyond expectation, and a sense of being rewarded out of proportion to the effort invested. See, for example, *Igrot Kodesh*, Vol. 17, p. 311; Vol. 18, p. 517; Vol. 21, p. 420; Vol. 26, p. 446; Vol. 27, p. 447.

In a 1956 letter to Zalman Shazar, who was then a member of Israel's parliament and later its president, the Rebbe shared a lesson on effort he gleaned from a seeming contradiction between two Talmudic statements (*Yevamot* 63a). One statement tells us that "whoever engages in building becomes impoverished," while another statement (on the same page) implies [see *Tosefot* ad loc., s.v. *"she'eiin lecha umanut"*] that "whoever hasn't a building is not a human." How can these two statements be reconciled?

"And I thought to answer this seeming contradiction: In order to put up a building—a true building that surrounds and individualizes a person and all his possessions, raising them to their highest level, that is, the human level, called *adam* from the word *adameh l'Elyon*, i.e., reflecting the Divine—[to accomplish this,] a person's overt strengths do not suffice, for not with them alone can one create an eternal edifice. Only when one 'becomes impoverished,' meaning, they invest all their overt strengths, and moreover draw on their hidden strengths, their essential strengths—only with this can one lay a foundation, build walls, and create an exalted ceiling, and it becomes "the beauty of a human (because they did their work, and toiled, and reached) to settle a home" [Isaiah 44:13].

This conclusion can be better understood in light of the spiritual meaning of the building components (foundations, walls, ceilings, etc.), especially as they are explained in the teachings of Chasidut, in the *maamar* of the Alter Rebbe titled *Mizmor Shir Chanukat Habayit*, printed in *Likkutei Torah, Parshat Vezot Habrachah*, pp. 98a-100d.

*

On the subject of effort, another principle from the Sages (see *Shir Hashirim Rabbah* 5:2; *Likkutei Torah, Parshat Korach*, p. 55a; *Likkutei Sichot*, Vol. 1, p. 191, in footnote) that recurs in the Rebbe's counseling is: "Open for Me like the eye of a needle, and I will open for you like the entrance of the *ulam* [the tallest and widest entranceway in the temple, leading into the Holy chamber]." This indicates that it is up to man to initiate and make an effort to open a crack. However, if you only make that first move—you are helped from above and the tiny crack is transformed into a large front-door opening. One letter (*Igrot Kodesh,* Vol. 9 p. 298) explains:

"There is entirely no need to feel down and dejected that you do not have consistent times for Torah study—because this is in your hands; at any given moment you can change this. In light of the approach in matters of holiness that 'little by little will I dispel [negativity],' it is not advisable to immediately accept upon yourself a few hours [of study]. Rather, in the beginning it should be a quarter of an hour or half an hour, preferably some of it in the morning and some at night.... However, you should insist on this quarter of an hour with determination. And once you break a path with this, over time it will become a well-trodden path, and you will be able not only to maintain this time commitment but also to increase it.

"Our Sages have taught us [See *Berachot* 61a, *Sukkah* 52b] that G-d stands at the right of every individual to help them in their divine service, and if only they create an opening like the 'eye of a needle,' they are given an opening from above like 'the entrance of the *ulam*.' And the significance of the word choice—'like the opening of the *ulam*'—is known: The *ulam* famously didn't have any doors [Middot 2:3], so that it was essentially always open. Thus, the work consists only of entering, which requires only breaking open a crack the size of a needle head."

237. *Petakim,* Vol. 1, p. 30.

See also *Otzar Hamelech,* Vol. 1, p. 320 ("Stop the self-pity; use your talents as detailed above—and *you will succeed...*"). See also ibid., p. 73 ("Crying and questioning the way the world operates only complicates all the above. This is only an *escape* (since crying doesn't take any effort at all) from fulfilling that which is your responsibility, for which you were given *all* the necessary capabilities, if only you truly resolve to do so.")

In a 1965 talk (*Likkutei Sichot,* Vol. 10, p. 148) the Rebbe pointed to a fascinating Talmudic source about the inadequacy of tears when action is called for.

After Joseph reunited with his younger brother, Benjamin, the Torah records (Genesis 45:14): "With that, Joseph embraced his brother Benjamin around the necks and wept, and Benjamin wept on his neck." The Talmud (*Megillah* 16b) points out that, peculiarly, the neck of Benjamin is referred to in the plural (necks), while Joseph's is referred to in the singular. "How many necks did Benjamin have?"

The great sage Rabbi Elazar (3rd century CE) explained that this discrepancy alludes to a broader meaning in the cries of Joseph and Benjamin. "Joseph cried over the two [plural] Temples destined to be destroyed in the tribal territory of Benjamin. Benjamin cried over the [single] tabernacle of Shiloh that was destined to be destroyed in the tribal territory of Joseph." The brothers cried for each other.

But, the Rebbe noted, this story is quite strange. While they surely cared about each other, "a person is their own closest relative," and the future of their own temples must have mattered to them too. Why were they only crying about the other's temple?

This captures a powerful idea: If you see a friend destroying their personal "temple," of course you must do what you can to help. You can talk to them, advise them, encourage them—but in the end, it's up to them. It's their choice. After you exhaust your efforts, the sympathetic heart is left to cry, helplessly watching a friend's temple going up in flames. But if your own temple is being destroyed? Don't cry—do something! That is in your hands to change—so don't wallow in misery, don't be satisfied with tears, get on it! Thus, Joseph and Benjamin cried for *each other's* temples. For their own temples, they weren't going to cry. They were going to do something.

Those present at this talk recount the emphatic vigor with which the Rebbe explained this, to the point that these words echoed vividly in their minds half a century later.

A related Chassidic dictum (from the Rebbe Rashab, repeated by the Previous Rebbe) referenced numerous times in letters is: "A single act is better than a thousand groans"

(*Hayom Yom*, entry for 8 Adar II). Some letters add, "All the more so a lot of acts."
238. *Igrot Kodesh*, Vol. 12, p. 315.
239. *Living Torah* (JEM), program 754.
240. The *Zohar* (Vol. II, p. 162b) says, "Everything in the world depends on nothing but will." Various sources point to this as the source for this known Jewish dictum, quoted in many letters of the Rebbe. In *Kuntreis Limud Hachasidut*, p. 29, the Previous Rebbe quotes the Mitteler Rebbe teaching this dictum to a Chasid in a private audience, and explaining the deeper meaning of it.
241. *Tanya,* beginning of chapter 2 (quoting Job 31:2).
242. English letter dated 4 Elul, 5739.

Essay
A Vision of Wholeness

What are the overarching themes in the Rebbe's counseling?

This question is larger than any one answer. Following are two ideas for consideration.

1: Outer Wholeness

CONVENTIONAL WISDOM ON EMOTIONAL wellness directs us to turn inward—to pay heed to the distressing thoughts and painful experiences that accumulated inside of us and give them proper voice.

The Rebbe's counsel points primarily elsewhere. He taught that the world, stripped to its essence, is a divine symmetrical organism. In G-d's holistic creation, each and every one of us plays a special role. Therefore, inner wellness is not achieved by retreating into our own minds, but by plugging into the larger, healthy whole outside ourselves.

This concept seems to be the common thread that runs throughout the many diverse themes found in the Rebbe's counsel. To recap from the chapters in this book:

- *To see other people's journeys and help them when they're in need (Chapter 1).*

- *To reflect that G-d is unconditionally at our side, no matter what's going on inside of us (Chapter 2).*

- *To fulfill the unique tasks we have been divinely selected to fulfill in our own particular circumstances (Chapter 3).*

- *To tend to our "external" selves—our bodies, schedules, occupations, and social environment (Chapter 4).*

- *To set aside time to study Torah and routinely practice spiritual deeds (Chapter 5).*

- *To refrain from denigrating our lives and characters and resolve instead to take up the divine calling of joy (Chapters 6 and 9).*

- *To pursue our endeavors with proactive faith that things will turn out well (Chapter 7).*

- *To utilize a bad mood as an opportunity for divine service (Chapter 8).*

- *To refrain from battling disturbing thoughts, and instead redirect our minds towards themes of "light" (Chapter 10).*

- *To see our problems and challenges not as factors that isolate us but as matters that unite us with others in similar circumstances (Chapter 11).*

- *To expand out of our subjective ruminations and consult with objective mentors and knowledgeable friends (Chapter 11).*

Taken all together, these points don't call for indulging in our own selves, our own problems, or our internal negativity—painful as they might be. Instead, they push us to actively engage with the vibrant world outside our own cocoon.

To be sure, Jewish wisdom does at times assign significant value to introspection in order to mend the past or develop one's character. In Chapter 2, we saw how the Rebbe helped someone heal from his debilitating traumatic experience—crash landing into enemy territory, losing a close comrade on impact, and being held hostage for three long years in horrible conditions—by having him revisit his haunting memories in a highly sensitive and supportive setting.

Yet, in most instances, the Rebbe's counsel did not recommend self-examination, instead encouraging people to transcend their limited reality and connect with something larger and infinitely greater.

The following 1963 letter to Zalman Shazar (a prolific writer, poet, and orator, who served as the third president of Israel) explains:

> Relative to the inner dimension of the world, its external dimension—as perceived superficially—is insignificant. In its inner dimension, the world is entirely good and beautiful.

And only through this [search and alignment with the inner layer of the divine] can a person find inner peace. And not the ideal of inner peace prevalent in India of disengagement and stillness, but rather the Jewish ideal of inner peace—to advance from strength to strength towards the whole, the good, and the beautiful.

2: Inner Wholeness

IN A TALK DELIVERED in 1958 the Rebbe said the following:

A newer method employed for psychological healing, that can already be found in the Torah many generations earlier, is to explain to someone who is suffering mentally or emotionally the reason that has led them to this internal state. By understanding how this ailment has latched onto them, they also see that they can get out of it, and this recognition is itself healing.

This approach is reflected in the teaching referenced in Chassidic and earlier Jewish sources that, "understanding an ailment is half its cure."

However, the innovative emphasis of Chasidut is not only to explain to a person the *reason* for their emotional ailment but, moreover, that at their very core, *they are entirely above their problems*. And just knowing this is already profoundly healing.

We all have a fundamental inner health, the Rebbe appears to say here. The darkness in our minds and hearts is not who we are. It is instead something that has *latched onto us* for one reason or another—broken relationships, childhood memories, societal expectations, financial stresses, loss of a loved one, or a myriad of other human hardships. These negative experiences certainly affect us, but they cannot break our essence. That place inside us remains forever complete, forever whole.

Counseling Method

THIS UNSHAKEABLE FAITH, THAT every individual has innate strength and wholeness, expressed itself in the healer-patient relationship the Rebbe advocated for and exemplified.

"Needless to say," concludes a letter to the father of a struggling child,
> the above is in addition to what we spoke
> about—the importance of his feeling that his
> parents and friends have the fullest confidence
> in him.

The Rebbe didn't construct his counseling ideas simply by judging their utility, and he didn't tell people of their undefeatable strength only because it would make them feel better. Rather, first and foremost—*he deeply believed it.* Immersed in the Torah's timeless teachings, he had a profound faith in the wholesome and resilient divine spark in every person, no matter their current state. He firmly believed in G-d's benevolent providence and that G-d only gives challenges to a person if they have the strength to overcome them. Thus, he didn't only empathize with people's pain—he also conveyed to them his complete confidence that they have it in them to persevere and triumph.

Diagnosing Vs. Empowering

INDEED, ONE OF THE most remarkable things about the Rebbe's counseling is the absence of character diagnosis ("you suffer from border personality disorder" "you are a manic depressive" "you have generalized anxiety disorder").

In a 1960 letter to an educator who asked how to deal with her students' problems, the Rebbe outlined an educational philosophy that perhaps sheds light on this absence:

> It is difficult to give advice from a distance, especially as the psychology of children may vary in certain aspects from one country to another. Nevertheless, I would like to make one general point which can be universally applied in educational problems, a point which is emphasized in the teachings of Chasidut. I refer to the effort to make the children aware that they possess a soul which is a part of G-d, and that they are always in the presence of G-d (as explained in chapters 2 and 41 of the *Tanya*).
>
> When this is done persistently, and on a level which is suitable to the age group and background of the children, the children come to realize that they possess a great and holy quality which is directly linked with G-d, the Creator and Master of the world, and that it would therefore be quite unbecoming and unworthy of them to do anything which is not good. At the same time they come to realize that

they have the potential to overcome temptation or difficulty...

As for the problem of some children having a habit to take things not belonging to them, this may fall into one of two categories: a. The attitude mentioned in the *Mishnah* in *Pirkei Avot* [5:10]: 'Mine is thine and thine is mine.' In this case, the effort should be made to educate the child that just as it is necessary to be careful not to offend or shame another person, so it is necessary to be careful not to touch anything belonging to somebody else. b. An unhealthy condition which should be treated medically by specialists who know how to handle such an aberration..

I would like to add one more point, which is also emphasized in the teachings of Chasidut, namely, to be careful that in admonishing children the teacher or parent should not evoke a sense of helplessness and despondency on the part of the child; in other words, the child should not get the impression that he is good-for-nothing and that all is lost, etc., and therefore he can continue to do as he wishes. On the contrary, the child should always be encouraged in the feeling that he is capable of overcoming his difficulties and that it is only a matter of will and determination.... "

A Different Effect

THE REBBE EMPHATICALLY CONVEYED this deep belief in a human being's potential to each person he came in contact with. An argument can be made that this was in many ways the overarching message he communicated.

Geulah Cohen (1926-2020), a notable writer and activist, eloquently articulated this after a private audience she had with the Rebbe in the 1960s:

> I have sat across the wise; I have sat across the intelligent; I have sat across the artistic. Sitting opposite a true believer is different.
>
> After meeting the wise you remain what you were—no less a fool and no more a sage. After meeting the intelligent you remain what you were—either knowledgable or ignorant. After meeting the artist you remain what you were—a creative or a handyman.
>
> Not so with the believer. After meeting him you are no longer the same. Though you may not have accepted his faith, you have nevertheless been embraced by it. For the true believer believes in you as well.

When the person sitting across from us feels that we *truly believe* that they are whole and strong and have it in them to completely overcome their current ailments—that is the most healing message we can possibly convey.

ACKNOWLEDGMENTS

I shall thank G-d with all my heart,
Guided by the counsel of the upright and the congregation.

—*Psalms 111:1*

It was a long and winding journey from sitting at a small wooden desk, peering at thousands of relevant letters and interviews, to completing the volume in front of you. It would not be possible to reach this destination without the many individuals who gave graciously of their time and talent.

Some of them assisted by sharing their knowledge, directing me in navigating the Rebbe's voluminous corpus and the subtleties of his Talmudic and Kabbalistic teachings. Many contributed with their insightful suggestions and honest feedback, gently letting me know when I was digressing to themes that belonged in the endnotes. Others helped this undertaking with their unwavering friendship and enthusiasm, urging me on when the awesome responsibility of purporting to accurately distill the Rebbe's ideas overwhelmed me.

To give each of the individuals mentioned below the full acknowledgment they deserve might well warrant a book of its own. You each know what you've done, and I—and anyone who might gain from this book—owe a debt of gratitude to you. (In alphabetical order:)

Tzvi Alperowitz, Rabbi Shmuly Avtzon, Mendel Banon, Rabbi Dr. Yosef Bronstein, Meir Brook, Sholom Brook, Menachem Caytak, Levi Deren, Mrs. Vivi Deren, Bentzi Duchman, Mrs. Faigy Duchman, Rabbi Zalman Duchman, Mrs. Johanna Ehrman, Rabbi Asher Federman,

Levi Feldman, Peretz Garelik, Mr. Josh Goldhirsch, Dovber Goldman, Mendel Goldman, Rabbi Ovadia and Nechama Goldman, Yosef Gorowitz, Richie Greenbaum, Rabbi Dov Greenberg, Mrs. Judy Gruin, Levik Gurary, Berel Gurevitch, Shmuly Gurevitch, Rabbi Shmuly and Toby Hecht, Yaacov Hecht, Rabbi Yossi Kamman, Yisroel Kaplan, Professors Bentzion and Lindsay Katzir, Mr. Harris Kligman, Mr. Eliezer Kornhauser, Sholom Laine, Mendel Levitansky, Rabbi Shmuel Lew, Dovid Margolin, Rabbi Mendel Mintz, Rabbi Judah Mischel, Chaim Muss, Eli Nash, Mrs. Baila Olidort, Zalman Pape, Elisha Pearl, Mendy Plotkin, Dov Popack, Yossi Rapoport, Mrs. Miriam Rhodes, Rabbi Josh Rosenfeld, Eli Rubin, Mrs. Lipa Schwartz, Bronya Shaffer, Levi Shemtov, Shammai Shemtov, Rabbi Mendel Shmotkin, Avraham Shneorsohn, Yisroel Slonim, Mendel Spalter, Ari Sperlin, Rabbi Shais Taub, Tzemach Weg, Orrel Weizman, Noach Wells, Menachem Wolf, Alex Zaloum, Rabbi Hirschy Zarchi, Jake Zebede.

The insight and mentorship of the following professors of psychology and practicing psychotherapists was important in clarifying to me the Rebbe's intent: Professors Ellen Langer and Kate Lowenthal, Drs. Yisroel King, Sonia Roitman, Dani Saul, Jonah Schrag, Yisroel Susskind, and Rabbi Dr. Tzvi Hirsch Weinreb.

This book could not have happened if not for others who toiled before me. The letters rely on the compilation (and some translations) of the Kehot team, the Sichos in English team (particularly the work of Rabbi Sholom Ber Wineberg), and the Chabad.org team. The first-person accounts rely on the tremendous work of Rabbi Elkanah Shmotkin and the JEM team in their "My Encounter" oral history project that has to date interviewed over 1700 individuals about their personal interactions with the Rebbe. The photographic reproductions of original letters—as well as tracking down many other English letters—owe to the diligent work of Shimon Gansburg who gifted this project with his wisdom, knowledge, and generosity of spirit.

There were several individuals who played key roles in shaping this book. During evenings of spirited discussion and long nights of painstaking work, my dear cousin, Shea Shmotkin, gave abundantly of his time, idealistic passion, and keen analytical skills to help formulate the core structure and narrative of this book. The tireless investment of Mrs. Nechama Golding helped bring the manuscript to another level. Her years of patient dedication, discerning advice, and meticulous editing were invaluable. The devoted work of Mrs. Musia Kaplan gave the book its final touch.

I would also like to thank Professor Susan Handelman and Rabbi Ari Sollish for their direction early on, as well as Rabbi Naftali Silberberg of the Rohr JLI for his guidance in translating some ideas from this book into a teacher-student curriculum.

Rabbi Yosef B. Friedman, Rabbi Mendel Laine, and the Kehot team lovingly oversaw the book's production. Among them, Rabbi Levi Raskin sensitively ensured every word remains true to the sources, and Rabbi Yirmi Berkowitz carefully formatted the text with attention to every detail. Moshe Muchnick and Alizah Chekroun from Spotlight Design thoughtfully created the cover and template.

Above all, I'd like to thank my dear parents, Rabbi Zalman and Malya Shmotkin, who were unswerving in their encouragement throughout this lengthy process, believing in the vision, sharing in its pains and delights, and serving as indispensable sounding boards and editorial guides. My grandparents, Rabbi Yisroel and Devorah Shmotkin and Rabbi Bentzion and Chana Stein, were a bedrock of support and living examples from the very beginning. Each of my siblings contributed in their own way as well.

Speaking of family, there are a few people who've been part of the fabric of our household since my earliest memories. This project has finally allowed me to experience their refined character, work ethic, and selfless devotion to the cause.

Chabad.org's Rabbis Meir Simcha Kogan and Motti Seligson enthusiastically threw their time and energy behind this effort from the get-go. The former, in particular, patiently but firmly nudged it forward, heaving it over the finish line. The Rohr and Tabacinic names have been similarly constant in my life since childhood. It was thus a particular delight to experience first-hand Mr. George Rohr's effervescent encouragement and support, along with his spot-on advice. Jared and Sondra Mehl have been forever an enthralling mix of no-holds-barred mentors and the most comfortable of friends. Their excitement for this project was truly touching.

Finally, I'd like to make special mention of my dear aunt Henya ע״ה Federman, Lubavitch emissary to the U.S. Virgin Islands, whose untimely passing occurred during the development of this manuscript. Henya lived by the lessons in this book—lessons she absorbed from her Chasidic parents: a mind liberated from ego, deeply aware of G-d's presence, and attuned to the needs of her children and others. Reflecting on her life granted me tangible words to describe certain ideals in the Rebbe's letters—making this volume yet another entity forever marked with her noble spirit.

I hope that the Rebbe's counsel shared in these pages uplifts you like it uplifted me, hastening the time when we will all be told:

> *Arise, my beloved; my fair one, go forth! For now the winter is past, The rains are over and gone. The blossoms have appeared in the land... Arise, my beloved; My fair one, go forth!*
> —*Song of Songs 2:10-13*

In loving memory of our mothers
Masha Shayna bat Yitzchak and
Zissel Shprintza bat Chaim Zev
and in honor of our parents and our children.

With deep gratitude for the spiritually elevated wisdom, understanding, knowledge, and love from the Shmotkin Family.

With deep gratitude to all of the Rebbe's Army and the members of the Israel Defense Forces who protect the mind, body and soul of the Jewish people.

Sondra and Jared

Stamford, CT & Ra'anana, Israel
2024

To our loves,

לילה, ראובן, אריאלה, יעל

May you all continue to be a blessing
to all those around you.

Let your light shine outwards always.

All our love,
Mommy & Daddy

Dedicated by
Rabbi Sholom Ber and Chani Levitin,
Shluchim in Seattle Washington,
in honor of their parents and grandparents.

In honor of the Rebbe
who envisioned a better world
and inspired us all to help create it.

Christopher Ruddy